SOUTHERN AFRICAN
BIRDS OF PREY

SOUTHERN AFRICAN
BIRDS OF PREY

Photographs by
Peter and Beverly Pickford

Text by
Warwick Tarboton

STRUIK

Struik Publishers (Pty) Ltd (a member of The Struik Publishing Group (Pty) Ltd)
Cornelis Struik House, 80 McKenzie Street, Cape Town 8001

Reg. No.: 54/00965/07

First published 1989
Second impression 1990
Second edition 1994

Copyright text © Warwick Tarboton 1989, 1994

Copyright photographs © Peter Pickford, with the exception of the Honey Buzzard on p.45 (P. Doherty: Aquila Photographics), the Longlegged Buzzard on p.92 (G.K. Brown: Ardea London), the Pallid Harrier on p.132 (P. Doherty: Aquila Photographics), and the African Hobby on p.148 (Peter Steyn). Copyright for these photographs remains with their owners 1989, 1994

Copyright maps © Warwick Tarboton 1989, 1994

Edited by Peter Joyce
Designed by Jenny Camons
Cover designed by Alix Gracie
Line illustrations by Duncan Butchart
Set by McManus Bros (Pty) Ltd, Cape Town
Reproduction by Unifoto (Pty) Ltd, Cape Town
Printed and bound by Kyodo Printing Co. (Pte) Ltd, Singapore

All rights reserved. No part of this publication may be reproduced, stored in a retrieval system, or transmitted, in any form or by any means, electronic, mechanical, photocopying, recording or otherwise, without the written permission of the copyright owners.

ISBN 1 86825 625 1

(Half-title page) An African Marsh Harrier pauses at the edge of its nest before adding a beakful of material to the lining.
(Title page) The Crowned Eagle has the build and manoeuvrability of a giant sparrowhawk with its broad, rounded wings and long tail.
(Below) The art of falconry is thousands of years old and a rich tradition has evolved around the training of hawks to catch wild quarry. Here, a Spotted Dikkop tries to escape a trained Lanner Falcon.

PHOTOGRAPHER'S PREFACE

*'Where is the thicket? Gone.
Where is the eagle? Gone.
The end of living and the beginning of survival.'*

The words attributed to Chief Seattle, in a speech to George Washington in 1855, have become more poignant with each passing day. To allow the eagle to become extinct would be tantamount to stripping the Earth of the last vestiges of its dignity – the bird of prey is the embodiment of free will and untainted liberty, representative of power and fierce, almost defiant, independence.

In his brief sojourn upon this earth, man is exposed to some unique and special experiences. For me, the flight of a falcon is one of these. I have found no rival for this most compelling and spiritual performance. It is a solo performance of joy, a masterpiece of effortless grace set to the subtle orchestration of the wind.

To treat the subject on a documentary level would have been an act devoid of sensitivity. My quest has been to photograph truthfully, to delve beneath the surface and explore the essence of my subject. I found aggression and indifference, condescension and curiosity, retiring fragility and blatant defiance. All of these I have sought to express but, above all, my desire has been to infuse the pages of this book with the indomitable spirit of majesty of the bird of prey.

ACKNOWLEDGEMENTS

Beverly and I wish to record our indebtedness to the following people, without whom this book would not have become a reality and to whom we are sincerely grateful:

Warwick and Guggi Tarboton for all that was given so unstintingly; Johan van Jaarsveld for his tireless support; Nico and Ella Myburgh for unparalleled friendship and hospitality; Dr Alan Kemp, whose empathy with birds is a source of wonder; David, Ester and Stephen Steyn for some memorable days; Ian Sinclair; Peter Steyn for his guidance; Richard and Bookey Peek for evenings of Rachmaninov and illumination on the Western Banded Snake Eagle; William Jonsson, whose home became our base in Zululand; Arthur Bowland, and Richard and Joy Alcock for sharing their eagles with us; Patrick and Jenny Shorten and all the staff of Sabi Sabi; Rob Filmer; Chris and Karen Olwagen for all their time and assistance; Walter Mangold, Stephen Fowkes and Christy Abrahams, whose co-operation was so unselfishly given; Ian Garland; Richard Brooke; Sally Klute and Joe Brooks; Tom Barlow for allowing us to pursue our quarry in the fair hills of Vergelegen; Hassner and Magda Pepler who shared their home with us; Isolde Mellet for her assistance; John and Sheila Nicholls for their kindness and hospitality; the staff of Entabeni Forest Station; Mr J. Dodds and the staff of Union Spring, who gave so generously of their free hours; Chris Pollard, who revealed to us the Taita Falcon; Dr Peter Mundy; Mr Harry Scott and his daughter, of Lawaan; Susan Ward and Mynhardt Bester of Bester-Ward films, who managed to sift through the dust of our frantic activity and emerge with a commendable documentary.

We are also most grateful to the following institutions: The National Parks Board and, in particular, Dr Salomon Joubert, Johan Kloppers, Elias le Riche and the rangers of the Kruger and Kalahari Gemsbok National Parks; the Natal Parks Board, particularly Dr John Vincent, Stewart Maclean, Don Unie, Richard Davies, Coen Albertyn, the Garnet-Jacksons and Mrs van Schoor; the Department of Nature Conservation of South West Africa/Namibia, with special thanks to Dr Chris Brown, Dr Tony Williams, Steve Bruyns and 'Reverend' Christopher Hines; Dr Johan Neethling and the Department of Nature Conservation of the Cape Province; Dr John Mendelsohn and Joris Komen of the Windhoek Museum.

The members of the Falconry Clubs of Zimbabwe and Natal were of immeasurable help, particularly Ron and Deirdre Hartley and the boys of Falcon College; Rudi Geisswein, Reg Querl, Peter Ginn and the boys of Peterhouse; and Dr Aase Huelin; in Natal, Tom Davidson, Rob and Jenny Booth, Neil and Morag Hulett, Dr Dieter Nischk, Alan Serfontein and Karl and Charmaine van der Merwe, all helped to make Natal one of our most successful 'birding' areas.

We are deeply grateful to those involved in the production of the book, and in particular to Peter Borchert, who tempered our dreams with reality; to Eve Gracie and Peter Joyce, and to Jenny Camons for an outstanding design.

Last, but by no means least, we would thank our parents, who have always been there.

Peter D. Pickford   Cape Town, June 1989

FOREWORD

Sasol is proud to be associated with the creation and publication of this fine volume which is dedicated to southern Africa's heritage of magnificent raptors.

It is sad that many of our birds of prey are themselves falling prey to poison and encroachment on their habitat. Indeed, some of the most majestic of the species are on the endangered list.

We trust that this book will stimulate awareness of and concern for our birds and their habitat, and so contribute to their conservation.

Johannes Stegmann
CHAIRMAN

SASOL

Sasol Ltd is strongly committed to conservation in South Africa

Contents

Photographer's Preface and Acknowledgements

Foreword

Author's Introduction 8

Secretarybird 11

Vultures 15
Bearded Vulture 16; Palmnut Vulture 18; Egyptian Vulture 20; Cape Vulture 21; Hooded Vulture 25; Whitebacked Vulture 26; Lappetfaced Vulture 29; Whiteheaded Vulture 30

Kites and Allied Species 33
Black Kite 34; Blackshouldered Kite 39; Cuckoo Hawk 42; Bat Hawk 44; Honey Buzzard 45

Eagles 47
Black Eagle 48; Tawny Eagle 52; Steppe Eagle 55; Wahlberg's Eagle 56; Booted Eagle 58; Lesser Spotted Eagle 60; African Hawk Eagle 61; Ayres' Eagle 65; Longcrested Eagle 66; Crowned Eagle 68; Martial Eagle 71; Western Banded Snake Eagle 73; Brown Snake Eagle 75; Blackbreasted Snake Eagle 76; Southern Banded Snake Eagle 79; Bateleur 81; African Fish Eagle 83

Buzzards 87
Steppe Buzzard 88; Forest Buzzard 91; Longlegged Buzzard 92; Augur Buzzard 93; Jackal Buzzard 94; Lizard Buzzard 96

Sparrowhawks and Goshawks 99
Redbreasted Sparrowhawk 100; Ovambo Sparrowhawk 103; Little Sparrowhawk 104; Black Sparrowhawk 107; Pale Chanting Goshawk 109; Dark Chanting Goshawk 113; Little Banded Goshawk 114; African Goshawk 117; Gabar Goshawk 118

Harriers and Allied Species 121
European Marsh Harrier 122; African Marsh Harrier 125; Black Harrier 126; Montagu's Harrier 131; Pallid Harrier 132; Gymnogene 133

Osprey 137

Falcons and Kestrels 141
Peregrine Falcon 142; Lanner Falcon 144; European Hobby 146; African Hobby 148; Taita Falcon 149; Rednecked Falcon 150; Eleonora's Falcon 152; Sooty Falcon 153; Grey Kestrel 154; Western Redfooted Kestrel 155; Eastern Redfooted Kestrel 157; Rock Kestrel 158; Lesser Kestrel 160; Greater Kestrel 161; Dickinson's Kestrel 164; Pygmy Falcon 166

Owls 169
Barn Owl 170; Grass Owl 173; Wood Owl 175; Marsh Owl 176; Cape Eagle Owl 178; Spotted Eagle Owl 181; Giant Eagle Owl 183; Pel's Fishing Owl 184; Scops Owl 187; Pearlspotted Owl 188; Barred Owl 190; Whitefaced Owl 192

Appendix 193

Further Reading 221

Glossary 222

Indexes
General 223; Common names 225; Scientific names 227; Afrikaans/English common names 228

AUTHOR'S INTRODUCTION

Birds of prey come in all shapes and sizes, from tiny Pygmy Falcons and Scops Owls that weigh a mere 65 grams to heavyweights such as the eagles and vultures that tip the scales at five kilograms or more. Some species are nocturnal, some are diurnal, and some live for the twilight zone that separates night and day; some hunt by stealth, others by sheer power, while many are scavengers. What does this wide-ranging group of birds have in common and why are not all predatory birds, like herons, cormorants, and even shrikes and warblers, included in the term 'bird of prey'?

The true birds of prey cover two orders. The first is the Falconiformes, encompassing the diurnal species such as eagles, vultures, kites and falcons which, despite their diversity, can all be traced back to a common hawk-like ancestor. The second group, the Strigiformes or owls, are nocturnal, and also evolved from a single ancestral species. There is no evidence that Falconiformes and Strigiformes are related in any way and it is thought that their often similar predatory habits are simply the result of convergence. Their complementary day and night roles as predators have led to their being collectively referred to as 'birds of prey' or 'raptors'.

The continent of Africa supports a remarkable diversity of birds of prey: a third of the world's 280-odd Falconiformes and a quarter of the 130-odd Strigiformes occur here. Southern Africa (that part of the continent lying south of the Kunene, Okavango and Zambezi rivers) supports some 69 Falconiformes and 12 owl species. This book discusses these 81 species, occurring in South Africa and its associated states, Namibia, Botswana, Lesotho, Zimbabwe, Swaziland and Mozambique (south of the Zambezi).

Only three of these raptors (the Cape Vulture, the Jackal Buzzard and the Black Harrier) are endemic, or restricted to the subregion. A further 48 are exclusively Afrotropical (i.e. restricted to Africa south of the Sahara Desert). The rest are found on other continents besides Africa, and of these, the Osprey, the Peregrine Falcon and the Barn Owl are among the most widely distributed of bird species and occur on most continents.

Europe and Asia are home to most of the species that extend their range beyond the Afrotropical region and no less than 17 of these have deeply forged links with Africa, breeding in the Palearctic and migrating south for winter. For many of them southern Africa is not only the terminus but also their main winter quarters and species like the Steppe Buzzard and Lesser Kestrel are plentiful here during this time. By contrast others, like the Longlegged Buzzard and Eleonora's Falcon, are very rare vagrants that have been noted here only once or twice.

There are a few other species, such as the Wahlberg's Eagle and the Yellowbilled Kite, which migrate to southern Africa but their biannual movement is contained within the continent: they fly south to breed and move back north of the equator to winter. Many others move about with no clearly defined seasonality, staying when conditions suit them and moving when food is scarce. Among these are the Brown and Blackbreasted Snake Eagles.

It is probably true to say that change is the keyword for the African birds of prey. A million or more transcontinental migrants move twice yearly back and forth from the Palearctic to Africa; trans-African migrants move seasonally, and nomadic species may be found in the central Transvaal one day and in northern Zaire the next. Even among the sedentary, territorial species there is change. Species that were once rare and restricted have extended their ranges remarkably: the Black Harrier, once thought to be endangered, is today much more widespread, and several sparrowhawk species have extended their ranges dramatically as a result of commercial afforestation.

By contrast, the numbers of many species have declined. The scavenging birds of prey, including vultures, some eagles, and the Black or Yellowbilled Kite, occur in fewer numbers and often within much smaller ranges today than they did a century ago. The most spectacular example is that of the Bateleur, which once ranged widely across southern Africa, but is now virtually confined to large game parks and remote, unpopulated areas. Such species are usually unable to adapt to the changes made by man in their preferred habitats, or are innocent victims of indiscriminate management practices such as poisoning campaigns against problem animals. In some species direct persecution has taken its toll, especially in those which occur at low density and have low reproductive rates. Currently 18 birds of prey species are listed in the South African Red Data Book of Birds. This is disproportionately high – whereas raptors comprise only nine per cent of the avifauna they make up 17 per cent of the threatened species. Herein lies a conservation challenge: to identify the threatened species, to unravel the causes of the problems facing them and to implement effective action before it is too late. Already one former breeding species, the Egyptian Vulture, has probably become extinct on the subcontinent.

Southern Africa is well served with good reference books on the identification and life histories of birds, and in this respect birds of prey have been admirably covered. This book makes no pretensions in this regard: it is an essay in pictures and words, nostalgic at times, about a spectacular group of birds which are coping, with varying degrees of success, with a fast-changing environment.

The nomenclature used in the book follows Clancey 1980, but the arrangement of species has been dictated by the needs of design. The main descriptive accounts of the species are followed by an appendix that summarizes the pertinent field information on each species, and gives the bird's distribution: either African in the case of resident species, or European in the case of the Palearctic migrants. The flight silhouettes in the appendix are shown to scale within each group; obvious sexual dimorphism has been indicated but, for reasons of space, it has not been possible to illustrate the wide variety of dark and light phase birds, and plumage development from non-adult to adult birds.

The brilliant orange eye and boldly patterned chestnut and black breast feathers distinguish the Cape Eagle Owl from the other large, long-eared owls found in southern Africa. The white feathers on its chin show briefly when the bird distends its throat to hoot.

SECRETARYBIRD

There is only one species in this family. The remarkable Secretarybird is a large, terrestrial bird that is endemic to the Afrotropical region. Although it looks and behaves like an eagle in many respects, its inclusion in the Falconiformes may not be correct. It has been suggested that it is more closely allied to a South American family known as the Cariamidiae, or perhaps has its greatest affinity with the crane family, the Gruidae.

This striking and distinctive avian predator of Africa's savannas and grasslands may be recognized by its long legs and short blunt toes, adapted for walking rather than for grasping and carrying prey; its long, wide wings which render it capable of tremendous soaring flight; its greatly elongated central tail feathers; its long neck; and its deep, croaking call.

(Left) The Secretarybird launches itself into the air after a short, flapping run. Although mainly a terrestrial species, it is capable of fine soaring flight matching that of a vulture. (Top) The unmistakable silhouette of the Secretarybird.

Southern Africa is so well endowed with unusual birds of prey that it is impossible to reach unanimity on which is the greatest oddity among them. The majority vote, however, would probably go to the long-legged, terrestrial Secretarybird.

From its name alone there is little clue to the identity and generic affinities of this remarkable bird, which stands 1,3 metres tall and lives on the ground, but behaves in many ways like an eagle. Its name is generally taken as an allusion to its crest, which is vaguely reminiscent of a bunch of quill pens tucked behind the ear of some medieval secretary. Another, less imaginative but perhaps more plausible, explanation is that the name is derived from the Arabic term *saqr-et-tair*, meaning hunter/hawk-bird. In any event the name avoids the inevitable disputes that would arise if the bird's chosen name attempted to pinpoint its taxonomic position (as, for example, would 'Crane-like Eagle' or 'Eagle-like Crane'!).

Secretarybirds occur throughout the savanna, scrub and grassland areas of Africa south of the Sahara, and in southern Africa they range from the fringes of the desert in the west to the montane grasslands of the east. Grassland in fact is the habitat in which they are most numerous, provided there are one or more suitable trees on which they can roost and build their nests. Their requirements in this respect are modest, and the birds often make do with a bush only two or three metres tall on which to construct a large flat platform of sticks, although their preference is for a bigger, flat-topped acacia in which access from below is virtually impossible.

Much of the Secretarybird's daily activity centres around the roosting or nesting tree. They are found in pairs throughout the year, and the male and female often forage in close proximity to each other, striding through the grassland, head inclined forward, and rolling from left to right with each step. In this way a bird will cover two or three kilometres in an hour and possibly 20 to 30 in a day. All their food is taken from the ground, and they eat virtually anything that they are capable of catching and overpowering. Thus grasshoppers feature very prominently in the diet, as do lizards and small rodents; small birds and birds' eggs are taken when found.

Although Secretarybirds have a reputation as snake-catchers, these probably make up less than one per cent of their diet. They certainly have the equipment and technique for killing snakes and do, on occasion, consume poisonous species like cobras and puffadders. Their long legs are covered with thick scales impregnable to snake bite, and they attack snakes in the same way that they attack other prey items – by stamping them to death with their feet. All prey, including large items, are swallowed whole, and nesting birds transport food back to their nests in their crops. Sometimes they arrive at the nest after a foraging sortie with crops bulging like a Father Christmas' bag, and the contents are then regurgitated on to the floor of the nest for the chicks to take their pick.

Nesting may occur at any time of the year and the breeding cycle, from nest-building to fledging, takes about five months. Some nests are used repeatedly, but more usually a new site is selected for each breeding attempt, perhaps because the tree's branches often grow up around the old nest, making access difficult for the adults. Sticks and weed stems are gathered from the ground nearby to build the nest and the centre is thickly lined with dry grass.

The female Secretarybird normally lays a clutch of two eggs (occasionally one or three), unmarked and white in colour, and she undertakes most or all of the incubation, being fed at intervals during the day by the male. Dry grass is continually added to the cup of the nest during this period. The incubating bird is completely exposed to the elements, and at times sits in searing heat, keeping cool by panting and raising her feathers. At other times she endures rainstorms and even hail. The eggs hatch after about 42 days, and once the chicks start to feather, the female assists the male in collecting food for the brood.

Unlike many birds of prey there is no aggression between the siblings, and Secretarybirds often rear two young, occasionally three. The nestling period is variable (10 to 14 weeks) but the chicks are fully developed, with long tails and head quills, by the time they fledge, although these appendages are somewhat shorter than those of the adults. The young are also distinguishable from their parents by their duller plumage and their yellow, rather than orange, facial skin. The young remain with the parents for a few months and the family often sleeps together on the same tree-top at night, but gradually the parental bond diminishes and they disperse and find their own patch of savanna or grassland in which to live.

SECRETARYBIRD

*A*t close quarters, the eagle-like bill and long eyelashes of the Secretarybird can easily be seen. The elongated feathers protruding from the back of its head are said to resemble a cluster of quill pens tucked behind the ear of a medieval secretary, and may have given the bird its name. It is more usually thought, however, that the name is derived from the Arabic for a hunting bird.
A young Secretarybird sitting in its treetop nest (above) shows the wide gape which enables it to swallow snakes and large rodents whole.

VULTURES

Eight vulture species are found in southern Africa. They are all large, powerful birds with massive wingspans, the largest being the Lappetfaced Vulture which weighs about seven kilograms and has a wingspan of 2,6 metres. All are scavenging species, living off carcasses which they locate from the air. Their large, broad wings enable them to remain aloft for most of the day and they use their keen eyesight to locate food. Two of the species, the Cape and Whitebacked, collectively referred to as griffon vultures, are sociable, foraging, roosting and nesting colonially and they may gather in hundreds at the carcass of a large animal where they jostle and fight for space. The other vulture species are more solitary in disposition but many of them also attend carcasses. They all have large, powerful beaks with hooked tips which they use for tearing off strips of meat or skin. Bearded Vultures are unusual in their behaviour of feeding mainly on bones, which they carry aloft and drop to break into fragments; the Palmnut Vulture is aberrant in having a mainly vegetarian diet.

(Left) Only at close quarters can the Bearded Vulture's black eye-mask, beard and red-rimmed eye be seen; at a distance its dark brown wings and tail and contrasting golden-brown body and head serve to identify it. (Above) Whitebacked Vultures jostle for the best pickings at a carcass.

Bearded Vulture

Throughout their range Bearded Vultures, or Lammergeiers as they are sometimes known, are associated with high mountain ranges, among them the Himalayas (where they have been observed at altitudes of 7 900 metres above sea-level), the European Alps (from where the last birds disappeared in the 1880s but to which they are now being reintroduced) and the various African highlands – from those in Ethiopia, where they are common, to the Maluti Mountains and the Drakensberg in southern Africa, where they are much scarcer.

Bearded Vultures are most often seen when they are in flight and, with their long, slender wings and falcon-like profile, they are easily recognized, even from a distance of several kilometres. Their wingspan is enormous – about 2,5 metres – and they have long, wedge-shaped tails. They fly with speed and great agility, usually cruising along ridges within 100 metres of the ground as they scan for food. Their wing and tail configuration enables them to fly effortlessly, using lift from hill-slopes, which enables them to be independent of the thermals needed by other vultures for gaining height.

These birds are called vultures, not because they are taxonomically closely related to other vulture species, but because they are primarily scavengers, living on the bones and carrion that they locate from the air. To a great extent they are dependent for food on mortality among domestic animals, and their strongholds (for example, the Tibetan and Ethiopian highlands) are regions where subsistence agriculture and stock farming are practised. Most of the Drakensberg Bearded Vultures are similarly reliant on the unsophisticated pastoral activities common on the high Lesotho plateau, where natural death among the free-ranging herds of sheep and goats provides a steady supply of carcasses. Bones make up the large part of a Bearded Vulture's diet, and there is usually a good meal to be had even after Cape Vultures have picked a carcass clean. The bird has a unique way of dealing with bones too large to swallow: it carries them high into the air, holds them lengthways in its talons and then drops them on to a rock surface, often repeatedly, until the bone shatters. Certain sites are especially effective for this purpose: they are called ossuaries, and are readily recognizable by the large numbers of bone fragments that accumulate at and around them.

The Bearded Vultures of the Drakensberg and Lesotho highlands live together in pairs year-round, their ranges centring on nesting sites spaced at intervals of five to 10 kilometres. Within the vicinity of the nest they are territorial, but when foraging they overlap with other pairs. A pair may cover an area of 5 000 square kilometres in search of food.

The nests – large, untidy accumulations of sticks, hair and wool, often well caked with excreta – are located in caves and potholes, and on sheltered ledges on high cliffs. The same nest is usually used year after year, some becoming impressively large structures. The clutch of two eggs is laid in winter and the parents share the incubation duties more or less equally, one attending the nest while the other forages. Incubation lasts about 57 days and the nestling period about 15 to 16 weeks. Although both eggs may hatch, and there is little or no aggression between the siblings, only one chick survives.

The bones and scraps of carcasses from successful forays often accumulate on the nest ledge, to be picked at at leisure. Even when the chick is on the wing it frequently returns to the nest to feed: only when the parents begin their next breeding cycle does it become independent of them. In the five or six years that these young birds take to reach maturity they range widely, sometimes living semi-communally with other young Bearded Vultures and often scavenging around villages and at refuse dumps, venues not usually used by adult birds.

The high plateau of the Maluti Mountains and the escarpment formed by the Natal Drakensberg form the stronghold in southern Africa of the rare and spectacular Bearded Vulture. Here, an estimated 260 pairs represent the remnants of a population that, a century ago, extended south-westwards along the mountain chains almost to the Cape Peninsula. The bird's straw-coloured head and shoulders and rufous underparts blend well with the winter landscape of its mountain environment. The rufous coloration of the underparts is not, in fact, feather pigmentation, but is caused by iron oxide which adheres to the birds when they settle on ledges, or perhaps when they bathe in mountain pools containing iron-rich water.

Palmnut Vulture

The Palmnut Vulture is ranked by many as the most curious of the African birds of prey and it is unique among them for being mainly vegetarian. It is also known as the Vulturine Fish Eagle and its true affinities – a vulture-like eagle, or an eagle-like vulture – are uncertain. This most distinctive species is placed in its own monotypic genus, *Gypohierax*, derived from the Greek for vulture hawk'.

Adult birds are mainly white with broad wings and short, rounded tails. In flight they show black secondaries and their tails are black with a narrow white terminal bar. The bare skin surrounding the eye is red; the cere is bluish, the bill yellowish, and the legs orange. The only other similar-sized bird of prey that is mainly white is the Egyptian Vulture, but the two are readily distinguished by their shapes and by the black parts on their bodies. Young Palmnut Vultures are also easily recognizable, for they are completely brown except for their facial skin, which is yellowish, and they have dull-white legs and feet. They become progressively whiter during the three to four years they take to mature and it is these intermediaries, with their blotchy brown and white colouring, that are seen most frequently beyond the breeding areas of southern Africa.

Palmnut Vultures breed along the Mozambique coast in as yet unknown numbers; elsewhere on the subcontinent the only known breeding population is the tiny one which is located in Zululand and which numbers, at most, six pairs. Most of these occur in the *Raphia* palm groves that grow around Kosi Bay, with another single pair located south of Richards Bay at Mtunzini. The latter occupy a grove of palms that was planted at the turn of the century by a local magistrate who had brought the seed down from the north. It has been suggested that the Kosi Bay palms were also artificially introduced, by the early Portuguese pioneers. Whatever the case, the Palmnut Vultures are only resident in the area because the palms are there.

Palm fruit is the species' staple food, but they also feed on other items, taking stranded fish and carrion generally, catching crabs, molluscs and snails, rodents and insects, and occasionally diving for fish in the manner of a Fish Eagle.

The birds that are observed from time to time in such unlikely places as the Kalahari Gemsbok National Park and southern Orange Free State are immatures. Just north of Tzaneen, in the north-eastern Transvaal, a collection of various palm species was planted long ago for ornamental purposes and from time to time young birds appear there, stay for a while and then move on. It is clear from this that Palmnut Vultures have the ability to find suitable habitat and if, for example, more *Raphia* groves were established in Zululand they would certainly be colonized by adult members of the species.

Most of what is known about the Palmnut Vulture's habits and behaviour is derived from observations farther north in Africa, where they have been studied in some detail. They are gregarious birds which roost at night in small groups and by day disperse among the palm trees to feed.

The nest is typically that of a bird of prey: a platform of sticks about a metre in diameter and placed high up in a tree. The duties of nest-building are shared, and the same nest is often re-used in successive years. They do not breed in colonies, but adjacent pairs may nest within a kilometre of each other. South of the Equator the birds lay their eggs during May to August (though in Zululand it may be a month or two later), the clutch being a single egg, which is white, marked with brownish blotches and smears. There is no accurate record of the duration of the incubation and nestling periods, nor are the parental roles in the breeding cycle known.

Perched atop a large seed-cluster growing out of a Raphia palm, an adult Palmnut Vulture (opposite, above) pauses between eating fruits. Each of these palms produces a single fruit crop when it matures at 35-40 years old, and then dies. The 2 000 or more fruits produced are each about 75 mm long and have a hard, scaly outer shell which the birds peck off to reach the fleshy inner layer. In parts of Africa where these, or the Guinea Palms, Elaeis guineensis, *grow in their thousands, Palmnut Vultures have a continuous, abundant food source and they are common birds. By contrast, in South Africa there are no more than a handful of resident pairs, and these depend on the isolated groves of palms that have been introduced by man.*
(Opposite, below) A Palmnut Vulture is playfully teased in flight by three Pied Crows.

Egyptian Vulture

The last-recorded active nest of an Egyptian Vulture in southern Africa was found in Transkei on 8 December 1923. It was on a high cliff ledge, and amid the collection of wool, bones, cow dung and other rubbish of its nest-lining lay two richly marked brown eggs. This is the only dated and reasonably detailed record of an Egyptian Vulture nest on the subcontinent, although reports from the last century, and even earlier, allude to its breeding in many localities. The same reports suggest that the bird was found in fair numbers and was widely distributed in southern Africa. What happened to it in the interim, and what its current status is, remains a mystery.

The nearest known breeding Egyptian Vultures occur in Tanzania, but every few years one or two tantalizing sightings are reported from Transkei or Griqualand East. These records are scrutinized by a 'rare bird committee' and, while some reports are rejected for lack of evidence or as misidentifications, others are indisputable, and they throw up a number of questions. Are these birds the last survivors of a population that has not been known to breed since 1923; are they vagrants from central and East Africa; or is there still a small, overlooked breeding population surviving in the inaccessible and remote gorges of this southern region?

An adult Egyptian Vulture is unlikely to be confused with any other African bird of prey. It is small by vulture standards, with a wingspan of about 1,6 metres, and is completely white except for its black primaries and secondaries. The Palmnut Vulture and the white colour form of the Wahlberg's Eagle are also mainly white and of similar size, but both these species have dark brown or black tails.

The petite Egyptian Vulture is known for its habit of using stones to break open the eggs of ground-nesting birds. It selects a suitably sized stone, which it picks up in its beak and throws repeatedly at the egg until the shell breaks. It is for this reason that it was not a popular bird in the ostrich-farming areas of the Cape when it occurred there a century or more ago.

CAPE VULTURE

A few years ago two schoolboys tragically fell to their deaths while trying to reach Cape Vulture nests in the Magaliesberg range, north-west of Johannesburg, and for a brief moment the media spotlit one feature of the species' biology – that it nests on inaccessible ledges on high cliffs. It is the only extant vulture in southern African to nest on cliffs and it is this habit that gives rise to its Afrikaans name, 'Kransaasvoël'.

Dependence on this type of nesting site means that breeding Cape Vultures are restricted both regionally, to landscapes in which cliffs have formed, and locally, to a radius around the colony (the limits are determined by the requirements for successful foraging). Not all cliffs, moreover, provide suitable nesting sites. For example, granite and dolomite cliffs seldom have the shelves that the birds need for nesting, in contrast to sandstone and quartzite formations, which, because of the bedded nature of the rock, have numerous ledges. Thus good sites that are inaccessible to potential predators tend to be few and far between, and those that are in use have probably been occupied by Cape Vultures for many generations and perhaps even for thousands of years.

There are two Cape Vulture breeding colonies along the Magaliesberg range, a quartzite formation with high cliffs and many suitable nesting ledges. The colonies are spaced about 50 kilometres apart, and the birds breeding here have been under observation by ornithologists for the past 40 years. In this time more than 5 000 of their chicks have been ringed, and it was the steady decline in the numbers of young being produced each year that alerted conservationists to the fact that all was not well with the species. Consequently there has been a great deal of research, and publicity, devoted to its future.

Sitting quietly above a Cape Vulture breeding colony is an exhilarating experience. Far below, and mostly out of sight from the top, innumerable vulture parents sit on their nests, grouped in clusters on the more spacious shelves but scattered about singly elsewhere. If it is July most of the birds will be brooding recently hatched chicks, patiently awaiting the return of their partners, who are away foraging. Throughout the day some vultures fly about in front of the cliff, and every now and again a bird will sail past so close that one can easily discern its beady yellow eye set in a woolly grey head. Occasionally a dust-devil on the ground hundreds of metres below will grow into a full-blown thermal, sweeping leaves high up into the air and signalling to the vultures that there is a free lift on offer. Suddenly the airspace is filled with birds as 20 or 30 peel off the cliff and spiral upwards. Some continue way beyond the top of the cliff and set off on a course to forage, while others wheel about for a while and then re-alight on the cliff. Frequently one will flap to catch up with another and then glide just above and behind it, and a third may join them to fly in tandem with the second. The vultures can be seen using their 'air-brakes' to slow down – dropping their legs and toes to increase wind resistance. There is no clear-cut explanation for the tandem flying behaviour: perhaps the reason lies simply in the pleasant sensation the bird gets riding in another's slipstream.

Adult breeding Cape Vultures are tied to their colonies for most of the year. In March and April pairs re-occupy their old sites and begin nest-building, bringing in tufts of grass, plants and sticks, stealing material from unattended neighbours' nests, and consolidating all these into a shallow, saucer-topped platform about 700 millimetres in diameter. On accommodating ledges nests may be a metre or two apart, just distance enough for the incubating birds to remain beyond pecking range of their neighbours. Most clutches (nearly always a single egg) are laid during May and the male and female share the incubation equally on a roughly day-on, day-off rota, the off-day being spent foraging. The incubation period lasts about 56 days and the nestling duties are similarly shared by the parents, one brooding or guarding while the other is away searching for food. The returning bird brings with it the baby food – a crop full of foul-smelling, decomposing flesh which is regurgitated and eaten by the chick.

The nestling period is lengthy, most chicks making their first flight more than four months after hatching, during November or December. The fledged chicks frequently return to their nests and are fed there by the parents, but in time they become more competent fliers and accompany the adults on foraging trips. However, their period of dependence may last another three or four months, after which the vulture's year has gone almost full circle, to the start of the next breeding season.

An adult Cape Vulture belonging to the southernmost breeding colony of the species was fitted with a radio transmitter and its movements tracked for eight months. The bird spent most of its time foraging within 10 to 15 kilometres of the colony and did not range farther afield than 28 kilometres. In East Africa, however, it has been estimated that Rüppell's Griffons (a cliff-nesting species much like the Cape Vulture) may forage up to 140 kilometres away from their colonies.

Young birds, of course, are under no such constraints and in the four to six years before they reach sexual maturity they may wander far from their birth-site. They do not need cliffs to roost on at night, and may instead use trees or electricity pylons. A number of the Magaliesberg-ringed chicks have been recovered, still as immature birds, up to 1 200 kilometres away. Some of the ringed chicks have returned to breed at their natal colonies while others have established themselves at other colonies.

The three largest Cape Vulture colonies are in the Transvaal and in recent years, during the period that their numbers have been monitored, each has supported between 600 and 900 breeding pairs. All three are in mainly cattle-ranching country and it is remarkable, considering the size of the vulture population, that animal mortality in the region has been high enough to provide sufficient food. If a vulture needs a daily intake of about 500 grams and the colony comprises 1 500 birds, together with their chicks, it means that they are consuming about a ton of meat a day, something like 1 000 dead cows a year. Every farmer wants to reduce stock mortality to the absolute minimum, and on many properties dead animals are burned or buried in order to reduce the risk of disease. Thus, as farming becomes more efficient so the birds face the prospect of a diminishing food supply. A more serious problem is the illegal practice of lacing carcasses with poison to kill scavenging dogs and jackals. Very often vultures are the victims of this irresponsible practice, and much of the conservation effort for the Cape Vulture today is devoted to preventing such needless slaughter.

A Cape Vulture peers warily from its nesting ledge behind a white-washed rock. The nesting cliffs of this species are invariably copiously white-washed, rendering them visible from a long way off. Even long-abandoned nesting colonies retain the trademark of their former occupation by vultures.

VULTURES

An adult Cape Vulture cruises slowly past its nesting colony against a flat bushveld backdrop in southern Botswana. Its very pale plumage distinguishes it from the darker, smaller Whitebacked Vulture which rarely, if ever, settles on cliffs. Young Cape Vultures wander great distances across the subcontinent in the five to six years before they attain adulthood. Some return to their natal colonies to breed, while others nest at more distant colonies. Once established, pairs tend to breed with the same partners and on the same ledges year after year.

HOODED VULTURE

Hooded Vultures occur widely in Africa, extending eastwards from Senegal, where the type specimen was collected in 1823, through the northern tropics to Sudan, Ethiopia and Somalia, and thence southwards into southern Africa.

West African Hooded Vultures are regarded as a subspecies of those in southern Africa, but if one compares the general habits and ecology of the two races, they could be quite unrelated species. In West Africa the birds' choice of habitat ranges from the arid desert fringes to the edges of lowland forest, where annual rainfall exceeds 2 000 millimetres.

From a West African perspective they are the most abundant vulture species on the continent. But this is in marked contrast to the situation in southern Africa: here they are scarce or rare (and are listed as such in the South African Red Data Book of Birds); they occur only in savanna habitats; they are mainly confined to the larger game reserves and national parks; they are usually solitary or found in pairs, and only rarely in groups of a dozen or more, and they are shy creatures that avoid rural settlements. In West Africa pairs breed semi-colonially in the tall trees that grow around villages, whereas in southern Africa they nest solitarily, their structure often well-hidden in foliaged trees along river edges. The contrast is indeed extraordinary, and it suggests that the two subspecies never mix.

Their commensalism with man in West Africa probably originated in the distant past when villagers acknowledged the usefulness of these free garbage disposers in their midst, and a kind of symbiotic relationship has endured to the present time. In southern Africa, and for reasons that have not been properly explained, no such relationship evolved, so here the birds remain shy and non-gregarious, and reliant for much of their food on the left-overs of carcasses provided by predators. Because of its small size, the Hooded Vulture tends to be dominated by other vulture species around the kill, and although it is sometimes the first bird to find the carcass, and is often the first to feed, it is soon displaced when the hordes arrive. It then has to wait, or to pick up scraps that are dropped in the mêlée, until the larger birds are satiated.

The Hooded Vulture with its 1,7-metre wingspan is one of the smallest African vultures, similar in size to the Egyptian Vulture and not much bigger than the smallest of all, the Palmnut Vulture. It is a mainly brown bird: juveniles are wholly brown except for the unfeathered dull white face and throat, but in adults the brown is relieved by some small white patches. The patches, situated on the thighs, the back of the head and around the crop, signal the birds' adulthood to other members of the same species in face-to-face confrontations or when flying in to land. The face and throat of the adult is bare-skinned, as it is in the juvenile. This skin is pale pink in normal circumstances but is capable of changing to crimson in moments of excitement.

Immature Hooded Vultures are fairly similar in appearance to the immatures of the Palmnut and Egyptian Vultures and, when there is no scale to show the size difference, may also be mistaken for the young of the much larger Lappetfaced and Whiteheaded Vultures. The slender bill shape and bare-skinned face of the Hooded Vulture will distinguish it from the Palmnut Vulture; the square rather than wedge-shaped tail will separate it from the Egyptian Vulture; and the two large vulture species have heavy powerful beaks which are quite unlike that of the young Hooded Vulture.

Their annual cycle is much like that of other vulture species. Pairs remain together and return each year to the same nest to breed, laying their single white egg during June or July. The parents take turns to incubate the egg, which hatches after about 51 days. The nestling period is variable, lasting three to four months, and the fledged chick remains dependent on the parents for up to six months afterwards, so that most Hooded Vulture pairs are preoccupied with the breeding process for most of the year.

The Hooded Vulture is distinguished from most other vulture species by its small size, its long, slim beak, its ruff of brown feathers and its pale throat and face. This species is usually found singly or in pairs, but occasionally larger numbers gather to feed on a large carcass. Hooded Vultures often associate with other vulture species, feeding alongside them on the ground or perching with them in tall dead trees. They are dependent on thermals for soaring flight, and wait in trees until conditions become favourable.

WHITEBACKED VULTURE

The similarity between an end-of-year sale at a giant department store and the average vulture feast is remarkable. In both cases the action begins with a free-for-all scramble for the doors, followed by shoving and jostling at the bargain counters and ends with the most robust and pushy customers staggering off with their spoils, leaving the store's depleted pickings to the timid and the latecomers.

Vultures are often led to carcasses by Bateleurs. These birds have a remarkable ability to locate carrion, and their low-circling descent is a signal to an armada of airborne scavengers that something of interest is down there.

The next arrivals are usually a Whiteheaded Vulture and a Hooded Vulture or two, planing in one after the other, alighting in the trees alongside the Bateleur, and eyeing the carcass warily. Another Whiteheaded Vulture arrives and, more courageous than the others, drops to the ground, pausing and looking around before sauntering towards the dead animal. Moments later the other birds flop down and approach. The little Hooded Vultures slouch in hurriedly while the two Whiteheaded Vultures start jostling for possession of the carcass.

The time they have for a relaxed meal is fast running out, however: already the real carcass-hogs are appearing in the sky above them. Moments later the first of the Whitebacked Vultures sails in and settles on a branch, and within 10 minutes there are 30 or so sitting in the nearby trees and others are drifting in by the minute. At first they look disinterested in the meal. Suddenly, as if responding to a dinner gong, a few drop to the ground and approach the carcass, and then a flood of Whitebackeds rush it in leaps and bounds, with pig-like squeals and flapping wings, and within seconds a mass of ravenous birds are jostling and fighting for space. The Whiteheaded and Hooded Vultures are swept aside by this Whitebacked Vulture phalanx, and for the next half hour they can do little more than hover about the fringes, snatching scraps that are dropped during sparring matches. As the Whitebacked Vultures are satiated, so one by one they emerge from the mêlée, bloodied and dirty, and with bulging crops. The gaps are immediately filled by newcomers. In minutes the carcass is reduced to skin and bones.

Almost too late, the first Lappetfaced Vultures plane in and land with a bounce on the ground. They bound up with spread wings, their sheer size and demeanour clearing a path before them, although they often get sidetracked from the business of feeding by engaging in disputes with each other.

VULTURES

Whitebacked Vultures have a remarkable ability to fill their crops quickly, doing this within two to eight minutes. A hundred of these birds can strip a 50-kilogram carcass in a mere three minutes. They have long beaks with a strong hooked tip and sharp cutting edges, and a serrated, stiff tongue which enables them to shovel food down their throats. Their heads and necks are not feathered but rather covered with short down, and their necks are long, enabling them to insert their heads deep into the carcass to feed on the intestines, organs and muscle of the animal. They do not have the strength or equipment to tear off and eat skin – and this is where the Lappet-faced Vulture scores: it is able to feed after the other vultures have finished.

Whitebacked Vultures occur in the savanna regions, extending from West and East Africa and southwards into Namibia, Botswana, Zimbabwe, the northern Cape, Transvaal and Zululand. They are by far the most numerous vulture species on the subcontinent, their populations being densest in the big national parks and game reserves, where large predators occur. In many respects they are a smaller version of the Cape Vulture, both being social foragers and both breeding colonially. In fact, the two species are often found together at carcasses. Whitebacked Vultures, however, do not nest on cliff ledges, as do Cape Vultures, but instead build a stick nest in the top of a tall tree. A colony of 10 or more pairs may be found in the tops of neighbouring trees.

These breeding colonies are sometimes located at the centre of lion pride ranges, and one assumes that the vultures are so positioning themselves to enhance their chances of finding prey. Whitebacked Vultures also occur in many cattle-ranching regions from which large predators have disappeared. In such areas their numbers and breeding success are affected by the vagaries of weather: in the rainy years times are lean, but in periods of drought they are favoured by the often high mortality of herbivores.

Like other vultures, this species breeds in winter and its single white egg is laid during April to July. The sexes share parental duties. The incubation period lasts 56 to 58 days and during the first 50 days of its life the chick is constantly attended by one or other parent. The off-duty mate spends its time away foraging and when it returns it regurgitates food from its crop to feed the chick.

A Whitebacked Vulture (opposite) broods its chick on its treetop nest. Breeding takes place in winter when the trees lose their foliage, rendering the nests very conspicuous.
(Below) Using its large feet as air-brakes, a Whitebacked Vulture planes in to land.

LAPPETFACED VULTURE

No vulture can really be described as attractive, but some are certainly impressive-looking – and the Lappetfaced, with its massive 2,6-metre wingspan, black plumage and wrinkly red head, is among the most imposing. The adult birds are mostly black but have white leggings (the tibia); white down on the breast and neck, which shows through to varying degrees; and a thin line of white feathers on the underwing near its leading edge, which is visible only when the bird is seen in flight from below. Males and females are similar in appearance, but immature birds lack the white features of the adults, have blackish-brown leggings, and at close quarters their bare heads are dull pink rather than red. The white plumage signifying adulthood is acquired over a period of four or five years. The lappets – lobe-like flaps – which give the bird its name are present from the day of hatching.

Lappetfaced Vultures are, typically, birds of the more arid areas, and in southern Africa their numbers are greatest in the Namib and Kalahari deserts, and in the low-rainfall Limpopo corridor between Zimbabwe and South Africa. Small numbers breed elsewhere on the subcontinent, the most southerly in the Umfolozi Game Reserve in Zululand.

The spatial and social arrangements of this species fall somewhere between those of the colonial vultures (like the Whitebacked) and those of the solitary, territorial Whiteheaded Vulture. The pairs tend to nest in clusters – not colonial to the extent of the Whitebackeds, as their nests are seldom closer than a kilometre apart, but near enough for neighbours to watch each other's movements. They join other vulture species to feed at carcasses but not in great numbers (no more than four or five, and usually only one or two, at a single kill), and are usually the last to arrive at the orgies, often finding only the leftovers – skin and bones – which, with their heavy beaks, they are better able to demolish than other vulture species.

The Lappetfaced Vulture's breeding cycle is protracted, and most pairs do not breed annually unless they have lost a clutch or brood. In normal circumstances they breed biennially. Their nests are flat platforms of sticks, up to two metres in diameter, placed atop and often covering the crown of a tree. In May or June they lay their single egg, larger than that of any other southern African bird of prey and often marked with reddish blotches. The incubation period is a lengthy 56 days or so. Both parents share the incubation, brooding and feeding duties.

The nestling period is also protracted, lasting at least four months, so that the chick fledges in November or December. Its last two months in the nest is a lonely time, with no more than a brief visit by a parent perhaps once a day. It is still dependent on the adults for food for some time after fledging, and young birds have been recorded visiting their nests as long as 293 days after fledging.

With their small, scattered breeding populations in southern Africa, their low recruitment rate, and the practice, employed by some farmers, of poisoning carcasses, the Lappetfaced Vulture is undoubtedly a threatened species.

The massive Lappetfaced Vulture is one of the world's most impressive birds of prey. When seen perched, it appears wholly black except for its red, wrinkled head, but seen in flight the characteristic white leading edges of the underwing and the white thighs become visible. Its 2,6-metre wingspan is amongst the largest of the raptors'. Although scarce over much of the subcontinent and confined largely to the large game parks and to semi-desert and desert areas, vagrants move about widely and may appear anywhere.

WHITEHEADED VULTURE

Seen at close quarters the Whiteheaded Vulture appears rather like a character out of the Rocky Horror Picture Show – almost comic in its multi-coloured ugliness. But observed from a distance, sailing high overhead, it is a dignified, very striking-looking bird of prey. At this range it presents a black-and-white chequered pattern, with white head and crop, black chest, white belly and thighs, black tail, black wings broken by a bold white line running their length and, in the female, a bold white panel in the secondaries.

Only from fairly close quarters can the oddly marked head be seen. The white, down-covered area which gives it its name is like a skullcap leading down the back of the head. In front, on the cheeks and throat, is bare skin, which can be pink or red depending on the bird's state of excitement. The bill is also reddish but is separated from the head by a blue cere. The eye is yellow. What purpose is served by this mix of colours is one of many unanswered questions about this unusual vulture.

Why, for example, is its social dispersion so different from that of other vultures? Nesting pairs are widely and evenly spaced and no more than two adult birds, a male and a female, may be seen together at carcasses with other vulture species, or indeed in any situation. This supports the conclusion that Whiteheaded Vulture breeding pairs are territorial. Adjacent nests are usually between eight and 15 kilometres apart and, based on this spacing, territories are at least 5 000 hectares and usually more than 10 000 hectares in extent.

The explanation normally given for the sociability of other vultures is that of collective benefit: the effort of defending an exclusive territory in which to forage is outweighed by the advantages to be gained by searching in groups for food which, when located, is sufficient for all. The same formula obviously does not apply to the Whiteheaded Vulture. Although they do join other vulture species at large carcasses, they often fail to get a meal there because of the fierce competition. The remains of prey found at their nests suggests that they often feed on carcasses of much smaller animals – a dead mongoose, for example, which would be too little for a flock of social scavengers but enough for a solitary Whiteheaded Vulture. Thus, if they are indeed largely dependent on small carrion, this may explain why the cost-benefit equation that prompts sociability among Whitebacked and Cape Vultures does not work for this particular species. But then another question arises: how do they come by these carcasses? A partial answer to this is that, on occasions, they pirate food from other predators.

The species appears to have much in common with the Bateleur. Both scavenge, both live in pairs, and both are territorial. Like the Bateleur, the Whiteheaded Vulture is confined mainly to southern Africa's large conservation areas. Another similarity – a curious one, though perhaps more than coincidental – is that they are both sexually dimorphic, males differing from females in the amount of white showing on the wing. In both species it is the female which has the more extensive white area.

Whiteheaded Vultures nest high up on the tops of tall trees, often baobabs or large acacias. Some pairs have two or more nests which they use alternately, and most breed annually, laying their single-egg clutch in May to July. The parents share the responsibility for incubating, brooding and feeding the chick. The precise incubation and nestling periods are not known but are thought to be as lengthy as those of the Lappetfaced Vulture.

Immature Whiteheaded Vultures take several years to acquire the distinctive plumage of the adults and during this stage are wholly dark brown, easily confused with other brown-plumaged vultures. When seen in flight from below they have a narrow whitish line running outwards along the centre of the wing and this is a useful identification pointer.

As illustrated by the laboured flight of this Whiteheaded Vulture, becoming airborne can be energetically expensive for these birds. However, once sufficient height has been gained and the bird can take advantage of warm rising air currents, its flight becomes almost effortless. This is one of the few vulture species in which the sexes can be distinguished at a glance: here, a female shows the diagnostic white secondaries in the wing. The bird's bare-skinned face is normally pink, but it flushes red during moments of excitement. Young birds have uniform brown down-covered heads.

VULTURES

Kites and Allied Species

The five species included in this group are very much a mixed bag, put together for convenience, and do not reflect any taxonomic affinity. Only one of the five, the Black Kite, is a true kite. This bird, like the other kites of the genus *Milvus*, is a bold, mainly scavenging species with a dexterous, graceful flight, and the ability to swoop quickly to the ground to snatch a food item. By contrast, the Blackshouldered Kite hunts mostly from a perch, and sometimes by hovering, and it lives largely on rodents; the Cuckoo Hawk and Honey Buzzard are lethargic predators, the first catching insects and small reptiles and the latter preying on the larvae and pupae of wasps which it locates by clambering about in trees. Only the Bat Hawk can be considered highly rapacious, hunting bats on the wing by hot pursuit at dusk and dawn. Honey Buzzards are non-breeding migrants to southern Africa and the other four species breed in the region, all building a stick nest in a tree.

When viewed head-on, the similarity between a Cuckoo Hawk (left) and the African (or European) Cuckoo is remarkable, and the reason for the name given to this bird of prey becomes apparent. Both are mainly grey with barred underparts, and yellow feet and eyes. (Above) An immature Yellowbilled Kite.

BLACK KITE

The Black Kites one sees in southern Africa during the summer months belong to two different populations, the one breeding in Europe and overwintering in Africa and the other resident in Africa but migrating within the continent. In the past they were treated as two species: the European birds were termed Black Kites and the African population Yellowbilled Kites. Today they are regarded simply as two well-defined races of the same species.

Both races arrive in southern Africa during August and September and depart again in March. The Black Kites follow the routes taken by many migrating birds of prey to and from Europe: they funnel through the narrowest land crossings of the Mediterranean Sea – the Straits of Gibraltar and the Sicilian channel – or go around the eastern edge of the sea and over Israel. These birds breed in the Palearctic and are non-breeding visitors to southern Africa.

The yellowbilled race of the Black Kite has a more complicated migratory behaviour than that of the Palearctic birds. This behaviour has not, to date, been explained adequately. This race is migratory right across its African range, which extends from East and West Africa southwards virtually to Cape Town. It moves into this area between August and March and breeds throughout the region during these months. However, many of the Yellowbilled Kites coming into southern Africa in this period are non-breeding visitors, and where and when they breed is uncertain. Where the population goes to outside of the breeding season is also speculative. Present opinion is that their main winter quarters are along the southern fringes of the Sahara Desert.

In southern Africa the two races often mingle in mixed flocks and, with a little care, can be distinguished from each other. In size, general body proportions and overall coloration they are very similar. The European birds have paler, greyish-streaked heads and less deeply forked tails than their African counterparts, and their bills (though not their ceres) are black, whereas Yellowbilled Kites, as the name indicates, have all-yellow bills, and their head colour is the same uniform brown as the rest of their plumage. Unfortunately the immatures of the two races are not as easily distinguished as the adults, as the distinctive forked tail and yellow bill and cere of the yellow-billed race are not well developed in young birds. There are also several other races of the Black Kite (found in Asia and Australia) and they have yet another suite of plumage characteristics. Occasional vagrants of these may find their way to southern Africa from time to time.

'Mystery' kites are occasionally reported on the subcontinent but whether they belong to one or other of these races or to the other European *Milvus* kite, the Red Kite, is uncertain. This latter bird is not known to migrate into the Afrotropical region but remains in Europe, breeding in the north in summer and moving southwards to the Mediterranean countries during winter. It has a deeply forked tail and is chestnut-coloured except for the pale head and large, almost white panels in the outer wings which are very conspicuous when the bird is seen in flight. Because of their localized occurrence the likelihood of Red Kites reaching southern Africa is remote.

The simplest approach in identifying the array of age and racial variations found in the Black Kite is to simply refer to them collectively as '*Milvus* kites', a term which also overcomes the ambiguous meanings of the black and yellow-billed adjectives.

The kite flocks one sees in southern Africa are nomadic. They are occasionally seen in great numbers (even in their thousands) but usually in groups of 10 to 20. They have a buoyant, easy flight, flapping and gliding at near-stalling speed, swooping gracefully down to snatch a food item, their long, forked tails controlling their movement. They often gather ahead of a bush-fire, flapping and soaring above the flames, seizing insects that are swept upwards, holding these in a foot and leaning forward to eat them while on the wing. They also forage along motorways, feeding on birds and small animals – and even other kites – that have been killed by the traffic. They are primarily scavenging birds, eating at carcasses when they can, living around refuse dumps and rural villages and, sometimes, thieving food morsels from visitors to game parks.

In past decades *Milvus* kites were far more abundant and widely distributed than they are today. As a group, the scavenging birds of prey – the Bateleur

KITES AND ALLIED SPECIES

When seen on the wing, the Black Kite (above) is easily distinguished from other similar-sized hawks by its easy, buoyant flight, long, thin wings and long, forked tail. It is less easy, however, to distinguish between the two subspecies of Black Kite that occur in southern Africa during the summer months: in comparison with the Yellowbilled Kite, the adult Black Kite (top) has a less deeply forked tail, a blackish bill with a yellow cere, and a streaky grey head.

and Tawny Eagle, the vultures, the *Milvus* kites – are extremely vulnerable to uncontrolled use of poison by farmers who lace carcasses or meat baits with toxins to kill jackals and other vermin. Usually the prime target, the wily jackal, evades the bait, which is taken instead by one of these birds, which have no defence against baits that have been poisoned.

The Black Kites that breed in southern Africa may associate at times with the non-breeding mixed flocks, but just as often occur solitarily. Pairs return to the same sites year after year, build their smallish stick nests, line them with dung, rags and other rubbish and lay their clutch of two eggs during September to November. The female undertakes most of the incubation, and she is provided with food by her mate. The incubation and nestling periods are about five and six weeks respectively. Often both the young are reared.

It is unusual to find birds of prey, such as this Yellowbilled Kite, drinking, as they usually obtain all their moisture requirements from their prey.

KITES AND ALLIED SPECIES

The yellow-billed subspecies of the Black Kite is restricted to Africa. It migrates within the continent, and comes to southern Africa to breed in the summer months.

KITES AND ALLIED SPECIES

The Blackshouldered Kite is one of southern Africa's commonest and most widespread birds of prey. It favours open or lightly wooded country and is most abundant in farming areas, where it preys on small rodents. Ringing has shown that it is a nomadic species, staying for a time in an area while conditions are favourable, then moving to new hunting grounds, perhaps hundreds of kilometres away. It breeds at any time of the year, and may take advantage of brief population explosions of rodents by nesting twice or three times in quick succession.

BLACKSHOULDERED KITE

Blackshouldered Kites can often be seen perched on telephone lines alongside roads – two innovations that have had as great an impact on the bird's ecology as on man's.

Blackshouldered Kites live for the most part on small rodents. They catch what is available and what they can handle, and in much of southern Africa this revolves around only two or three suitable prey species: the diurnal Vlei Rat and Three-striped Mouse, and sometimes the nocturnal Multimammate Mouse. These weigh about 50 grams, 28 grams and 25 grams respectively, and one Vlei Rat or two of the smaller species constitutes a day's meal for an average non-breeding Blackshouldered Kite. Where they have the choice, the diurnal species live in areas with good grass cover, whereas the Multimammate Mouse, perhaps because it is nocturnal, is not so fussy. In much of southern Africa, roads have fences running along the sides and almost everywhere, but especially in lower rainfall areas, fences usually mean a denser grass cover in the road reserve than beyond the fence, where the land may be cultivated or heavily grazed. The fringes also benefit from extra rain runoff from the road. Rodents find road reserves particularly attractive to live in, and consequently so do Blackshouldered Kites.

The kites hunt by watching the ground below for movement, either from a perch or by hovering. The latter choice clearly involves much more effort, and all things being equal the birds will opt for perching. In many suitable hunting terrains (such as vleis) there are no perches, but along road reserves, there are almost always telephone lines and poles, affording them a low-energy means of exploiting the terrain.

When a kite leaves its roost in the morning, it takes up position on a perch and watches the ground below. For the first half hour this may be a rather desultory business but as time passes its concentration becomes sharper. On some mornings it is lucky: a fat little Vlei Rat will soon offer itself and, after a moment of head-bobbing and intent peering, the kite lifts itself off the perch and, with a few quick wingbeats, plunges into the grass and dispatches the animal with its sharp talons. This happens infrequently, but when it does the bird's real activity for the day is over. After a leisurely meal, ending with an awesome gulping down of the rodent's hindquarters, tail and all, the Blackshouldered Kite takes itself off to the interior foliage of a shady tree. Perhaps later in the afternoon it will soar about for a while, but for four or five hours it will put up the shutters.

More usually, though, it takes several hours to find prey. The kite changes perch every five or 10 minutes, either moving along the lines or to other vantage points, or it takes to the wing, soars up to a height of 30 or 40 metres and, facing the breeze, begins hovering, wings flapping rapidly, body angled according to the wind speed, head down, watching the ground below. It hovers for a short time – 10 or 20 seconds over one point – then breaks off, soars to another position, and repeats the process. When it spots a rodent it begins its dive in gentle fashion – wings held above the body, feet below, parachute-like – but in the last few metres it tilts forward and plunges in head first.

Not all strikes, either from perches or from hovering, are successful: the success rate is only about one in five. The difference between these techniques is that the reward comes much sooner from hovering. On average a hunting bird acquires its meal after 40 minutes in the air, but has to wait for more than two hours when perching. Thus hovering is a quicker but more energy-consuming way of obtaining prey and, in the final energy cost-yield equation, the one technique is about as profitable as the other.

The kite is something of a gambler and it will not start the day hovering when it may get a meal simply by sitting on a pole. As the day wears on, and as it gets hungrier, it will resort to the high-cost method. In consequence kites are seen hovering much more frequently in the afternoon than at other times. When they need more food than usual they hover more often than usual – so a breeding male, busy feeding his mate and offspring, hovers twice as much as a non-breeding bird.

Hunting kites have an effective way of warning intruding birds off their territory – they wag their tails up and down. This has the effect of a flashing white spot when viewed from above and is usually sufficient to prevent a confrontation.

While the adult Blackshouldered Kite is mainly white with black shoulders and wing-tips, and a grey back, the immature bird (above) is less attractive, being dull white, streaked with brown. (Right) A near miss! A sharp-eyed Blackshouldered Kite aborts a strike at a small rodent whose movement it detected in the grass moments before. These kites are successful in only about one in five attempts.

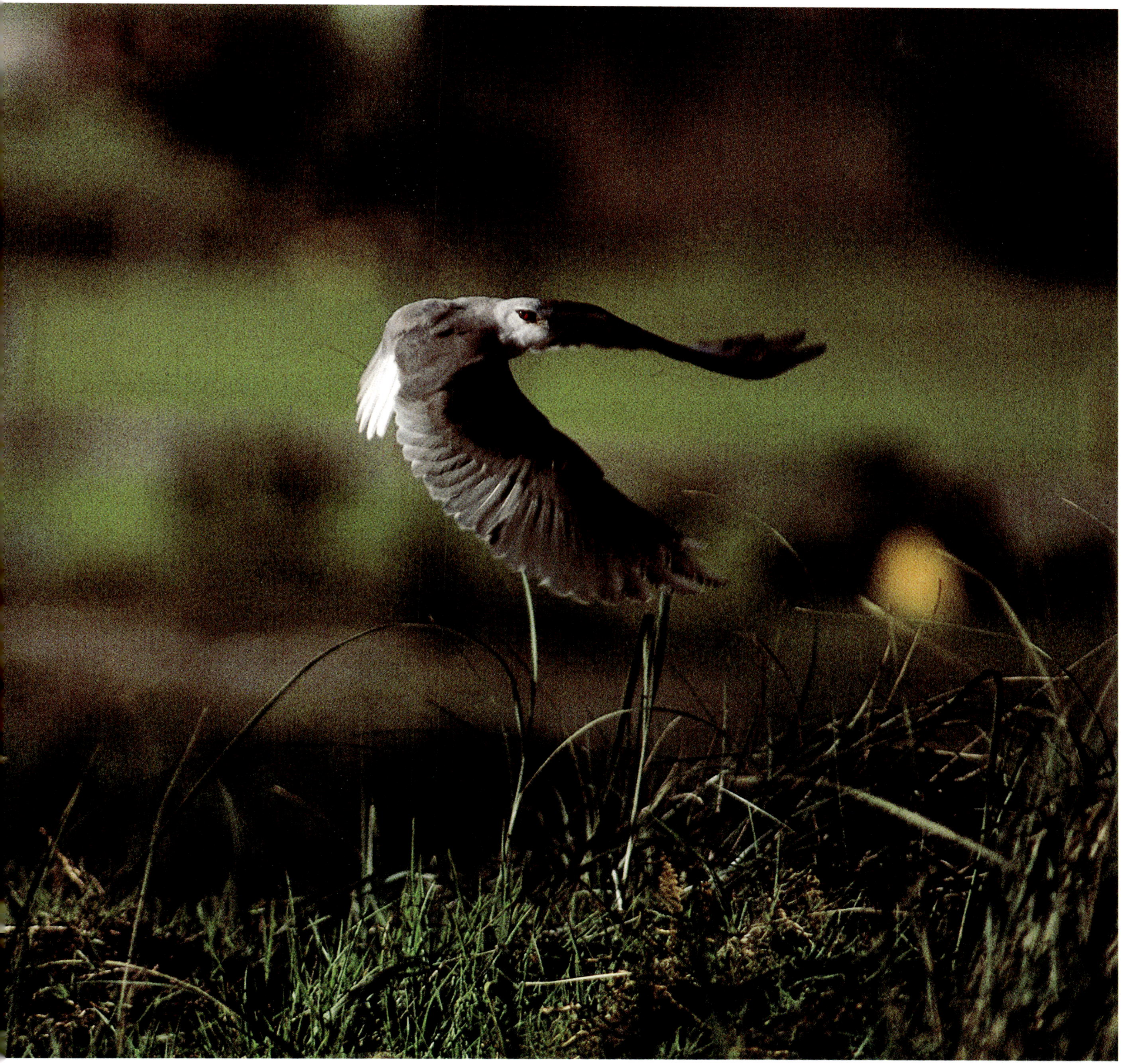

Cuckoo Hawk

The Cuckoo Hawk is the African member of a group of four closely related birds which are known as Bazas in Asia and Australia. They are long-winged, short-legged species with crests and boldly barred underparts and, superficially, most closely resemble goshawks. But despite their looks they are not closely related to accipiters. Rather, they are thought to have their nearest links with the kites. In the past they were called Cuckoo Falcons because of their notched bill, which is like the toothed bill found in the falcons, but their relationship to this family is even more remote and, in southern Africa, the latter name has been abandoned.

Cuckoo Hawks are found in the higher-rainfall, eastern side of southern Africa and nowhere are they common birds. It is difficult to put one's finger on what precisely constitutes their preferred habitat. They frequent tall, broadleaved woodland such as miombo; they use eucalypt plantations (at least for nesting purposes), and they are also regularly found in the galleries of tall trees that fringe some of the east-flowing rivers that extend northwards from Natal. Their hunting techniques almost belie the fact that they are birds of prey, for they often flop around in the crowns of leafy trees, or drop to the ground and walk about in the grass – looking for insects! The latter – and especially large green grasshoppers, mantids and hairy and hairless caterpillars – comprise much of their diet, though they also take chameleons and lizards, chicks from any birds' nests that they happen across, and the occasional rodent. Between foraging points they fly with a lazy wingbeat reminiscent of the flight of a harrier.

In many respects Cuckoo Hawks are unusual birds. Their plump appearance, short legs and bulging yellow eyes are incongruous for a hawk, and their habit of peering about myopically while foraging enhances their Billy Bunter image. They cannot easily be mistaken for any other species – their crest is a giveaway, and the broad bars on the chest and belly of the adult birds are very conspicuous. The sexes are alike in plumage and size. They are often found in pairs, even when they are not nesting. In spring the male, and sometimes the pair, soars above the nesting area uttering a clear whistling note. On such occasions one can see their chestnut underwing coverts (or 'armpits'), which is one of the diagnostic features in identifying the bird.

The pair share in the construction of the nest, which is positioned in a high fork of a foliaged tree. The materials they use are rather unusual: broken-off leafy branch ends, which they collect with much flapping and manoeuvring, and the eventual structure looks more like a fallen branch that has become entangled in the tree than a bird of prey's nest. One such nest took 11 days to build and consisted of 144 pieces of leafy twig. There must be a reason for such concealment; perhaps it is because they are ineffectual at defending their brood from predators and a disguised nest offers them some protection.

In October or November the clutch of two handsomely marked eggs is laid and incubation begins, a function also shared by the pair. Unlike most other birds of prey, each off-duty bird forages for itself and males have not been observed feeding their mates. Usually both the chicks are raised, and as they grow larger so they become more noisy, soliciting food with a loud, repeated 'ki, ki, ki, ki...' note that may be audible from half a kilometre away.

The young Cuckoo Hawk's markings are quite different from those of its parents. It is brown above with a white front, boldly spotted with dark brown, and, just as the adult resembles an adult African Goshawk, so the immature resembles an immature African Goshawk. There has been speculation about this similarity: has it happened by accident or by design – and if by design, what led to such mimicry?

Outside the breeding season, when the Cuckoo Hawk is not circling and calling or feeding its nestlings, it is an unobtrusive bird and is easily overlooked. At this time of year it often wanders away from its breeding site, sometimes extending into areas beyond its normal range and even straying on occasion into cities like Johannesburg and Pretoria.

The Cuckoo Hawk occurs singly or in pairs. It is usually seen flying with lazy wingbeats from one perch to another, or sitting quietly on a vantage point, surveying its surroundings. The boldly barred underparts and crest are distinctive features and, when the bird takes to the wing, its rufous 'armpits' are another clue to its identity.

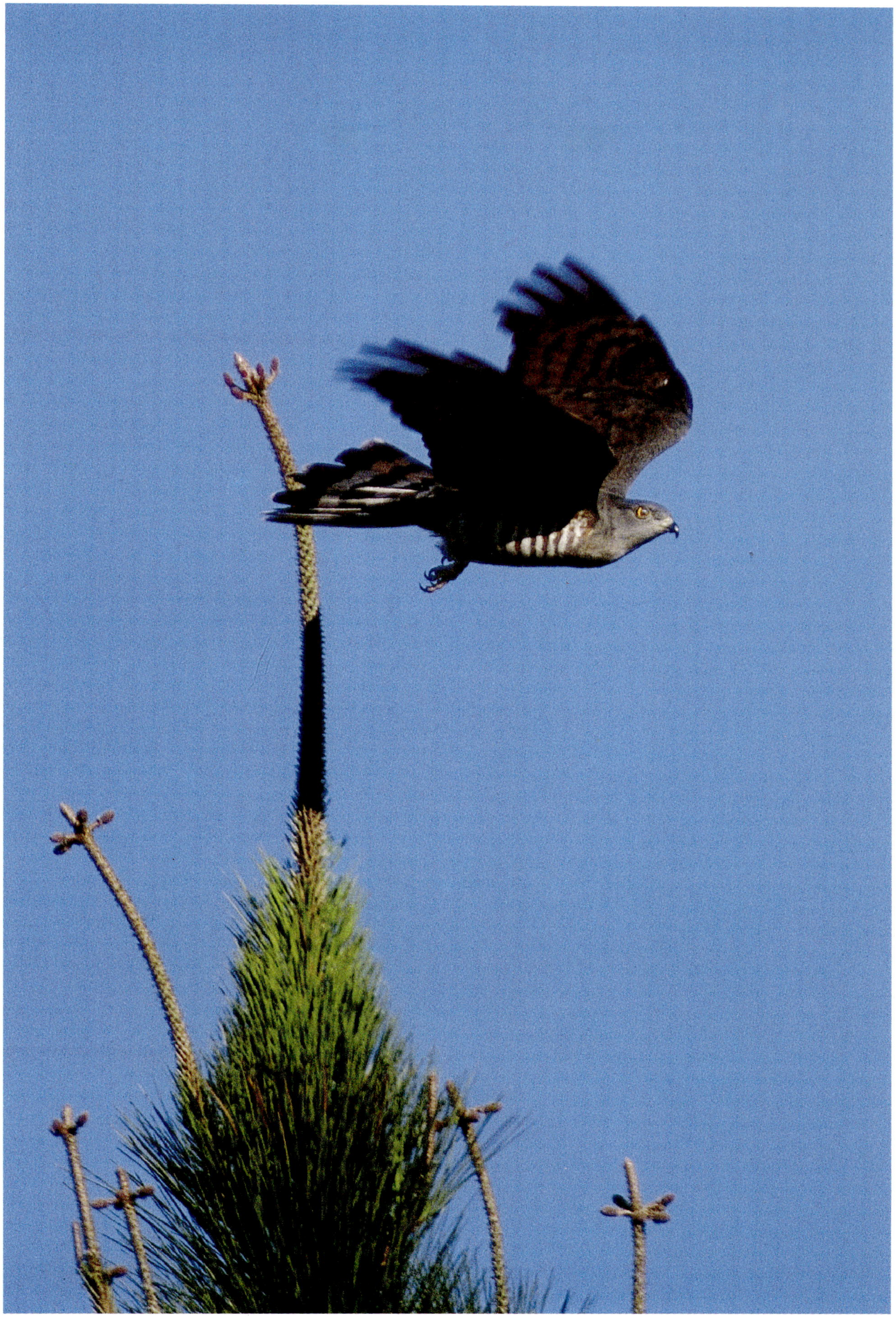

KITES AND ALLIED SPECIES

BAT HAWK

By day the Bat Hawk is a rather unspectacular bird, usually to be found sitting immobile, hunched up with head sunk into shoulders, eyes closed, high up in the foliage of a tall tree – a sombre brown, squat bird with striking white eyelids, a white chin and two white eye-spots on the nape.

This rare bird has an unusual lifestyle. During the day it is dead to the world, but as dusk approaches, the Bat Hawk starts taking an interest in its surroundings, preening and grooming. Then, without warning, it takes to the wing to hunt. As its name implies, it is a specialist in hunting bats and it does so in the short period of twilight between the time these flying mammals emerge and the time when it becomes too dark to hunt. This may last from 15 to 30 minutes, during which time the birds need to secure enough food to meet their requirements for the next 12 or 24 hours. Although their feeding behaviour is obviously difficult to observe, circumstances occasionally enable someone in the right place at the right time to make a detailed study. One such study was undertaken in Zambia, at a cave which the Bat Hawk visited for six successive nights in 1973. The bird arrived after sunset and hunted the emerging bats for, on average, 18 minutes each evening. It caught between four and 11 bats a night, rapidly subduing each with its talons before (usually) swallowing it whole. While bats comprise the main prey, the remains of small birds – swifts, swallows, martins, a nightjar, doves, a cuckoo and several others – have also been recorded in the hawks' pellets.

In southern Africa Bat Hawks are found widely but very sparsely, and with regularity only at their breeding sites: away from these, sightings are a rare and lucky event. Nesting occurs in summer, the single plain white egg appearing between September and November. Both sexes incubate the egg but the female's share of this duty is the larger. While one of the pair incubates, its off-duty mate perches quietly in a nearby tree. At dusk, when they need to hunt, both may leave the nest unattended for up to half an hour. This brief absence could expose the egg to predators, but it would not be long enough to chill the embryo at that time of the year.

The incubation and nestling periods of the Bat Hawk are 42 and 67 days respectively, but relatively little else has been documented about other aspects of the breeding cycle. When it hatches, the chick is covered in white down, which is gradually replaced with brown feathers as it gets older.

A Bat Hawk at its daytime roost, high up in the leafy canopy of a tall tree. This crepuscular species is rarely seen in southern Africa, the whereabouts of no more than a handful of nesting pairs being known from the region.

HONEY BUZZARD

Every autumn, upwards of 200 000 Honey Buzzards pour out of Europe through the sea crossings of the Mediterranean to spend their non-breeding season in Africa. Arriving in such large numbers one would expect them to be as commonly seen as, say, the Steppe Buzzard, but this is not the case: where they go to and what they do in Africa is little known. In southern Africa, no more than a handful are recorded each year. They are regarded, at best, as a scarce migrant on the subcontinent.

The paucity of records may in part be attributed to the difficulty often encountered in trying to identify the species: no two Honey Buzzards look precisely alike. Some are almost entirely white below, some dark brown and others intermediate in colouring; some have heavily barred underparts, others are streaked, and still others are unmarked. Thus, unless one knows exactly the diagnostic features of a Honey Buzzard and checks for these when observing the species, it is unlikely that the mystery bird will be identified by subsequent references to a bird guide.

To narrow the field, however: Honey Buzzards are buzzard-shaped and buzzard-sized hawks with small, pointed heads and rather large eyes. A few other raptors, including the Gymnogene, share these features. The Honey Buzzard's tail-barring pattern is its most distinctive characteristic. If you suspect that a particular bird could be this species, get into a position where you can clearly see its tail. If it has three dark bars across a lighter tail, two narrow and near the base and the third broader and at the end, it is definitely a Honey Buzzard.

'Wasp' Buzzard would perhaps be a more appropriate name for the species (and indeed it is so-called in German and Afrikaans) as these birds do not, as their English name suggests, rob beehives. In Africa, they live primarily on wasps and their larvae and pupae. Where there is an abundance of these insects in an area one or more Honey Buzzards may arrive and spend the entire season in residence, moving unobtrusively through the trees looking for, and eating the contents of, wasps' nests.

The Honey Buzzard has one of the most variable plumages of all birds of prey, ranging from almost white and speckled, like the individual shown here, to dark brown and heavily barred. All, however, have the characteristic three bars on the tail.

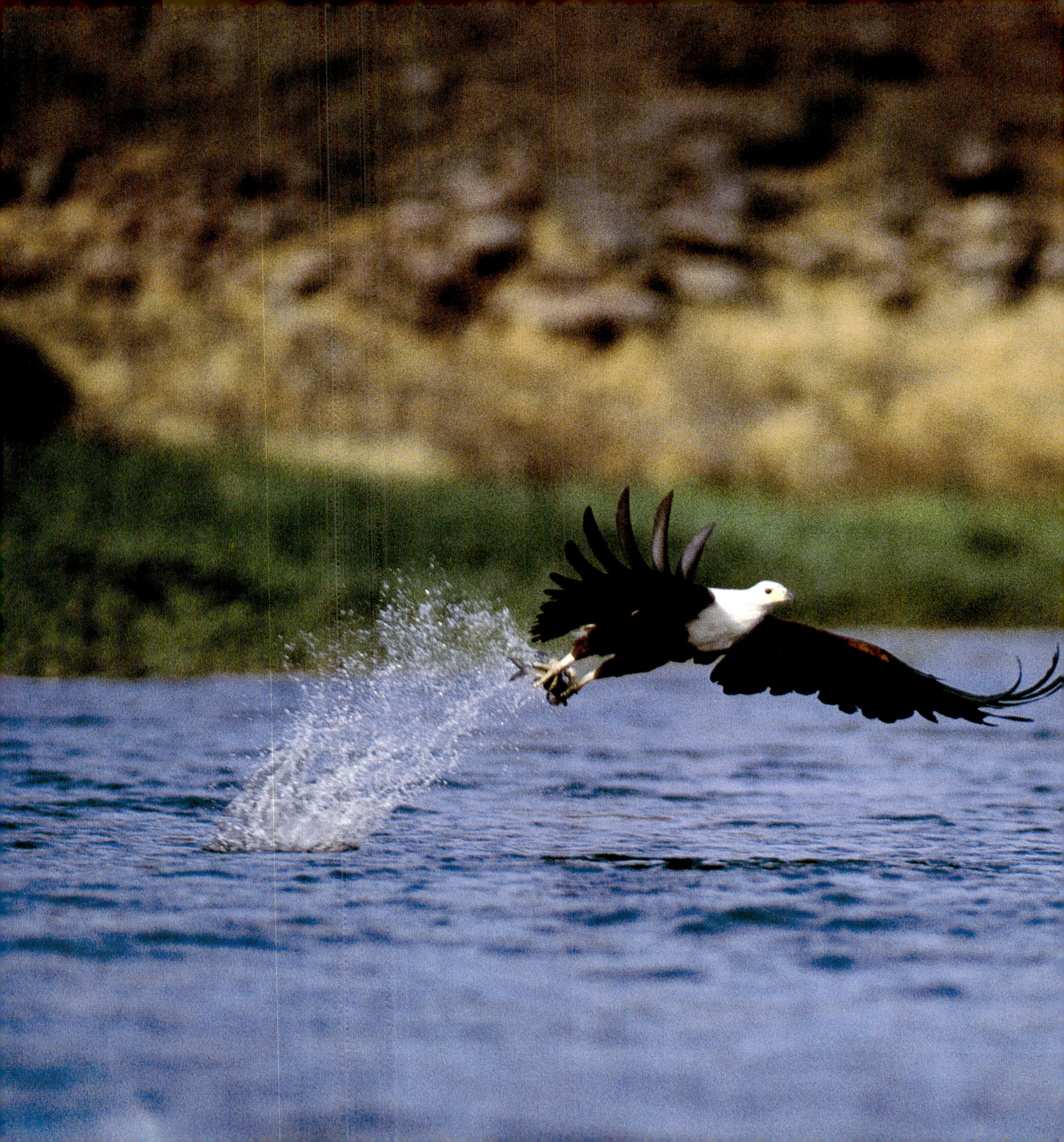

EAGLES

Like vultures, the eagles include several taxonomically unrelated groups of birds which have nothing more in common than their large size and predatory nature. Seventeen species are found in southern Africa: five 'true' *Aquila* eagles; three species of *Hieraaetus* ('hawk-eagle'); four types of snake eagle (once called Harrier Eagles for their harrier-like flight) and a fifth, 'honorary' member, the Bateleur; and finally a mixed bag comprising the Longcrested, Martial, Crowned and Fish Eagles. The smallest of the 17 is the Booted Eagle of the group *Hieraaetus*. This species may have only recently become established as a breeding bird on the subcontinent – it was first recorded doing so in 1972. The largest are the Martial and Crowned Eagles, the two most impressive and powerful avian predators in Africa. The African Fish Eagle is a *Haliaeetus* ('saltwater') species, and is closely related to the famed American Bald Eagle. This genus, dare it be said, is regarded as a derivative of the thieving, scavenging kite family, very distantly removed from the noble and dashing *Aquila* group.

(Left) Its slippery prey securely grasped, an African Fish Eagle lifts itself away from the water's surface. (Above) Ayres' Eagle, a denizen of the woodland.

BLACK EAGLE

Black Eagles, rocky hills and rock dassies go together. Find some boulder-strewn hills with a good population of dassies and a suitable nesting cliff and one is almost certain to find a pair of these magnificent eagles in residence too; and as likely as not it will be the shrill bark of a dassie that first alerts one to their presence. Black Eagles, known also as Verreaux's Eagles farther north in Africa, are among the aristocrats in the eagle world. They are true-blue *Aquila* eagles, large, powerful and so distinctive in shape and colour that they cannot be mistaken for anything else. Perched, they are entirely black except for yellow feet, yellow cere and a contrasting white V showing above the wings on their back. In flight the unfolded wings expose a completely white back, of which the V is the top end, and whitish panels in the outer wings which are visible from above and below. The wings have a characteristic spoon-handle shape, narrow at the base and broad towards the ends, a shape that must, somehow, facilitate their cruising slowly past a cliff face with wingtips almost brushing the rock or maintaining aerial control when accelerating in to snatch a dassie off a boulder.

Rock dassies, which share the Black Eagle's mountain habitat, are the bird's main, and often only, prey. There are two species of these furry, tailless little animals which are so common in some areas. Both live in colonies from a few individuals to hundreds, and they are often to be seen scurrying about on the rocks or sunbathing in exposed positions. They are diurnal and feed on grass and leaves, and sleep and shelter in holes. They weigh two to four kilograms and are conveniently sized food parcels for a Black Eagle weighing four to six kilograms. A pair of eagles would need to take one dassie every two or three days to sustain themselves and perhaps one a day when they are feeding a growing nestling. They appear to be able to catch these surefooted, sharp-eyed creatures with no difficulty, sometimes swooping down on them from a perch higher up the mountain, sometimes sneaking around a corner and catching them unawares. Black Eagle pairs are often seen flying together and they probably also hunt in tandem, the one distracting the victim while the other attacks. To be consistently successful, however, probably requires that the Black Eagles know the location of every dassie family in their territory and the whereabouts of every dassie sunning spot and every dassie escape route.

Black Eagle territories probably vary in size according to the availability of prey. In the Matobo National Park in Zimbabwe where the Black Eagles have been the subject of a long-term monitoring programme that began in 1964, pairs occur at a higher density than has been recorded anywhere else in their range, at about one pair per 1 000 hectares. Most of the Matobo territories and nest-sites have remained unchanged year after year. The pairs that live year-round in these territories recognize and respect the boundaries of their neighbours and chase out intruding Black Eagles that violate their airspace. Actual physical clashes are uncommon and pairs occupying territories advertise their presence by perching conspicuously, soaring and performing their breathtaking display flights.

At the end of summer pairs start repairing their nests and the long breeding cycle gets under way. Not all pairs breed regularly and some breed much less frequently than others; on average breeding occurs in two years out of three. The same nest is often used year after year, or there may be two or three nests which are used alternately. Nests are almost invariably placed on a cliff ledge and with successive years of sticks being added, they often become very large. The biggest recorded nest was 4,1 metres high and it dwarfed the incubating parent.

During April to June the clutch of two eggs is laid and these are incubated by the female with some assistance from the male. They hatch after about 44 days and the chick makes its first flight some 13 to 14 weeks later, usually during September or October. Because the eggs are laid three to four days apart and because incubation starts when the first egg is laid, the hatching of the eggs is similarly spaced. This leads to cainism, which occurs in many birds of prey and is exemplified in the case of the Black Eagle. The larger, first-hatched chick attacks its younger sibling and eventually kills it. For this reason it rarely happens that Black Eagles raise two young, despite their normally laying two eggs. If events are manipulated and one of the chicks is removed and later returned then two young can be raised. Why lay two eggs if only one chick is going to be raised? One explanation is that the second egg is an insurance against infertility; another is that the chicks fight to compete for food. However, the 'Cain-and-Abel' struggle often goes on in nests literally heaped with dassie carcasses. Also, many other raptors lay one-egg clutches and these have as high a hatching success as Black Eagles. Neither of these explanations is convincing, and the subject therefore offers an interesting research challenge.

Unaware of the impending danger, a dassie crouches on its rocky perch. Moments after the Black Eagle has swooped in and snatched it, the lifeless animal will be presented at the nest, where a half-grown eaglet keenly awaits its parent's return. Black Eagles prey almost exclusively on dassies, and in bountiful times nests may be surrounded by half a dozen or more carcasses of this species, waiting to be eaten.

An adult Black Eagle is unlikely to be confused with any other bird of prey. Its jet black plumage is offset by its yellow feet, eyering and cere, and by its broad white back and barred inner primaries. The white back is almost concealed by the wings when the bird is perched, when only a narrow white V protrudes above the wings. Black Eagles are found throughout Africa wherever rocky, hilly habitat exists, and they reach their northern limits in the Middle East. They live in territorial pairs. In areas of optimum habitat they may be spaced at intervals of two to three kilometres; more usually, however, the spacing between neighbours is between five and 10 kilometres.

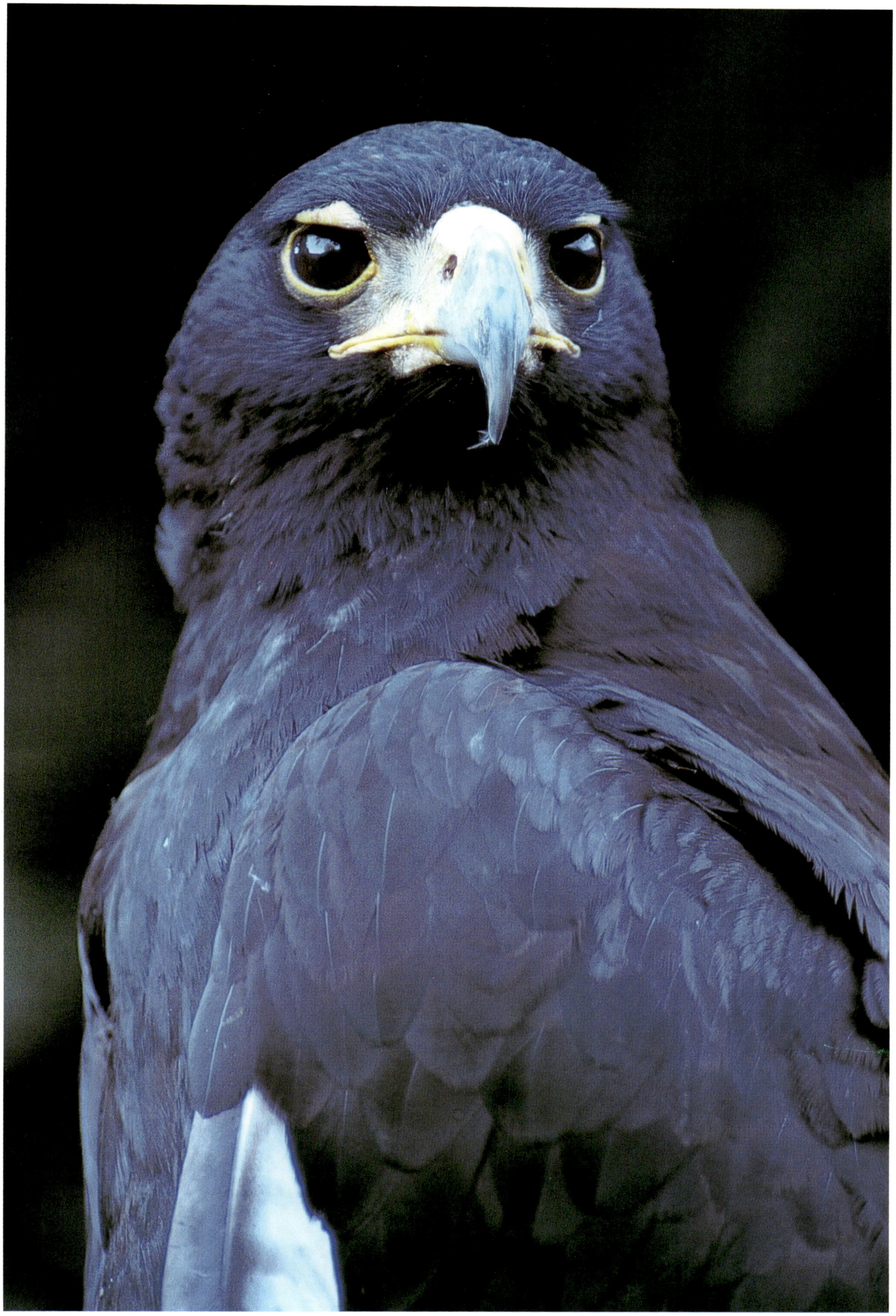

TAWNY EAGLE

The appropriately named Tawny Eagle is a medium-sized bird that is a characteristic species of the open acacia savannas of southern Africa. It is common in those national parks in which this habitat is represented (Kruger, Etosha, Kalahari Gemsbok and Hwange all have good populations) and it is still fairly frequently found in some rural areas. Its numbers have taken a knock in many of the more intensively farmed pastoral regions such as the northern Cape and Transvaal bushveld, where poisoned baits are used routinely in carnivore control. Because Tawny Eagles are partly scavengers in their feeding habits, they often become victims of this practice.

They are in fact particularly versatile birds of prey, scavenging and pirating when they can, and hunting when they cannot. They will eat anything from dead elephants to termites, their preference dependent on where they are and what is available. In the Karoo, for example, they prey mainly on suricate and yellow mongoose, which are common in the region; in the south-western Transvaal they take ground squirrels, yellow mongoose and guineafowl. At a number of savanna localities they have been recorded as primarily bird hunters, for the most part taking guineafowl and francolin. Reptiles, especially monitor lizards and snakes, sometimes feature significantly in a particular pair's diet, and occasionally termites are picked up off the ground during their brief emergences. The bird is also a notorious pirate, stealing from other raptors and especially from the Bateleur. In the Kruger National Park Tawny Eagles have been observed harassing Bateleurs to the extent that they succeed in pirating about one fifth of the Bateleurs' prey.

The Tawny Eagle's breeding cycle starts in early winter, and the clutch of two eggs is usually laid in May. Pairs tend either to re-use the same nest year after year or build another close by. These are placed, like those of many vulture species, on the very top of a large thorn tree, open to the sky. The structures are large and conspicuous and easily visible from the air. Because of this the nests can be located with the aid of aircraft, and their contents monitored. Such a study was conducted over a number of years in Zimbabwe's Hwange National Park, where some 177 breeding pairs are known to occur. In a total of 1 044 pair-years monitored, young were reared at an average of 0,6 per pair per annum. Not every pair attempted to breed each season, and the actual success of different pairs varied greatly. Hwange National Park is underlain in the north by nutrient-rich basaltic soils and in the south by nutrient-poor Kalahari sands; the Tawny Eagles occurred in both areas, but their density in the nutrient-rich habitats was much higher than in the poorer areas. They bred with equal success in the two areas but pairs required larger areas in which to secure their food in the nutrient-poor habitats.

The two eggs hatch after about 42 days, the second following two or three days after the first. Most of the incubation is undertaken by the female. The smaller, second-hatched chick is almost invariably eliminated by the cainistic behaviour of its older sibling; very rarely are both chicks raised. The young make their first flight when 11 or 12 weeks old and disperse to fend for themselves after a few months. Ringed chicks have been recovered up to 267 kilometres from the nest less than a year after hatching.

The plumage variation found in Tawny Eagles is often a source of confusion as they range in colour from blondes through tawnies and ginger-browns to dark browns, and some are streaked while others are plain. To some extent these colour variations reflect sex and age. For instance, young birds, on leaving the nest, are usually ginger-brown but the plumage fades to a pale brown or blonde colour. Over three or four years they gradually moult into adult plumage which, in males, is typically 'tawny' or golden-brown and, in females, is most often dark brown and streaked.

A Tawny Eagle nestling (opposite, above) adopts a threatening pose on its treetop nest. Despite its formidable-looking beak, such a young eagle will normally use its talons in defending its nest against an intruder. The eggs were laid in early winter when the surrounding bushveld was becoming brown and bare. Now, four months later, with the eggs long hatched and the surviving chick close to fledging, early rains have transformed the landscape and brought out the first blossoms on the knobthorns.
(Opposite, below) Tawny Eagles are variably plumaged birds, ranging from blondes and tawnies to gingers and dark browns.

EAGLES

EAGLES

STEPPE EAGLE

The Steppe Eagle is considered by most authorities to be a race of the Tawny Eagle rather than a species in itself, as it is treated here. From a southern African perspective the distinction between the two birds is obvious but elsewhere in their ranges, especially in Asia, the two forms interbreed to produce a spectrum of birds of intermediate plumage.

In contrast to the resident Tawny, the Steppe Eagle is a migrant that comes to Africa outside its April to August breeding season in eastern Europe and the Soviet Union. It is not to be confused with the Steppe Buzzard, which has a similar migratory pattern: the eagles even follow the buzzards' same north-bound and south-bound routes, avoiding the seas and funnelling around large waterbodies during their transcontinental journeys. At Eilat, in Israel, as many as 29 000 migrating Steppe Eagles have been counted, flying north to their breeding grounds, in a season – perhaps small beer compared with the flocks of Steppe Buzzards moving through but, for an eagle, an impressive number. It has been suggested that the adults and immatures have different seasonal ranges, the adults spending their winter months north of the Equator and the immatures moving south as far as southern Africa. This is partly borne out by the fact that most Steppe Eagles seen on the subcontinent are non-adult birds.

The immatures are easily distinguished from adults by plumage differences, and they are likely to be confused only with immature Lesser Spotted Eagles. They are generally a tan colour with two long, pale stripes running the length of the wing, one at the junction between the coverts and the remiges and the other along the trailing edge. These whitish bands are visible from both above and below. Moreover, they have a broad white rump and a pale rim to the tail, and these paler areas combine to produce a strikingly patterned bird. Adults, seen in small numbers in southern Africa, are a uniform dark brown with yellow feet and cere. One of their most distinctive features – by which they can be differentiated from Tawny Eagles – is their elongated gape. This extends beyond the eye, whereas that of the Tawnies stops short of the eye.

In southern Africa, Steppe Eagles are found mainly in the northern areas, in northern Namibia, Zimbabwe, and the northern and eastern Transvaal. They occur erratically, being common in some years and scarce in others and, during the months they are present (October to March), they move about widely. They are nearly always to be seen in groups, from three or four birds to flocks exceeding a hundred. They are often found in association with other raptors, especially Black Kites and Lesser Spotted Eagles.

The Steppe Eagle's nomadism and flocking behaviour is related to an unusual diet for so big a bird. In their breeding range they prey on small mammals, birds and reptiles, but in southern Africa they seem to feed mainly on termites. In drought years, when termite emergences are infrequent, the species is scarce; in wetter years, when the massive outpourings of termites from the ground are a common phenomenon, it is much in evidence. A bird of its size and nutrient requirement needs to eat about 2 000 of these insects each day. At first glance it is hard to imagine that termites are the best option available for so large an eagle. On the other hand, in good years termites are an abundant food source, easy and safe to catch and predictably located after rainstorms. Not only do they survive on this unusual diet in Africa, but they often put on a large amount of fat, which fuels them during their northward migration. Because they are not tied to the vicinity of a nest-site while in Africa they are able to move about widely in response to changing conditions.

The Steppe Eagle generally appears to be a darker brown version of the Tawny Eagle, and has a greatly elongated gape, clearly visible in the bird illustrated here. It is a non-breeding visitor to Africa from the Palearctic; most of the individuals reaching the subcontinent are immatures, easily distinguished from adult birds by their paler colouring and the presence of whitish panels and lines in the wings and on the rump. They are nomadic and often associate in flocks, mixing freely with Lesser Spotted Eagles and, sometimes, Black Kites. When not perched in trees or flying, they are often seen on the ground foraging for termites.

WAHLBERG'S EAGLE

In most people's minds the term 'eagle' conjures up an image of an enormous bird with a fearsome eye and a formidable pair of talons. In reality eagle species are many (no less than 17 in southern Africa alone) and varied, differing greatly in shape, size, colour and diet.

The Wahlberg's Eagle is a lightweight among the eagles and tends to be overlooked or regarded by the casual observer as 'just another brown hawk'. It is in fact the most numerous eagle species in southern Africa, and probably in Africa as a whole, and it is the most commonly seen eagle in the savanna regions. It weighs about a kilogram and has a wingspan of a little over a metre. It is brown from head to ankle, with contrasting yellow feet and cere, and it has a brown eye. The shade of brown, though, varies greatly, some being dark chocolate, most being 'medium', a few russet- or honey-coloured and about five per cent 'blonde' or almost white in colour. One occasionally encounters 'two-tone' birds with pale heads and dark bodies, or vice versa, and the identification of these can be problematical at times.

Wahlberg's Eagles migrate to southern Africa in August and depart again in March. Where they come from and where they go to is one of Africa's best-kept secrets. Many have been ringed, but so far there have been no recoveries from their winter quarters, which must lie north of the equator. In early spring, pairs return to their previous year's nest-sites, and either make repairs to their old structures or begin a new nest close by. In extensive suitable habitat pairs are spaced two to three kilometres apart and each ranges over an area of 10 to 20 square kilometres. They can be heard calling while they soar high above the woodland, uttering a plaintive 'kleeeeu' note. Because of the variability in their plumage it is often possible to recognize individuals, and some of these distinctively marked birds are known to have returned to the same nests and mates over a period of at least 14 successive seasons.

The nest is small by eagle standards: about 600 millimetres in diameter and less than half a metre thick. It is built high up in a tall tree and lined with green leaves, which are supplemented daily throughout the incubation period and well into the nestling time. Most clutches are laid in the two to three weeks around the end of September and beginning of October. Usually only a single egg is laid, though occasionally a particular pair will consistently produce two. In addition to the varied plumages, females can often be recognized by their egg markings – some lay white clutches, lacking any coloration or pattern, while the eggs of others are richly marked with dark red blotches. Most, however, are white with a scattering of reddish-brown speckles.

Incubation is usually undertaken by the female with minimal assistance from the male, who hunts and brings her food. The egg hatches after about 44 days. In those rare cases when there is a two-egg clutch, the second-hatched chick is killed by its older sibling. Most chicks are covered in dark brown down when small and are endearingly attractive. If, however, one of the parents is a blonde, there is a good chance that it will have pale offspring, off-white in colour right from the downy stage. They begin to feather when they are about three weeks old and make their first flight at about 10 weeks, usually in early January. In contrast to most eagles, Wahlberg's do not go through transition plumages from juvenile to adult, recently fledged young being similar in appearance to the adults. They rapidly become self-sufficient and leave southern Africa at the same time as their parents, in March.

Wahlberg's Eagles take a great variety of prey, and hunt in a number of different ways. They spend a lot of their day on the wing, soaring 100 metres or so above the ground. Depending on what kind of prey is sighted they make either a swift plunge or a gentle parachuting descent for the kill. With these techniques they catch bush squirrels, rodents, small mongooses and young hares, a great diversity of birds (but especially young gamebirds), many lizards, small snakes and frogs. There seems to be much regional variation in their prey preferences but, generally speaking, the most frequently taken prey are birds, followed by small mammals.

Wahlberg's tend to be understated eagles, often sitting quietly for long periods, lacking the verve of the larger, more spectacular species, but, in their own distinctive way, are both rapacious and elegant.

EAGLES

The Wahlberg's Eagle is a variably plumaged brown eagle, ranging from dark brown in colour, like the one illustrated above, to almost white. Sometimes the jizz of the bird is the only ready means of identifying it: the rather squat shape and the slight crest which gives the head a squared-off appearance are characteristic. However, despite the wide range of plumage coloration, the brown eye and yellow cere are constant.

Booted Eagle

The Booted Eagle's situation in southern Africa is both interesting and perplexing. It is essentially a Palearctic species which breeds in Spain, Morocco, France, Greece, Turkey and westwards into the Soviet Union. It frequents hilly, wooded country, nesting during the northern summer (May to August), then migrating to Africa to spend winter. A few of these migrants probably reach the southern end of the continent each year.

Booted Eagles have been known to occur in southern Africa since the first specimen was collected here in 1830. The birds were, understandably, always taken to be non-breeding migrants from the Palearctic. In 1917, however, a nest was found in the southern Cape which, with the wisdom of hindsight, must have belonged to this species but at the time was incorrectly ascribed to the Ayres' Eagle and so no further attention was paid to it. Then in 1972 a pair of Booted Eagles was discovered nesting in the western Karoo and, with the gates opened, a flood of hitherto unknown nesting pairs were discovered in the southern Cape.

The question arose whether this marked the start of a breeding colonization of the Cape by Booted Eagles or whether their nesting here had previously been overlooked; in view of the 1917 report the latter became the generally accepted opinion. No sooner had ornithologists revised their ideas – that there were two populations in southern Africa, one migrating here from the Palearctic during its non-breeding period, the other breeding at the Cape during August to December and moving north to overwinter – when, in 1983, two pairs were found nesting in northern Namibia in the supposed 'winter' quarters of the Cape population!

Despite other uncertainties, it is clear that the Booted Eagle has established itself as a breeding species in southern Africa in comparatively recent times. This species is now regarded as being relatively common in the southern Cape and its population here is thought to number at least 100 pairs.

Booted Eagle nests are very easily overlooked. In the southern Cape they breed in remote kloofs and ravines in the hilly country along the interface between the karoo and maccia biomes or between karoo and grassland. The nest is small by eagle standards and inconspicuous, usually positioned on a narrow ledge, and often tucked behind a shrub or tree growing from the cliff. Before laying their eggs the birds soar and call in the nesting area and perform impressive undulating display flights. They are conspicuous at this time of year, but once incubation begins they are much less in evidence. The incubating bird sits tight and does not flush easily from the nest. The Cape's Booted Eagles are taxonomically identical to those found in the Palearctic but they do differ in choice of habitat and nest site. European birds frequent more wooded country, and they almost always nest in trees.

Both the Palearctic and southern African Booted Eagles occur in two colour forms, the pale form having a dirty-white plumage and the dark form being brown; in both regions the pale form predominates. This species is one of the world's smallest eagles, males weighing 700 grams and females about one kilogram. The 'boot' refers to the heavily feathered legs but this is not a useful field identification character. A better one is the small white area found along the leading edge of each wing close to the body. Most birdwatchers rely on these so-called 'landing lights', present in both pale and dark birds as well as in immatures, to identify the Booted Eagle.

The clutch usually comprises two white, unmarked eggs. The female undertakes most of the incubation, during which time she is fed by the male. Incubation lasts about 40 days. Two young are sometimes raised in the same nest, although more often one dies at an early age: sibling aggression may account for some of the chick losses. The nestling period is unusually short for an eagle: it lasts from seven to eight weeks, and the young become independent within two months.

Booted Eagles take a variety of prey, with birds – larks, buntings, starlings, sandgrouse and others – forming the bulk of their diet. Lizards are also taken in number and rodents feature to a small extent. It is quite remarkable how, in the short space of 15 years or so, this bird has emerged from almost total obscurity in southern Africa to become a species whose population status and biology are now well known.

EAGLES

The Booted Eagle occurs in two colour forms, the more common (above) being brown above and whitish below, streaked with pale brown. The less common form is entirely brown. This species, about the size of a Steppe Buzzard, is the smallest eagle in Africa and one of the smallest in the world. Its 'boots' are its feathered tarsi, a feature shared by many eagle species.

LESSER SPOTTED EAGLE

This is one of two similar-looking Spotted Eagle species that breed in the Palearctic region and overwinter in Africa. It is the commonest eagle of the deciduous and coniferous forests of eastern Europe, and one of the smaller members of the family, the adult weighing about 1,5 kilograms (about the size of a Wahlberg's Eagle).

Many nestlings have been ringed in eastern Europe and several have been recovered in Africa, including one ringed in 1952 (in Latvia) and found in Zimbabwe in 1954, and an adult ringed in the Kruger National Park in November 1972 and recovered 11 months later in the Soviet Union.

At least 90 per cent of the birds coming to southern Africa are immatures, which are strikingly patterned when seen in flight and thus unlikely to be mistaken for the Wahlberg's Eagle. They resemble most closely the immatures of the much larger Steppe Eagle but, because the size difference is not a good field character, one needs to look carefully at the flight pattern to distinguish the two. Lesser Spotted Eagles have a line of bold spots, seen as a ragged white line, along the upper wing coverts. There is also a thin white line along the trailing edge of the wing and whitish panels at the base of the primaries. They have a U-shaped white rump. These pale areas occur on the same parts of the body as on the Steppe Eagle, but in the Lesser Spotted they are less extensive and consequently less striking.

While in Africa, Lesser Spotted Eagles share many of the Steppe Eagle's habits. The two species often occur together in mixed flocks; both are nomadic, moving about the country in response to changing conditions, and they both feed largely on termites. In some years Lesser Spotted Eagles are common whereas in others they are scarce or absent. They arrive in late October and depart again in March and, like the Steppe Eagle, the Lesser Spotteds are confined to the northern regions – northern Namibia, Botswana, Zimbabwe and the northern and eastern Transvaal. In Europe they prey mainly on small mammals such as voles, rats, mice and ground squirrels, but also take amphibians, reptiles and birds. In southern Africa they catch rodents and frogs but are most often observed at termite emergences and sometimes at quelea breeding colonies.

A brown bird of prey perched on a branch can be difficult to identify to species level. In this instance, the feathered tarsi show that it is a species of eagle, while the narrow 'stove-pipe' appearance of the legs, together with the absence of any crest on the head, indicates that it is a Lesser Spotted Eagle.

AFRICAN HAWK EAGLE

The savanna belt of Africa, beginning in somewhat straggly fashion in the eastern Cape and extending northwards up the continent to the edge of the Sahara, is home to a number of eagle species, but none is more characteristic of the biome than the African Hawk Eagle.

The belt includes the tall teak woodlands of northwestern Zimbabwe and northern Botswana, the climax miombo of eastern Zimbabwe, the marula-knobthorn parkland of the Transvaal lowveld, and the carpet of mopane in northern Namibia and the hot low-lying river valleys of the east. All of these habitats are occupied by the African Hawk Eagle. In the Transvaal lowveld, the average population density is one pair per 55 square kilometres; in Zimbabwe's Matobo National Park the figure is one in 36 square kilometres, while in the Waterberg plateau of the Transvaal the birds are much sparser, one pair occupying an area of 110 square kilometres. The pairs probably stay in the same territories throughout their lives, and the differences in regional density are probably linked to the availability of prey.

This highly rapacious species is medium sized, the male weighing about 1,2 kilograms and the female about 1,6 kilograms. They prey mainly on gamebirds, especially francolin, but also take guineafowl, which outweigh them, and sometimes catch such mammals as scrub hares and dassies, which may weigh two kilograms or more. Since they favour gamebirds, it is not surprising that they also take domestic chickens on occasion.

Pairs are often seen together, either perched near one another in a tree, or drawing ever-widening circles in the sky as they soar aloft. They often hunt in pairs, one bird diverting the attention of the intended victim while the other swoops in low and fast to make the kill. If their quarry escapes into a thicket the eagles are not averse, figuratively speaking, to rolling up their sleeves and going in on foot after the terrified francolin or guineafowl.

In the breeding season the nest becomes the focus of their activities. It is almost always placed in a tree (in fact there is only one record, from Kenya, of a cliff nest-site) and usually high up, either in the upper branches of a tall riverine species, or in a baobab, or in a hillside tree where the bird has a sweeping view from the nest. Some pairs re-use the same nest season after season, and these become very large over the years. One well-known nest on the hill behind Punda Maria camp in the Kruger National Park has been occupied for a very long time and is quite enormous. Other pairs may chop and change between nests from year to year. Recently the species has been observed nesting for the first time on electricity pylons and it will be interesting to see if this is the beginning of a new trend.

Egg-laying occurs during May to July, which is a month or two later than other winter-nesting eagles. The clutch normally comprises two eggs and, like most eagle species, the second-hatched chick usually succumbs to an early death from sibling aggression. The female undertakes most of the incubation, being relieved by her mate for short periods, when he brings prey and she leaves the nest to feed. The incubation period is about 43 days, which is short for an eagle of this size. Comparatively, the nestling period is even shorter – 60 to 70 days – and to date there has been no satisfactory explanation for these unusually short durations. For a few months the young African Hawk Eagle, recognizable by its brown plumage, can often be seen soaring with its parents in the vicinity of the nest, but it will have left by the start of the next breeding season. Pairs do not breed every year; on average they miss out one in three.

Adult African Hawk Eagles are easily identified. They are essentially black and white, black-backed and white in front with black streaks, the latter accounting for their scientific name *spilogaster* (spotted stomach). Females are invariably more heavily marked in front than males, and can be distinguished both by this feature, and by their larger size. The smaller Ayres' Eagle is somewhat similar in appearance but is darker, usually much more heavily marked in front, and lacks the African Hawk Eagle's white panels on the outer wings. Young African Hawk Eagles are rufous brown in front and dark-brown on the back, and in colouring resemble young Black Sparrowhawks. However, they have the typical eagles' feathered legs while the sparrowhawks' are long, thin, bare and yellow.

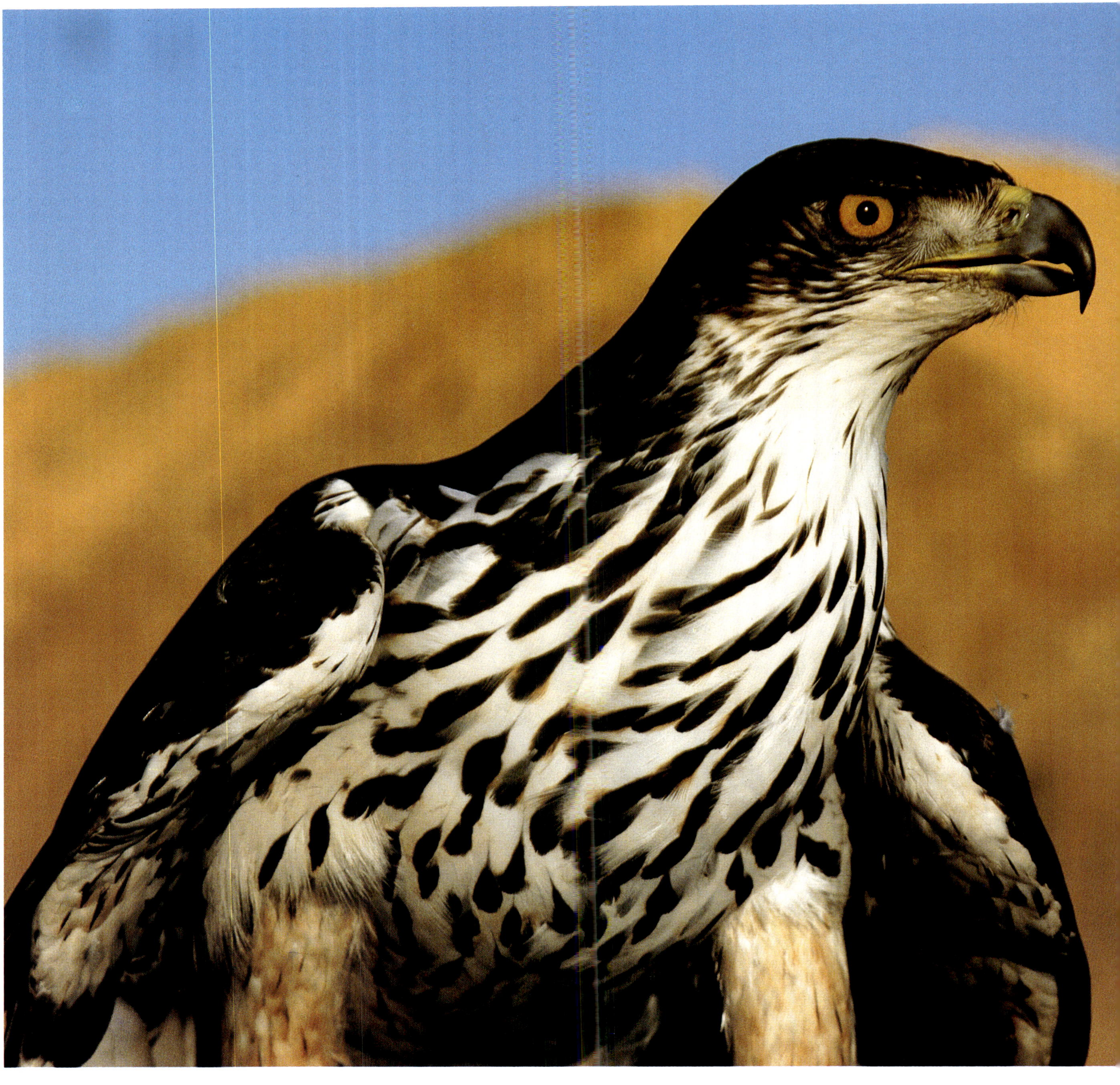

At a distance, the African Hawk Eagle appears to be black above and white below but, when seen at close quarters, its more intricately patterned plumage becomes apparent. The white front is boldly streaked with black, the female's more so than the male's. The upper wings are dark brown, with a contrasting pale panel towards the extremity of each. The male is noticeably smaller than the female and this is obvious when the birds are seen perched or soaring together, as they often do. African Hawk Eagles are more frequently encountered in pairs than any other eagle, and they often hunt as a team, one bird distracting an intended victim while the other makes the strike. These bold, rapacious eagles are often used for falconry.

EAGLES

AYRES' EAGLE

In an age when honouring people in birds' common names has become unfashionable, Thomas Ayres, the renowned 19th century bird collector, has fared better than most. Three southern African species are named for him and two of them – this eagle and the flufftail that carries his name – are rarities that are greatly sought after by birdwatchers.

Very little is known about the Ayres' Eagle on the subcontinent. It has a mystique all its own, created partly by its rarity and partly by the lack of information about it. It was dubbed 'the most dashing predator in Africa' by the late Leslie Brown, who conducted a 30-year-long nesting study of a pair in Kenya, and most of what has been written about the biology of this species is based on his work. The 'pair', which nested each year on a forested hillside, actually consisted of a succession of birds which were individually recognizable by their distinctive markings. The first male survived for eight years and his mate was replaced by a new bird, after six years. The longest surviving bird, a male called 'Old Whitey', occupied the territory for 11 years.

The Kenyan eagles nest in winter, laying their single-egg clutch during June to August, which is rather later than the few southern African recorded instances, in which eggs have been laid during April to May. In Kenya the entire incubation is undertaken by the female without assistance from the male, who hunts and brings her food at irregular intervals. The incubation period lasts for 45 days, and the female stays with the chick until it is well grown. Only then does she start hunting and helping the male provide for the nestling. The chick leaves the nest for the first time when it is about 75 days old and remains in the vicinity, where it continues to be fed by its parents for another month.

Ayres' Eagles prey almost entirely on birds, which they catch by hot pursuit, either from a perch or by soaring. They are formidable predators, described as having the speed of a falcon and the manoeuvrability of a goshawk, and adventurous ones, too, sometimes coming into towns and cities in southern Africa during the summer months. Between September and March in Bulawayo, for example, individuals are sometimes found loafing in the city's tall gum trees or sowing terror among flocks of pigeons. Of 176 prey items taken by Ayres' Eagles recorded in Bulawayo, nearly half consisted of Laughing Doves and two thirds were doves or pigeons of some sort. In Johannesburg a similar summer influx of non-breeding birds is recorded from time to time.

Ayres' Eagles are not known to nest in South Africa, and the few breeding records documented on the subcontinent are from eastern Zimbabwe. Just where the birds that visit towns and cities like Bulawayo, Johannesburg, Mutare and Nelspruit come from remains uncertain.

The species is superficially similar to the African Hawk Eagle, at least in published illustrations. In fact it is much smaller, proportionately shorter-legged, less aquiline and more like the Booted Eagle in build. Ayres' Eagles are generally dark above and heavily blotched below, with heavily barred wings and tail, and they do not have the pale panel in the outer wing that is so characteristic of the African Hawk Eagle in flight. The extent of the blotching on the Ayres' Eagle's front is variable and can be so extensive that the chest appears black. The amount of black and white on the head is also variable, individual birds ranging from being virtually white-headed to virtually black-headed (these were the variations that enabled the specimens at the Kenyan nest to be distinguished). They also have a white area on the leading edge of the wing, where it meets the body, giving it the 'landing lights' feature shared by the Booted Eagle. Young Ayres' Eagles are rufous to buffy brown, scaled on the back by pale edgings to the feathers and streaked with darker brown on the front. They resemble young Booted Eagles but are more extensively barred on the wings and tail.

It is an odd situation that this rare and little-known eagle is probably more likely to be seen flying over the Johannesburg Zoo or downtown Bulawayo than anywhere else in southern Africa.

The rarely encountered Ayres' Eagle superficially resembles the African Hawk Eagle, but is a smaller, darker bird, boldly barred on the underwings. It is heavily blotched, rather than streaked, in front, and lacks the pale wing panels characteristic of the larger species. Head colour is variable, some birds being dark brown and completely hooded (lower bird), others being partly hooded (upper bird).

LONGCRESTED EAGLE

Some people could find it difficult to be serious about an eagle with a comical, floppy, Woody Woodpecker-like crest. And it is not even a crest that can be raised or lowered: it simply hangs there, tousled by the breeze and flopping back and forth as the bird turns its head. Males and females both have crests and even young birds, just out of the nest, are characterized by this sprout of long feathers. It is not known whether, or to what extent, the odd-looking protruding feathers play a role in the species' daily life, or in its courtship or mating displays. Whatever the case, this curious feature renders the Longcrested Eagle unmistakable, and one of southern Africa's most easily identifiable birds of prey.

When the bird is in flight the crest is not visible as it lies along the nape. Identification is still easy, however, as these eagles have strikingly conspicuous white panels in the outer wing and bold white bars down the tail, both features contrasting strongly with their otherwise chocolate-coloured plumage. Most Longcrested Eagles also have contrasting white legs, but this is not invariable as brown-legged individuals do occur. Young Longcrested Eagles are similar to the adults in plumage.

Breeding Longcrested Eagles are restricted to the higher-rainfall eastern parts of the subcontinent, and inhabit well-wooded or forested country. Here they are likely to be seen perched quietly on a telephone pole alongside the road. They are buzzard-like in their habits, spending much of their time hunting from perches, scanning the ground below for prey. They are primarily rodent eaters, more so than any other eagle: 98 per cent of their recorded prey consists of rats and mice. The common, diurnal Vlei Rat, which weighs up to 200 grams, is the single most frequently taken species, and one or two of these fat little creatures each day satisfies the eagle's food requirements. A variety of other prey items has also been recorded – small reptiles, insects and even fruit – but these are incidental to the main diet; an unusual prey item recorded was a young Wood Owl, which was pursued in flight and killed.

In the past Longcrested Eagles were probably restricted to the edges of riparian and montane forest and to the woodlands fringing dambos in the higher-rainfall savanna areas. Now, with millions of hectares under plantation, the Longcrested Eagle has vastly more nesting habitat and a greater number of hunting perches available. This means that, though still restricted in range, it is probably commoner than it ever was. Only in the southern and eastern Cape do its numbers appear to have diminished. Outside the breeding season Longcrested Eagles occasionally wander beyond their normal range.

At times Longcrested Eagles can be noisy birds, making their shrill, whining 'keeeee-eh' call while soaring above the forest. These periods of frequent vocal activity are probably related to the onset of breeding activity. Breeding occurs erratically, with pairs sometimes missing a year and then raising two broods the following year. Egg-laying is also erratic, occurring any time between July and January. Most often, however, the eggs are laid during early summer, and especially in September.

The nest is a flat, leafy platform of sticks built high in a tree. One of the loftiest raptor tree-nests recorded in southern Africa belonged to a Longcrested Eagle. It was built 45 metres up in a massive eucalypt close to Tzaneen in the eastern Transvaal. The normal clutch comprises two white eggs, often marked with dark red blotches. Most of the incubation, which lasts about 42 days, is undertaken by the female. The nestling period, at around 55 days, is unusually short. Although only one of the young normally survives, there seems to be none of the sibling aggression so prevalent among other African eagles; the second-hatched probably dies of starvation.

As a consequence of its disappearance from the southern Cape forests, it was once thought that the Longcrested Eagle was a threatened species, and it was listed as such in an earlier edition of the South African Red Data Book of Birds. Farther north, however, it is doing well, albeit restricted to the relatively narrow breeding range described.

No explanation is needed as to why the Longcrested Eagle is so named. What purpose is served by the long, floppy crest, so at the mercy of every breeze, is not certain. Buzzard-like in nature, these eagles perch for long spells on telephone poles or in dead trees watching for a movement in the grass below. They prey almost entirely on rodents. Most birds have the white 'leggings', illustrated in the bird shown here, but a few differ by having dark brown tarsi. In flight they exhibit conspicuous white wing panels which contrast strongly with their otherwise chocolate brown plumage.

EAGLES

CROWNED EAGLE

Crowned Eagles are more likely to be heard than seen, their evocative call as much a signature tune of the forests as the African Fish Eagle's is of the wetlands and rivers.

In a forested area like Karkloof, Sabie, Magoebaskloof or Zimbabwe's Vumba, the Crowned Eagle's ringing 'koo-wie, koowie, koowie....' sound, rising and falling and emanating from somewhere high above, will be familiar. In the areas where these birds are common you will hear them almost daily – most often around mid-morning – as they soar over the forest. If they can be located in the sky you will also be treated to a fine performance of undulating flight. Pairs sometimes fly and call together, the male's note higher ('kewee') and the female's deeper ('koi'). You may on occasion hear the same sound coming from the undergrowth – not that of a grounded Crowned Eagle but of a resourceful Chorister or Natal Robin mimicking it!

Crowned Eagles are formidable predators. They have enormous feet, larger than those of any other African bird of prey, and, with their broad, rounded wings and long barred tail, exhibit the proportions of a giant sparrowhawk. They do not match the Martial Eagle in size or wingspan and yet they consistently take larger prey. Their accipiter-like structure, it is assumed, gives them manoeuvrability and speed while flying below the forest canopy. There have been a number of eye-witness accounts of kills made by Crowned Eagles, the largest recorded prey taken being a young bushbuck ram which weighed an estimated 30 kilograms. Antelope, especially young ones, feature prominently in the diet of some pairs. Monkeys are also taken, including the large, forest-loving samango – and the difficulty in catching these primates can be imagined.

A preference for this kind of prey has been offered as an explanation of the well-documented habit Crowned Eagle pairs have of breeding biennially. Throughout their range these birds are associated with forest, ranging from the vast lowland areas of Zaire, through the discontinuous montane forests down the eastern side of Africa, to Zimbabwe, the eastern Transvaal, Natal and the Cape as far as Knysna. They also range out into drier country where there are only fragments of forests or narrow galleries of trees along the larger east-flowing rivers.

In regions of continuous forest (especially in Uganda), monkeys, or monkeys and antelope, are the main prey. By contrast, in more arid environments dassies often comprise the bulk of the eagle's diet. It has been suggested that these little animals are easier and less dangerous to catch than the larger prey, and in areas where they are available young Crowned Eagles can soon become proficient hunters and be independent of their parents within a few months. On the other hand, when the young are forced by circumstances to learn to catch monkeys and antelope, the hunting skills take longer to acquire, and they remain reliant on the adults for a year or more after fledging. In these instances the pair is unable to breed annually (unless the clutch or chick is lost) and biennial breeding is the norm.

The information currently available corroborates this, for where dassies feature prominently in the diet, annual breeding occurs more frequently. But there is also an alternative explanation: that eagle predation has a greater effect on antelope populations than it does on those of dassies, and eagles dependent on the former are inhibited from breeding annually because of the depressed prey base.

Although they have a fairly restricted range in southern Africa, Crowned Eagles are not threatened. Most of them occur in timber-producing areas where they do not harm livestock and are therefore not persecuted by man. Indeed many forestry officials regard them as beneficial since they keep in check the various animals that damage young pine trees. This is taken to the point where it is common forestry practice, when the time comes to fell a block, to leave standing the group of trees in which the birds are nesting. To find a large eagle faring so well in the face of man's general onslaught on the environment comes as a welcome change.

It is only during threat display, as shown here, that the Crowned Eagle exhibits the feathers that give rise to its name. This is one of several eagle species that have elongated crown or nape feathers, and these are usually raised and become briefly conspicuous only during moments of fear or anger. The Crowned Eagle is considered to be the most powerful African eagle and it commonly preys on young antelope and monkeys.

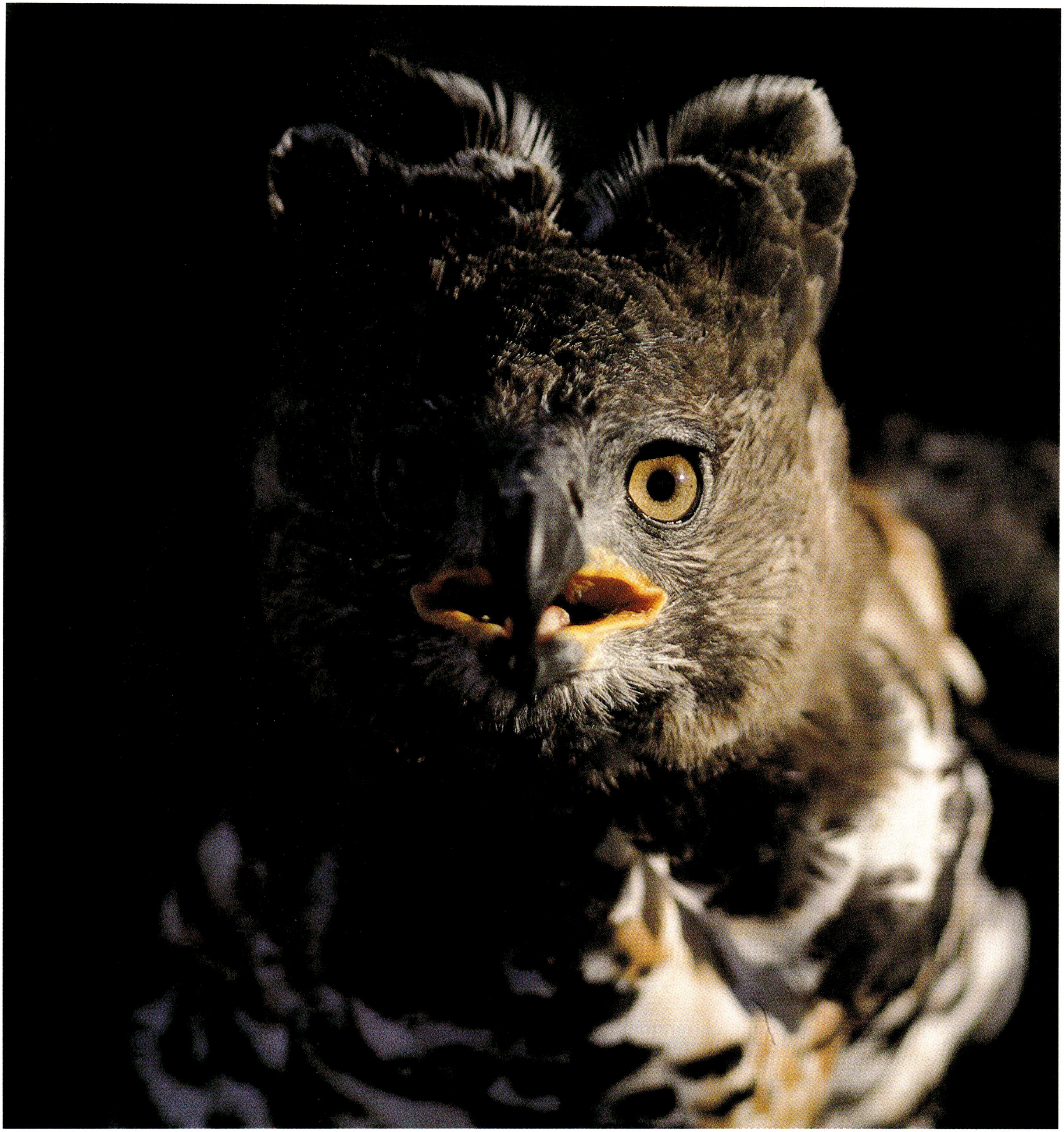

EAGLES

*T*he adage 'safety in numbers' works for a troop of Helmeted Guineafowl that have filed down to a bushveld waterhole to drink. One of the flock spotted the approaching Martial Eagle and its shrill alarms thwarted the eagle's attempt to catch one of its favourite food items. Martial Eagles have many such disappointments before becoming skilled hunters.

MARTIAL EAGLE

Imagine spending a large part of your day cruising a kilometre or so above ground and having eyesight several times more acute than that with which you have been endowed. Very little of what went on far below would escape you. You would, for example, know where the scattered groups of guineafowl that came out on to the harvested lands to feed, went to drink; where the banded mongooses and ground squirrels had their burrows and young; and you would probably know exactly how far the chickens that were scratching around the dusty kraal would range beyond the safety of the huts. And if these were the kind of animals that provided your daily meal you would soon learn to match your skills as a hunter against their skills in evasion. Experience would tell you how and where and when to launch a successful attack. You would not simply parachute down to try and snatch the prey, because it would see you coming. More likely, you would go into a shallow dive and use the 1 000-metre drop to gain speed, making the final approach skimming above the trees so that the quarry could not reach cover from the time it saw you to when the impact of your swoop broke its body.

This is the world of Africa's largest eagle.

The female Martial Eagle weighs up to six kilograms and has a wingspan exceeding two metres. The male is slightly smaller. Much of their time is spent in a lofty world safely beyond human vision. It is exhilarating to watch a Martial Eagle leave its nest and begin soaring, become smaller and smaller as it gains height until, even through powerful binoculars, it becomes indistinct and disappears in the haze.

Because of its size and bold pattern this species is unmistakable: dark brown on the back, wings and chest, and white in front with scattered dark spots. The sexes can be distinguished by their size, the female being larger, and by the female's overall darker colouring and more heavily spotted front. Juveniles take about five years to mature and are initially pale, being white below and on the underwing, and grey above. Like adults they have a slight crest at the back of the head. When they are about a year old, brownish feathers start forming a collar across the throat, gradually extending across the upper chest, and the back and underwings become dark brown. Adulthood is signified by the appearance of brown spots on the lower parts.

Martial Eagles are widely but very sparsely distributed across southern Africa, their choice of prey varying according to region. In the Karoo they are primarily mammal predators, taking suricates, mongooses, ground squirrels and dassies. In savanna areas their prey can range from almost exclusively gamebirds to a diversity of mammal, bird and reptile species. In some localities monitor lizards feature prominently in their diet, and in parts of Kenya the small antelope, the dikdik, is the preferred prey. The largest recorded animal taken by these eagles is a young impala. In many regions gamebirds, especially guineafowl and francolin, are taken, and free-ranging poultry is seized when the opportunity presents itself. The most frequent villains of these poultry thefts are young eagles that are independent of their parents, inexperienced and hungry: domestic stock is so much less wary and easier to catch than its wild counterpart. Consequently Martial Eagles are sometimes regarded as a pest and many are shot.

The Martial Eagle's reproductive rate is low, with about one young being reared every two years. Low too, even in optimum habitat, is its density, at an average of one pair per 100 to 150 square kilometres. When mortality in a population exceeds the recruitment there is an inevitable decline in numbers. Exactly this situation is thought to have overtaken the Martial Eagle in many parts of its range on the subcontinent as a result of persecution by farmers, and it has become a very scarce bird outside all but the largest conservation areas. If the decline is not halted the populations of the bigger reserves may become the last outposts of this magnificent bird, and even these may be at risk because of the inherent low density of the species – the Kruger National Park, for example, is home to fewer than 150 pairs, and Hwange in Zimbabwe has an estimated 110 pairs.

Martial Eagles normally make their nests in forks high up in tall trees, though in 1972 they were reported nesting for the first time on electricity pylons near Kimberley and since then this habit has become commonplace. In a study currently being undertaken in the Karoo, for example, all 18 nests under investigation are on pylons, and there are many similar nests dotted about the Transvaal. In trees their nests are added to over the years and develop into enormous stick structures, whereas those on pylons tend to remain shallow, quite flimsy affairs.

Egg-laying occurs in early winter (mostly during April to May) and the single-egg clutch takes about 48 days to hatch. In some cases it is incubated by the female alone and in others the male provides some assistance. The breeding period is the only time during which Martial Eagles make much noise: the food-begging call is uttered by either the female or the chick. It is a far-carrying, melodious 'ko-wee-oh' sound, repeated at intervals. In one recorded case an incubating female started calling while looking intently in one direction. Exactly two minutes later the male skimmed in from that direction, bringing prey. If we reasonably assume that she first called when she caught sight of her mate, and that he flew in at 60 kilometres per hour, we can deduce that they were in visual contact when he was still two kilometres away – an indication of just how phenomenally sharp the eyesight of the species is.

The Martial Eagle is Africa's largest eagle species. It is a powerful bird with a massive wingspan, large feet, a broad, flat head with a short crest, and piercing yellow eyes set below craggy brows. Over much of its southern African range it has become a rare sight and it is only in the larger national parks that it is likely to be encountered with any frequency.

Western Banded Snake Eagle

This species (also called, in some textbooks, the Smaller Banded Snake Eagle, or simply the Banded Snake Eagle) is a tropical African bird which appears only in the northernmost parts of southern Africa: along the Caprivi Strip, in northern Botswana and in northern Zimbabwe. It then ranges northwards through Zambia, Malawi and Angola into East and West Africa, extending as far west as the Gambia and Senegal. It is a bird of the galleries and ribbons of forest and tall woodland that fringe the larger rivers of the continent, and in southern Africa is found in the riparian forest fringes of the Zambezi, Chobe, Okavango and a few other major watercourses. It is a resident species, and quite likely to be encountered in the right areas.

A solitary bird for the most part, it spends much of its time perched quietly on an upper branch of a dead tree overlooking open ground or wetland. It may sit, inactive, for hours on end and, as it is not shy, can be approached quite closely. When pressed to take to the wing it flies with rapid, shallow wingbeats before scooping up to alight on another perch. In true snake eagle tradition it preys mainly on these reptiles, taking venomous as well as non-venomous species, but also frogs, fish, insects and other species which it spots from its observation perch. Its single most important field identification character is its tail pattern, which is black except for a single broad white bar across it near the end. It utters a crowing call very similar to that of the Southern Banded Snake Eagle: a staccato 'kok-kok-kok-kok-ko-ho', which it emits both while sitting on its perch and while on the wing.

Its breeding habits are only sketchily known: to date only one nest of the species (in which the contents could actually be checked) has been recorded in southern Africa. This was found in early May 1984 by a fishing group who, fortuitously, camped under the nest tree near the edge of the Zambezi River upstream from the Victoria Falls. It was a small stick nest about half a metre in diameter and lined with leaves, and it contained a single, week-old chick. The adults reached the nest by swooping into the clump from below, the chick calling whenever its parents were in the vicinity of the nest. The adults were seen bringing in a variety of snakes, the largest 75 centimetres long. In the nest were found the remains of a herald snake and a water monitor.

Buzzard-like in looks and demeanour, a Western Banded Snake Eagle takes to the wing along a floodplain in northern Botswana. The single broad white bar on its brown tail and its geographic location serve to distinguish it from the Southern Banded Snake Eagle.

EAGLES

Brown Snake Eagles like to perch conspicuously on high vantage points such as the tops of dead trees or electricity pylons. The large, cowled head and big yellow eyes are obvious from a distance but, in flight, it is the mainly white underwing that identifies them.

Brown Snake Eagle

Snake eagles are particularly interesting birds of prey. They are not closely related to true eagles at all, but are so called because of their relatively large size. In the earlier bird books they were referred to as 'Harrier Eagles' (and their generic name, *Circaetus*, is the Greek word for this) but the old name has been abandoned in favour of one which more aptly describes their feeding habits. They are a typically African genus comprising four species, all occurring in southern Africa. The snake eagles are distinguished by their disproportionately large heads, big yellow eyes, shortish tails and unfeathered legs, which are armour-plated with hard round scales.

The Brown Snake Eagle is the largest member of the group, weighing about two kilograms and having a wingspan of about two metres. It is usually seen perched conspicuously on a high vantage point, often an electricity pylon. Even from a long way off it is recognizable by its large, cowled head and by the way it perches, the body held away from the perch so that the unfeathered legs are visible. From behind, however, it could just as easily be a Blackbreasted Snake Eagle, and only when one sees its all-brown front can its identification be certain.

The species does most of its hunting from a perch, watching the ground for prey and then gliding or parachuting down and swiftly dispatching the victim with its strong claws. It takes a variety of snakes, including poisonous ones, the largest recorded being a mamba nearly three metres in length. The bird is not immune to snake venom, but is well protected by its scaled legs and feet and by the thick undercoat of feathers on its body. Errors in judgement or lack of skill, though, may have fatal consequences, and there have been reports of Brown Snake Eagles succumbing to their intended prey. A Brown Snake Eagle ringed in the Transvaal in 1974 was recovered seven years later, apparently as a result of such an incident. The report was sent in by a Belgian schoolteacher working in Kabinda Province of Zaire. He had bought the ring from some villagers who, in turn, had taken it from a bird (which they ate) that 'had been killed by a big snake'.

The Zaire ringing recovery is remarkable, for it shows that an individual of this apparently sedentary species had travelled a distance of 2 100 kilometres. Brown Snake Eagles are a familiar sight in some areas and one takes it for granted that they are resident. The recovery, however, and the indication that the species' abundance in a given region does fluctuate, suggest that they are nomadic birds that move widely about the savanna belt of Africa, stopping where the pickings are good and moving on when conditions deteriorate. Further evidence of this is that they seldom use the same nest twice and do not seem to breed annually in the same area, as do many of the territorial eagles.

The breeding season is unusual, though similar to that of the Bateleur. Egg-laying occurs in midsummer (January to March) and the chick fledges some five months later, in the dry winter months. Relatively few of the flimsy stick nests of the species have been found in southern Africa, probably because they are small and inconspicuous and difficult to locate. They are built on the top of a leafy tree, but sometimes the bird takes over the nest of another eagle species. A single egg is laid and the nest is kept lined with green foliage throughout the incubation period. Most or all of the incubation and care of the chick is undertaken by the female, the male providing the family with prey. He arrives at the nest at intervals and regurgitates various lengths of snake, sometimes with a little assistance from his hungry mate, who helps pull them out! The nesting cycle is remarkably prolonged for the size of the bird, with incubation lasting 50 days, followed by a nestling period of about 100 days.

In terms of plumage, young Brown Snake Eagles are very similar to the adult birds from the time they leave the nest. Some have a mottling of white on their fronts, though, and can be confused with young Blackbreasted Snake Eagles, which are entirely brown to begin with but gradually assume the white fronts that mark adulthood. A look at their respective underwings should, however, be sufficient to distinguish them: the young Brown Snake Eagle has brown underwing coverts (and white primaries and secondaries) whereas the young Blackbreasted has all-white underwings (with faint barring on the primaries and secondaries).

Blackbreasted Snake Eagle

The Blackbreasted Snake Eagle is the largest known bird of prey that hovers regularly. A few other big species, such as the Martial Eagle, the Brown Snake Eagle, and even the African Fish Eagle, do so very occasionally, but the Blackbreasted Snake Eagle is often to be seen holding the air rather like a giant Blackshouldered Kite, wings gently winnowing, tail spread and head facing down.

Especially when there is a breeze to assist them, these birds hunt by hovering, scanning the open ground below them for snakes. At other times, though, and like other snake eagles, they hunt from high perches – including electricity pylons, to which they are very partial (as is the Brown Snake Eagle). When prey is sighted they parachute gently down to the ground and, if the victim is a small snake, they take to the air again quickly, carrying the writhing reptile in their feet. As they gain height and the snake is subdued they bring it forward and swallow it while in flight. Larger prey is subdued on the ground and then carried aloft to be swallowed on the wing. Most of their diet consists of small snakes, though a cobra 1,8 metres in length has been recorded as a prey item and, on occasion, they take rodents, frogs and insects. One of the finest eagle photographs ever taken – by Peter Steyn – is of a female Blackbreasted Snake Eagle about to alight on its tree-top nest, wings spread, feet dangling and the back end of a cobra hanging out of its bill. Although they are regarded as a diurnal species that roosts at night there was a recent observation of a bird that spent 20 minutes hunting by hovering, long after dark, in the floodlights at Harare airport.

Blackbreasted Snake Eagles often occur alongside the Brown Snake Eagle and, indeed, the two may even perch on the same or adjacent pylons. Generally, though, the former – the smaller of the two – frequents more open country than its cousin. Adult Blackbreasted Snake Eagles are a handsome black (actually very dark brown) and white in coloration. Seen from above they are uniformly dark, but from below they appear almost white, for they have a white front and underwings, and show only a black throat and narrow black barring on the underside of the primaries and secondaries. Young birds are entirely brown when they leave the nest, and progress through a blotchy brown and white intermediate stage until eventually, over a period of about three years, they assume the adult colouring. At the intermediate stage they resemble a snake eagle, found in the Middle East, known as Beaudouin's Eagle and this bird, in turn, in its immature plumage, is akin to the Shorttoed Eagle of southern Europe. This rather complicated pattern of similarity has been interpreted in various ways, some authorities regarding the three forms as races of the same species and others according each a specific status (as done in this book).

Pairs build their small stick nest in a tree-top, as often as not selecting a nondescript little tree for this purpose and concealing the nest in a cluster of mistletoe or a thicket of twigs. It is usually inconspicuous and decidedly un-eagle like. The breeding season is centred in late winter, the single white egg usually appearing during June to August. The incubation is undertaken by the female, to whom her mate brings prey from time to time. The nesting cycle is prolonged, with incubation lasting about 52 days and the nesting period about 90 days.

Relatively little is known of the Blackbreasted Snake Eagle's pattern of social dispersion. It is common in many parts of its range but is not continuously present at any one locality. Similarly, it may breed in a particular area one year but not the next. At times it is gregarious to the extent that as many as six birds can be seen hovering in the sky and as many as 30 found roosting together in the evening. It is a relatively easy bird to trap and a fair number of the species have been ringed over the years. So far, however, there have been no recoveries to confirm the suspicion that these birds are nomadic and capable of widespread movement across the subcontinent.

The Blackbreasted Snake Eagle has the characteristic upright stance and bare legs of a snake eagle. In adult plumage it is an unmistakable bird, with a white front and almost black back, head and throat. In the two to three years the young birds take to acquire adult plumage, they change from entirely brown in colour to black and white, and the varied plumages of the intermediates can cause identification problems. The bird illustrated on the right presents no problem: it is nearing the end of its moult and the last vestiges of immature plumage are disappearing.

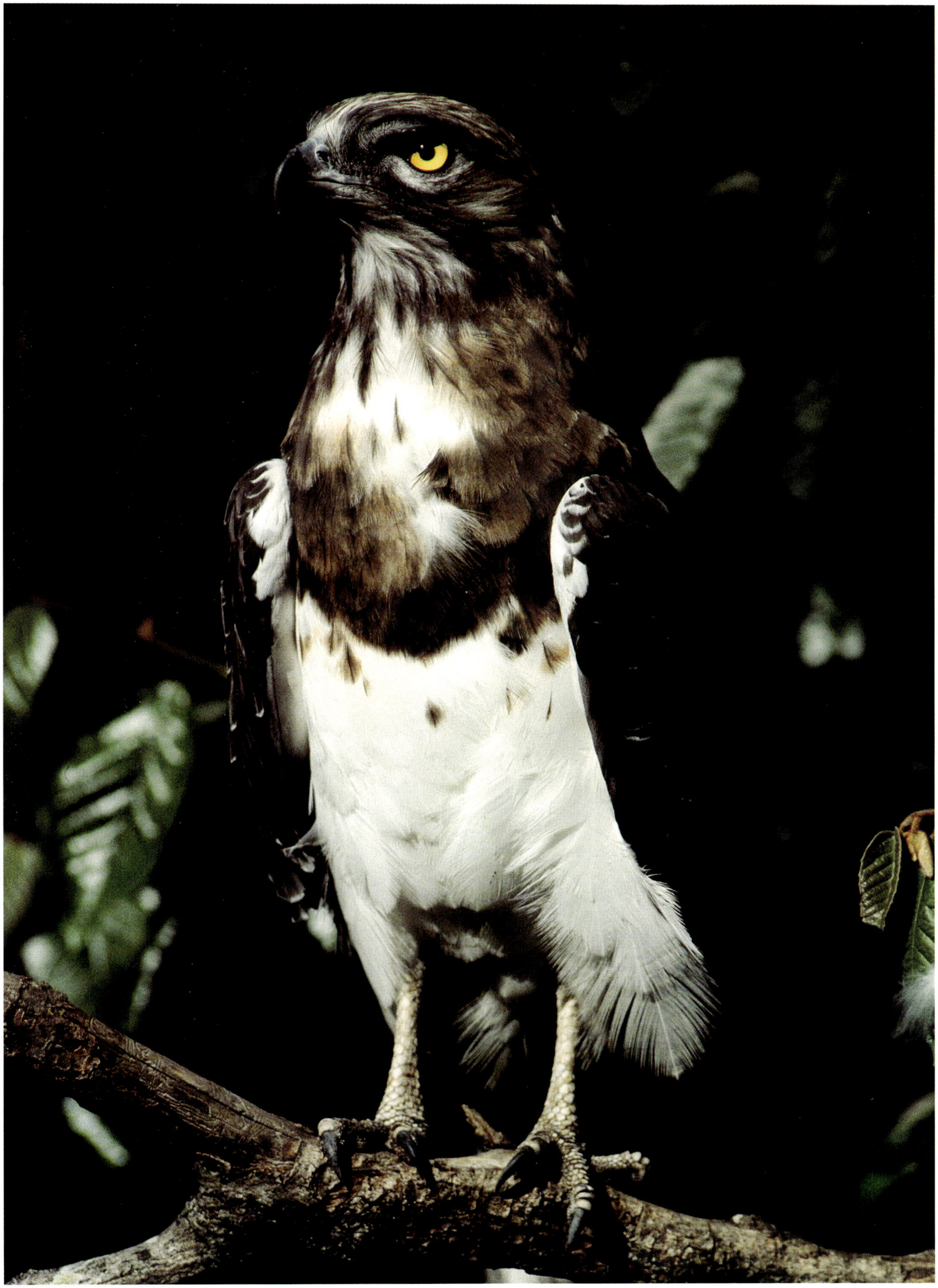

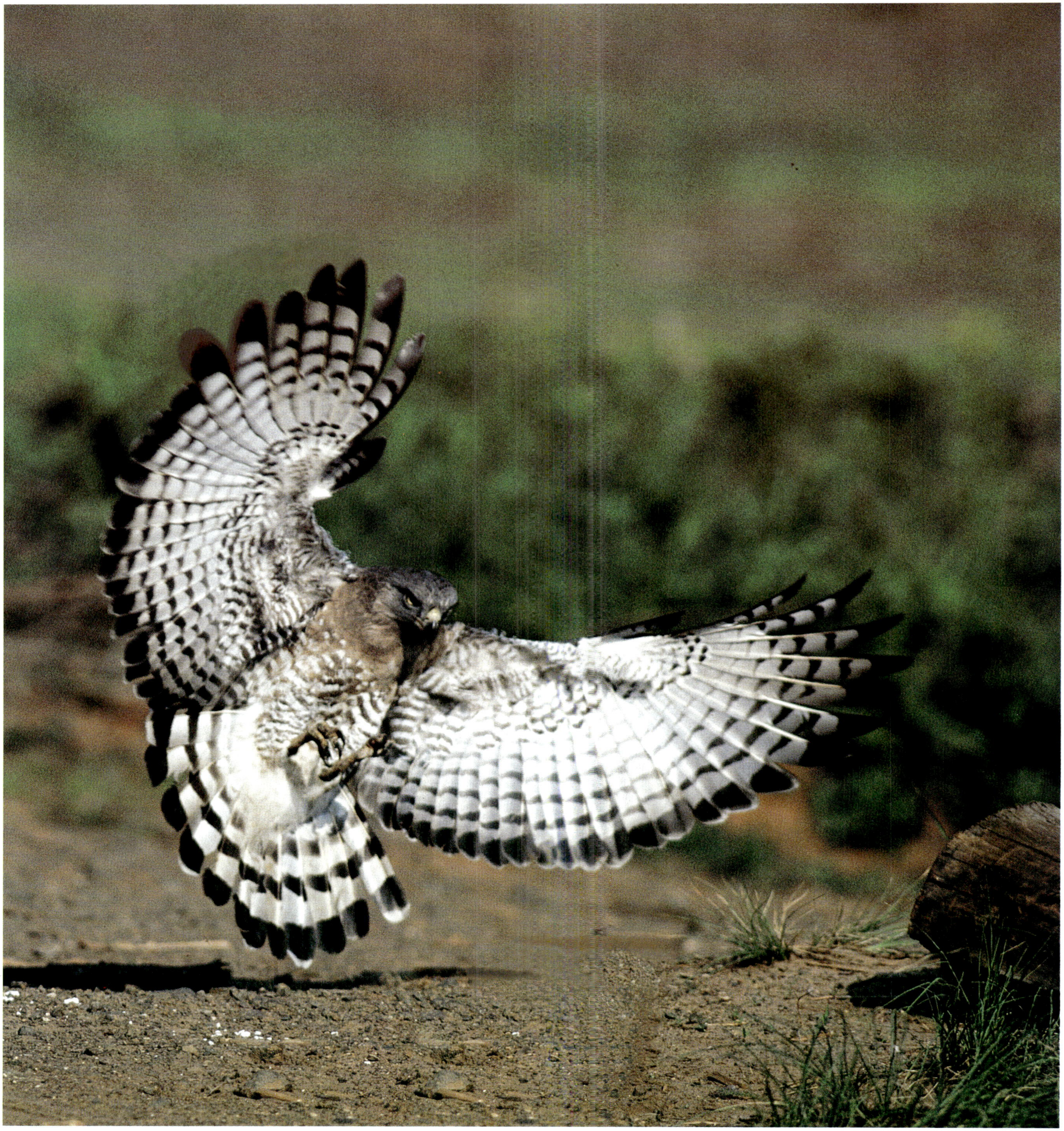

SOUTHERN BANDED SNAKE EAGLE

Considering the degree of interest in birds of prey in southern Africa it is surprising that there should be one that is as little studied and poorly known as the Southern Banded Snake Eagle.

The species has a restricted range on the subcontinent, being confined to the narrow coastal plain of Zululand and Mozambique and to the low-lying south-eastern edge of Zimbabwe. From here it extends northwards along the eastern coastal plain of Africa through Tanzania and Kenya and into southern Somalia. It is not a rare bird in Zululand and, for example, is often encountered in the vicinity of Lake St Lucia, or along the Pongola River floodplain. The type specimen was collected in Durban in 1850, but it has long since retreated northwards from this area where increasing human population pressure and spreading farmlands have eliminated most of its preferred habitat. Because its range has shrunk and because of its small population size it is listed in the South African Red Data Book of Birds.

Less is known of the breeding biology of the Southern Banded Snake Eagle than of any other eagle species in Africa. The one and only active nest to have been recorded in southern Africa dates back to September 1907, when a male bird was shot near Beira (Mozambique) as it left its nest, which contained one egg. It is hard to credit that not a single nest has been located in the 80-odd years since then. In Kenya two nests have been reported, both in trees tangled with creeper. At this stage, therefore, little more can be said of the species' breeding habits than that it builds a nest in a creeper-covered tree and lays one egg in early summer.

The bird's diet and hunting behaviour are almost as poorly known. It hunts from perches, scanning the ground below, and it has been recorded catching snakes, lizards, a mouse, small birds and insects. At times it utters a raucous crowing call, a 'ko-ko-ko-kaau', which often betrays its presence.

The bird's barred belly and greyish brown plumage give it the looks of a goshawk or, perhaps, a Cuckoo Hawk, but its typical snake eagle-like stance – perched upright, with legs showing – and its broad, cowled head reveal its true identity. It is very like the Western Banded Snake Eagle in size, shape and colouring, but is more extensively barred on the belly and has three tail bars, in contrast to the other's single tail bar. The two species do not overlap in range and this alone will prevent confusion.

Anyone holidaying or living in Zululand who can put in a few hours' observation of this little-known species would almost certainly be rewarded by discovering something that will add to the slender body of our knowledge.

The boldly barred underwing and undertail of a Southern Banded Snake Eagle are visible as it swoops down to snatch a prey item from the ground; when seen perched it appears much less dramatically marked. It is very like the Western Banded Snake Eagle in appearance, being distinguished principally by its triple-barred, rather than single-barred, tail. The two species have much in common, both living in tropical wetland habitats, and both hunting frogs, small reptiles and rodents from perches.

EAGLES

*T*he flamboyant Bateleur inhabits the savanna regions stretching from West Africa to South Africa, although on the subcontinent its range and numbers have been greatly reduced in the past 40 years. The sexes differ in plumage, the male having black secondaries, and the female, like the one illustrated above, having greyish-white secondaries. Pairs live permanently together and share the same territory. On rainy or overcast days they remain grounded but when it is sunny they may spend up to six hours on the wing, and fly as much as 300 kilometres, coursing back and forth in their unique manner, in search of food.

Bateleur

With its extravagant colours, odd shape and renowned flying skills, the Bateleur must be one of the most remarkable of all birds of prey. Its head and front are velvet black, its back and almost non-existent tail a rich chestnut, and its cere, legs and feet bright red. All in all, it has, for an eagle, a most extraordinary mix of colours. When seen perched, it is stocky-looking and, with its wings extending far beyond its body, appears to have no tail. But in flight it is transformed into a graceful, delta-winged glider with a two-metre wingspan.

The mechanism of the Bateleur's flight and the function it serves has been the subject of much speculation. It flies fast, at about 50 to 60 kilometres per hour, and at a low altitude, keeping a steady course for long distances with scarcely a wingbeat, the only movement being a gentle rocking motion from one side to the other. Periodically it sights something of interest on the ground, and banks and returns to pass again over the spot. Bateleurs, waiting for the atmosphere to warm up, take to the wing from about nine in the morning onwards and are likely to remain in the air until mid-afternoon. In the course of an average day they probably travel 300 kilometres or more.

Rick Watson, who spent three years studying Bateleurs in the Kruger National Park, has suggested that their aerodynamic design is specialized to enable them to keep gliding in one direction, getting lift from the small, weak thermals they encounter and dropping gently between them. It is for this reason that they make such a late start in the morning, for the earth needs the sun's heat to create bodies of rising air. On rainy, overcast days they remain grounded, and are unable to hunt.

With this mode of flying Bateleurs cover large areas without expending much energy, and are thus likely to have numerous chance encounters with temporarily vulnerable prey. Rick Watson suggests that they are highly specialized opportunists: the Lilacbreasted Roller that drops down to snatch an insect is vulnerable to predation at that particular moment; so is the lizard basking on an exposed rock, and the nocturnal hare that has been flushed from its sleeping place by a herd of wildebeest. Birds such as rollers, hornbills and Longtailed Shrikes that go down to the ground for food feature prominently in the Bateleur's diet. In a sample of more than 2 000 Bateleur prey items from the Kruger Park about a third consisted of live food. The other two-thirds comprised carrion, either in the form of small dead animals, reptiles or birds – often road casualties such as nightjars – or pieces of meat and bone that were gleaned from large carcasses. By experimentally putting out meat baits Rick found that Bateleurs have a remarkable ability to locate small carrion. Most of the baits were located by the birds before any of the other numerous scavengers in the area came on the scene.

The Bateleur's high dependence on carrion is considered to be the reason for its almost total disappearance from South Africa outside the largest conservation areas, and for its widespread decline in Zimbabwe. Today it is almost inconceivable that the first Bateleur specimen was collected – in 1800 – close to George in the southern Cape. Now the nearest place it is likely to be seen is hundreds of kilometres to the north, in the Kalahari Gemsbok National Park. In most stock-farming areas poisoned baits are routinely used to kill predators such as jackals. Poison, usually strychnine, is placed inside small pieces of meat and these are laid out along farm roads. Bateleurs have been designed by evolution to locate such objects and, as a result of taking these baits, have disappeared from a large part of their former range. On the other hand – and ironically – the wily jackal, after decades of poisoning, is still with us in undiminished numbers.

In the large conservation areas Bateleurs occur at relatively high densities. The Kruger National Park, for example, supports an estimated 400 to 500 breeding pairs. Here the birds live throughout their lives with the same mate in the same territory, which may be 20 to 30 square kilometres in extent.

The species has a protracted breeding cycle and, unusually for an eagle, the birds lay their single egg in midsummer. The nest is usually centrally located in the territory – a stick structure often built in an upper fork of a knobthorn – and for five to six months activity centres around it, first during the incubation period, which lasts about 55 days, and then during the lengthy nestling period, which can take anything from 101 to 194 days. Both these time spans are longer than those for any other African eagle. Both male and female share the incubation, brooding and feeding of the nestling, another unusual feature for an eagle. The chick is a uniform dark brown when it fledges and it remains so for a long time, attaining full adult plumage only in its seventh year.

The bird's slow reproductive rate and the deferred maturity of the young means that it would take many years for this magnificent and harmless species to re-establish itself in its former range, even if the scourge of poison could be eliminated.

Beginning life as uniformly brown birds, Bateleurs pass through successive moults, each bringing them nearer to the bright plumage of adulthood. The young bird below is probably in its third or fourth year.
(Bottom) A soaring male shows the distinctive Bateleur wing shape.

African Fish Eagle

With a little help from the media the African Fish Eagle, characterized by its gleaming black, white and chestnut plumage and its ringing 'WHOW, kyow kow-kow' call, has become the best-known bird of prey in Africa, familiar to millions of people, if not in the flesh then from its frequent appearances in nature features on television.

Pairs are most vocal at the start of the breeding season and calling is often related to territoriality. In places where the species is numerous, for instance at Lake St Lucia in Zululand and along the Chobe or Botletle rivers in Botswana, the habitat is partitioned into territories, and neighbouring pairs regard infringements of their space in much the same light as do human suburban residents.

These birds prey mainly on live fish, which they catch by swooping down to the water at a shallow angle, grasping the victim in their talons, then lifting off again and carrying it to a perch to eat. Many photographers have filmed this sequence in the Okavango, using as bait a tiger fish stuffed with papyrus to make it float, and some African Fish Eagles there have become so accustomed to their star roles that they seem to be waiting to perform 'on set' whenever a boat appears. The fish most frequently taken are surface-living species. Those weighing up to one kilogram are handled with ease. A two-kilogram fish can still be lifted out of the water but the bird has to bring heavier prey ashore by flopping across the water, using its wings as oars. African Fish Eagles are also notorious pirates, robbing other species such as herons and cormorants of their prey. They also scavenge when the opportunity arises, and take nestlings from heronries, and young waterbirds. These alternative food sources are probably exploited when the fishing is unrewarding.

A remarkable photograph was published a few years ago showing a concentration of more than 100 adult Fish Eagles gathered around a small pan in the Okavango, squabbling for the fish stranded in the receding water. These normally resident birds may have congregated in this extraordinary way because the channels in their territories had dried up. In permanent wetlands, where conditions remain stable, African Fish Eagle pairs probably live their entire life in the same small territory and spend very little of their time actually seeking food. In a study made in such conditions in Kenya the birds spend on average just eight minutes a day fishing!

In southern Africa, Fish Eagles breed in winter, laying their eggs during April to June. The nest is a large structure of sticks usually placed high up in a tall tree although, occasionally, cliff-ledge sites are used. The same nest is reoccupied year after year; some are known to have been in use for at least 30 years. The normal clutch is two plain white eggs, but one more or less is laid on occasion. Most of the incubation, which lasts 42 to 45 days, is undertaken by the female, to whom the male brings food. The young hatch asynchronously and sibling aggression often leads to the death of the last-born chick, though the species raises two young more frequently than most other African eagles, and on occasion even three chicks survive. The young make their first flight when they are about 70 days old and soon start imitating the hunting habits of their parents. For the next four years they are easily distinguished from the adults by their mottled brown, rufous and white plumage. After spending two to three months in the vicinity of the nest they begin moving farther afield.

Fish Eagles are generally much admired birds of prey and it is rare to hear of people persecuting them. On the other hand they are very vulnerable to indirect attack from poisons and pollutants entering the aquatic systems that support them. A number have been killed by eating fish which carry lethal doses of dieldrin, and many more have been adversely affected by fish contaminated by organochloride pesticides. One of the consequences of this contamination is that the shells of their eggs become thinner than usual and a higher breakage results. There is clear evidence that, in southern Africa, Fish Eagles' eggs are thinner-shelled today than they were a few decades ago, a trend directly attributable to the contamination of fish populations.

More than any other species, the African Fish Eagle represents a barometer of the quality of our wetlands, dams and rivers. Where the bird continues to fare well we can be confident that water systems are clean; where they do not, there is cause for concern.

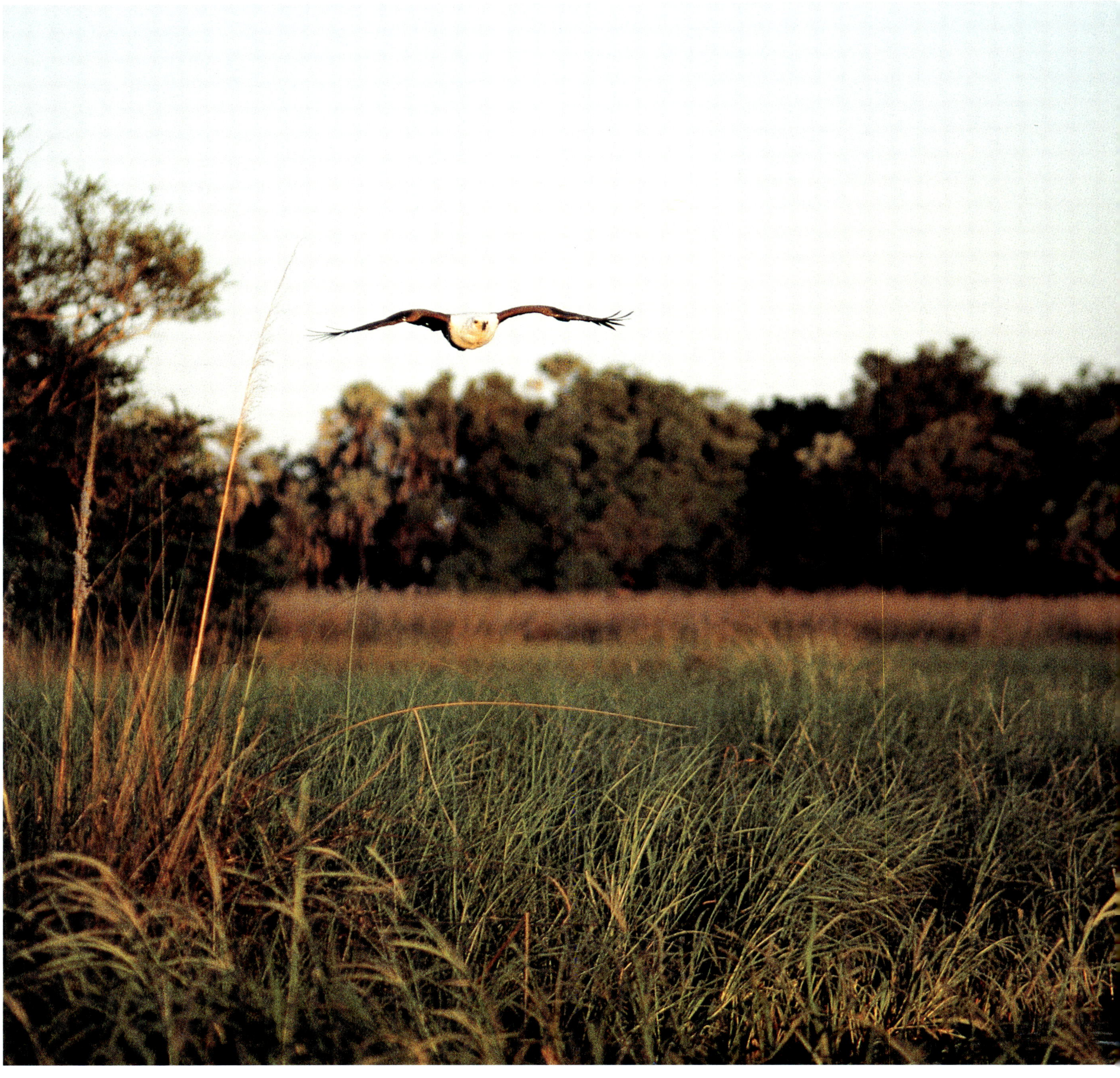

The African Fish Eagle belongs to the genus Haliaeetus, *which is represented by other species elsewhere in the world. One of these is the famous Bald Eagle of North America which, like the African species, has a white head and tail. African Fish Eagles inhabit Africa's larger waterways, estuaries, lakes and dams, where they hunt fish from perches overlooking the water.*
(Above) Females, like the bird on the left sunning itself, are slightly larger than males; it has been suggested that they can also be distinguished by having a more squared-off white bib on the chest. Females have a lower-pitched call than males, a difference which becomes obvious when a male and female are heard calling in duet.

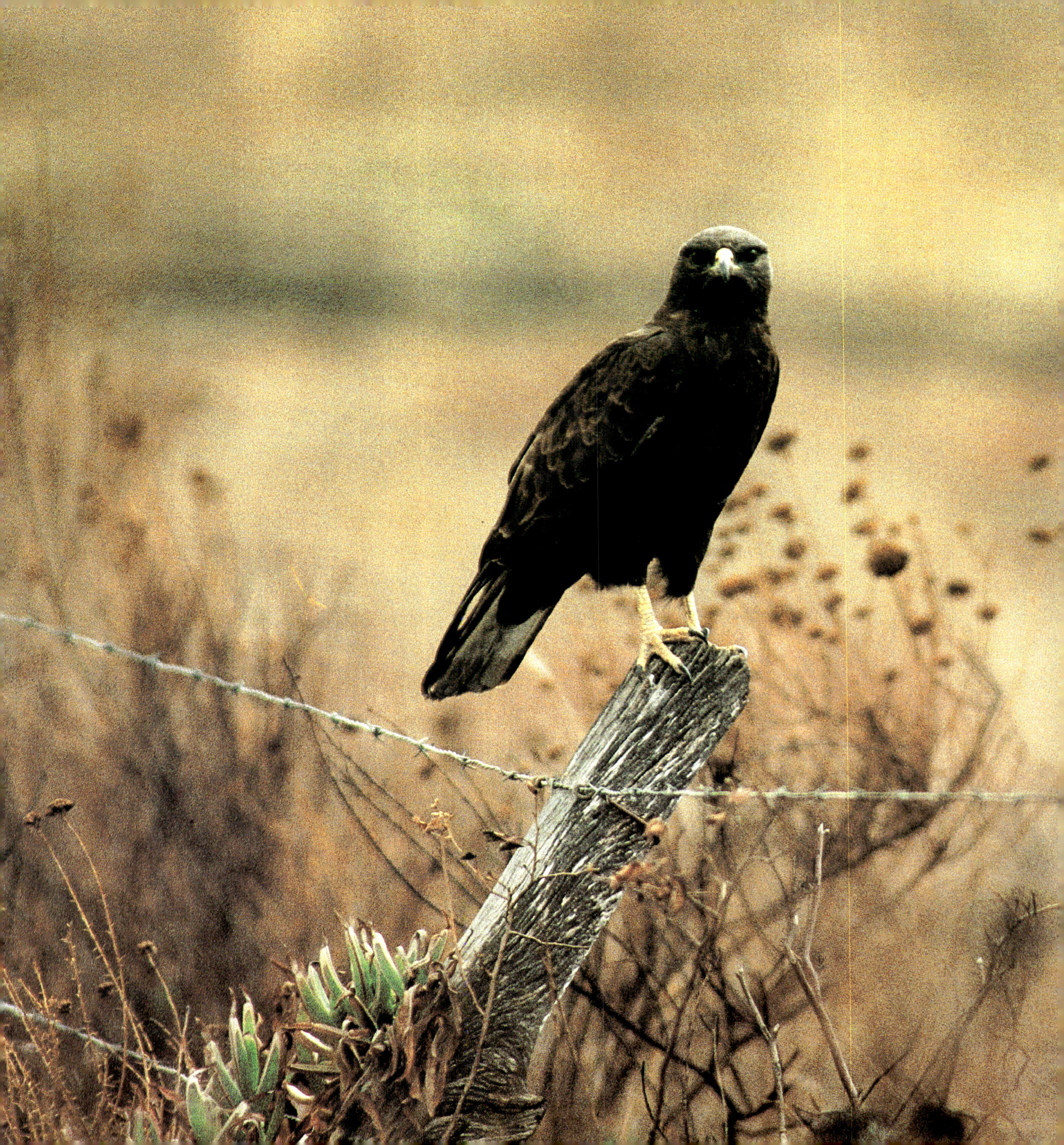

BUZZARDS

Seven species going by the name 'buzzard' are found in southern Africa. The Honey Buzzard is not really a buzzard at all and is included with the kites, while the Lizard Buzzard, though included in this group, is perhaps misplaced and should be grouped with the chanting goshawks. The typical buzzards are medium-sized, broad-winged hawks that like to perch conspicuously, often on a fence or telephone pole next to a road. They soar in warm weather and some hunt on the wing by hovering above ridges. They prey mainly on rodents and small reptiles. Most of the species occur commonly in southern Africa; the Steppe Buzzard, a non-breeding migrant from the Palearctic, is probably the single most numerous raptor during the summer months. It is closely related to and scarcely distinguishable from the resident Forest Buzzard. Four of the species breed on the subcontinent and two of them are non-breeding visitors.

(Left) Using a fence post as a hunting perch, this dark-plumaged Steppe Buzzard is well situated to detect the movement of a lizard or small rodent, animals which form its main prey. (Above) A Jackal Buzzard soars over its hilly terrain.

STEPPE BUZZARD

For those people just starting their acquaintance with birds of prey, the Steppe Buzzard is the species most likely to provide the first encounter. The chances are, though, that the beginner will have a problem with its identification as this is one of the most variably plumaged and nondescript raptors, appearing in a range of browns from a pale sandy colour through ginger and chestnut to dark brown, with an equally variable amount of streaking or barring on its front. Field guides face an unequal challenge in attempting to illustrate it in all its forms, and it is the bird of prey whose identification probably causes the most head-scratching.

Most Steppe Buzzards are medium brown with an indistinct whitish band across their chest. Immature birds tend to be streaked whereas adults are usually barred on the front. Young birds are also distinguishable from adults by their pale yellow eyes (brown in adults) and by the terminal bar on the tail which is the same width as the other tail bars (adults have a terminal bar twice as wide as the other tail bars). The sexes look alike, though the females are a little larger than their mates.

The term 'buzzard' is often applied indiscriminately to hawks, and the use of the word even extends to such unlikely birds as Ground Hornbills (or 'Turkey Buzzards', as you may hear them being called in the Kruger National Park). In fact 'buzzard' refers specifically to raptors in the genus *Buteo*. The nominate race is *Buteo buteo buteo* and is resident in western Europe, where it is called simply the 'Buzzard'. Its sister race, *Buteo buteo vulpinus*, or Steppe Buzzard, breeds from Finland eastwards into Mongolia during the northern summer and in winter moves to Africa. Large numbers reach the southern subcontinent during October to March.

Their migratory pattern has been studied in some detail in recent years. It is a remarkable phenomenon to witness, especially in those areas where the birds concentrate in order to avoid crossing large waterbodies. Their reluctance to do so is understandable, for extensive stretches of water do not produce the thermals on which the birds depend for easy flight. For a species the size of a buzzard it would be impossible to make the annual round trip by flapping all the way, and so they 'leapfrog' from one mass of rising air to another, sailing their way north and south, soaring up high in the thermals and then gliding gently downwards until they find the next lift. From an energy conservation point of view it is thus more economical for the birds to make a 500-kilometre detour to stay over land, using its rising air, than to make a 50-kilometre flapping flight over the sea.

So they funnel around the edges of the Black, Caspian and Mediterranean seas and are counted on passage by teams of birdwatchers. In Turkey, as many as 204 000 have been counted flying around the eastern rim of the Black Sea in spring, while at Eilat, in Israel, the highest spring tally (in 1977) totalled a staggering 315 800 birds. When they get to Africa they also tend to keep close to the lines of hills and escarpments that offer them lift. The great central African Rift Valley is one such route. In South Africa the same phenomenon occurs along the eastern escarpment in the Transvaal, and on a warm day in mid-March the stream of migrating Steppe Buzzards sailing northwards, on the first leg of what may be a 13 000-kilometre journey, can be seen from several points. It is a spectacle well worth looking out for.

Over the years many Steppe Buzzards have been trapped in southern Africa and fitted with numbered aluminium rings, and several have been recovered en route to the breeding grounds or in Eurasia itself, the easternmost report having come from longitude 93°E. Ringing has also shown that these birds may live for up to 25 years.

In southern Africa Steppe Buzzards tend to occur solitarily, and often remain in the same territory throughout their stay, even returning to the same place in successive years. They like open country and often hunt from telephone poles or fence posts, or from the branches of dead trees. They take a wide variety of prey, including rodents, lizards and insects, which they catch by simply watching for movement from their perch and then gliding down to pounce. On warm days, though, Steppe Buzzards are often seen soaring, and they may locate some of their food from the wing. Their call is seldom heard on the subcontinent, but when it is, the sound is a typical buzzard-like 'kee-oo'.

BUZZARDS

*T*he Steppe Buzzard is one of the most numerous birds of prey during the summer months when it visits the subcontinent. Its preferred habitat is open savanna or grassland and it is especially common in crop-growing areas where telephone and fence poles provide it with ideal hunting perches. It occurs in a variety of plumage forms, some dark brown and others rufous brown, but most resemble the individual illustrated above. The extent of streaking and barring on the front also varies, as does the amount of white on the chest.

BUZZARDS

A typical buzzard pose and a typical buzzard perch – a Forest Buzzard catches the evening sun in an open field. This species is very similar to the Steppe Buzzard and the two species have in the past been treated as conspecific. The Forest Buzzard is boldly blotched in front, and lacks barring on its underparts. In its immature plumage the front is almost completely white. These features, and the fact that it breeds in the southern Cape, distinguish it from the migratory Steppe Buzzard.

FOREST BUZZARD

This species is difficult, if not impossible at times, to distinguish from the Steppe Buzzard. It is found in the forested high-rainfall areas of southern Africa, ranging from the Cape Peninsula through the southern and eastern Cape into Natal, the eastern Transvaal escarpment region and as far north as the Soutpansberg. It has not been recorded in Zimbabwe, but it does occur in Malawi and in isolated populations in the pockets of highland forest through East Africa and into Ethiopia. At one time it was thought that the southern African birds were migrants from central Africa but they are now known to be resident on the subcontinent.

Although the Forest Buzzard is recognized as a distinct species it has, in terms of classification, had a chequered career. It was first collected at Knysna in 1830, at which time it was described as a distinct species. Subsequent taxonomists have sometimes retained this classification and sometimes relegated it to a subspecies – as is the Steppe Buzzard – of the European Buzzard *Buteo buteo*. Its current scientific name is also under dispute, with some textbooks referring to it as *Buteo tachardus* and others as *Buteo trizonatus*. Even its common name has undergone a change in recent times, from Mountain Buzzard to Forest Buzzard. This uncertainty reflects that little is known about the bird, its behavioural patterns and similarities to and differences from other buzzards.

On what grounds, then, is the Forest Buzzard distinct as a species from the Steppe Buzzard? The two look much alike. However, Steppe Buzzards breed in Eurasia and Forest Buzzards in Africa. Steppe Buzzards frequent open country; Forest Buzzards inhabit forests and plantations of exotic trees. Steppe Buzzards are found in southern Africa during October to April; Forest Buzzards are resident. These features are not in themselves diagnostic, however, as Steppe Buzzards may wander into forests and occasionally overwinter in southern Africa.

The clues to distinguishing one from the other are related mainly to plumage, are subtle and may even be masked by the variability that is found in the two species. The adults of both differ from immatures in terms of eye-colour (adults have brown eyes, immatures have yellow) and in the width of their tail's terminal bar (the same width as the other tail bars in young birds but twice as wide in adults). Forest Buzzards are never barred in front, and this distinguishes them from adult Steppe Buzzards. Forest Buzzards have large, tear-shaped streaks on their fronts, and the shape of these also distinguishes their immatures from those of the Steppe Buzzard. In the latter the streaks are thin and not tear-shaped. Thus, if a buzzard is seen in winter in, say, an eastern Transvaal escarpment forest, the chances are that it is a Forest Buzzard. But if it is barred on its flanks then it is an adult Steppe Buzzard away from its normal habitat. On the other hand if its front is streaked and not barred at all then we must look carefully at the shape of the streaks. If they are tear-shaped we can conclude that the bird is the elusive Forest Buzzard.

The first recorded breeding by Forest Buzzards in southern Africa occurred near Port Elizabeth in 1939, and probably fewer than a dozen nests have since been located, all of them in the southern Cape, where the bird is relatively common. Here breeding takes place in summer. During the early stages of the cycle the birds soar and call frequently from the nesting area, uttering a high-pitched, clear, buzzard-like 'keee-oo' note. Most of the nests found to date have been in commercial pine plantations, placed high up in a fork of a tree against the main trunk. This preference for nesting in plantations has led, on occasions, to the loss of nests when trees were felled while the birds were breeding. On the other hand the widespread establishment of these plantations has undoubtedly extended their breeding range greatly, and Forest Buzzards are probably more numerous now than they ever were.

The clutch usually comprises two eggs, pale green with scattered red-brown markings, laid in September or October. However, more than one chick is seldom raised, the younger one succumbing, it is believed, to sibling aggression, or cainism. The nestling period is about 50 days, which is in line with other *Buteo* species. Forest Buzzards hunt in and on the fringes of forests and plantations and take a variety of prey, which they catch on the ground. Rodents, lizards, birds, frogs, chameleons and insects have been recorded in their diet.

LONGLEGGED BUZZARD

This large, pale brown buzzard originates from eastern Europe, the Middle East and the Mediterranean countries, where it inhabits open, semi-arid country and desert fringes. Here it is resident in some areas and migratory in others.

Although the nature of its movements has not been well documented it is probable that the migratory population overwinters in the Sudan and along the southern edge of the Sahara. There have also been scattered records of the species occurring elsewhere in Africa, including a few from southern Africa, but, because of the difficulty of distinguishing it from the smaller Steppe Buzzard, few of the reports have been confirmed. It is, at best, a rare vagrant to the subcontinent. The areas where it is most likely to be found are those that match its breeding habitat, namely the semi-arid regions of Botswana, Namibia and the northern Cape.

If seen alongside a Steppe Buzzard its larger size – it is about 20 per cent larger – will distinguish it immediately. It is also a longer winged, longer tailed and more gangly bird with a slower, more 'elastic' wingbeat. The adult Longlegged Buzzard has several quite distinctive plumage features which, if taken in combination, will also distinguish it from the very variably plumaged Steppe Buzzard.

The Longlegged Buzzard usually has a pale head, which contrasts with the rest of its body, and a pale rufous, almost unbarred tail. Its underwing shape and pattern are also subtly different. There is a more extensive black patch on the carpal joint and the white areas on the primaries have a translucent appearance. In shape its wing is not as indented as the Steppe Buzzard's at the trailing edge, where the primaries meet the secondaries. The immature birds lack most of these features, though, and are usually indistinguishable from Steppe Buzzards except in terms of size and wing shape.

Any new sightings of the Longlegged Buzzard in southern Africa would be of great interest to raptorphiles, but would have to be well supported with photographic evidence to satisfy the sceptics.

The Longlegged Buzzard is a non-breeding visitor to Africa but it seldom migrates south of the equator and very rarely reaches southern Africa. It resembles the Steppe Buzzard but is larger, has longer wings and tail, and is generally paler.

AUGUR BUZZARD

This species is similar in many respects to the Jackal Buzzard. Its striking white underparts set it apart immediately, of course, but if it were not for this obvious difference one would be pressed to make a firm distinction between the two. They are similar in size and shape and are virtually identical in behaviour, habits and choice of habitat. Even their calls are not dissimilar. The Augur Buzzard's range, however, begins where the Jackal Buzzard's ends. Not all current textbooks treat the two as different species, some simply regarding them as two races of the same bird. This issue can be resolved only by studying them in an area where they overlap and determining to what extent, if any, they interbreed. If they are reproductively isolated, they are separate species, whereas a high incidence of interbreeding would show that they are conspecific.

The Augur Buzzard's range extends northwards from the Limpopo River and from central Namibia, and continues through East Africa to Ethiopia. However, if there is a single locality most closely associated with the species, it is the Matobo National Park in Zimbabwe. In this rugged, granite-hilled country the birds are common, and many of their nests have been found and monitored over the years. Their density in the area is about one pair per 2 000 hectares, with nests of adjacent pairs, on average, about 3,5 kilometres apart. Pairs live year-round in territories. At the end of winter, the start of the breeding cycle, they are noisy and demonstrative in their territories, soaring and often uttering their loud, distinctive cry: 'kow, kow, kow...'.

Most nests are positioned on the inaccessible, narrow ledges of cliffs, but occasionally they are built in trees, especially where these grow out from a rock face. Both sexes build the nest or repair the old one, and both bring sprays of green leaves to line it throughout the nesting cycle. In August or September the female lays her clutch of two blotched eggs, and she takes on most of the incubation. The eggs hatch after about 40 days. With rare exceptions, the younger chick dies a few days after hatching as a result of sibling aggression, and the surviving one makes its first flight when about 50 days old.

The bird's diet is typically buzzard-like in its variety. Reptiles are the most frequently taken items, but rodents, insects and birds, especially young gamebirds, also feature. The largest prey recorded have been a young dassie and a young scrub hare.

Augur Buzzards share the Jackal Buzzard's marvellous ability to hang motionless in the air, riding a strong wind slicing off a hillcrest, and often hunt in this way. They also hunt from perches.

The sexes can be told apart by their difference in size (females are about 10 per cent larger); in call (females' are lower pitched), and colour pattern (females have black bibs on their throats whereas males' throats are white). Young birds are streaked buffy brown below and darker brown above, and attain adult plumage at about one and a half years.

From behind, the Augur Buzzard is virtually indistinguishable from the Jackal Buzzard, both having the same slate-grey upperparts and rufous tail. However, unlike the Jackal Buzzard, the Augur Buzzard is wholly white below. The sexes can be distinguished by the extent of white on the throat: the male Augur Buzzard, illustrated here, has a white throat, whereas in the female, the dark grey on the head wraps around the throat.

Jackal Buzzard

Jackal Buzzards are cast in the typical squat, thickset buzzard mould, not overly exciting to look at when perched but lovely to see on the wing, especially when displaying their mastery at hanging motionless high above the lip of a windy ridge. Here they ride the turbulent air with rigidly held horizontal wings and tail, rocking gently now and again, head down, intently scanning the grassy slope below for movement. When a potential prey item is spotted, down the bird goes, not in a dramatic power-dive but in a gentle parachuting descent.

These are birds of the hilly and mountainous country and their bulging, broad-winged design, shared by some of the other mountain-inhabiting raptors, must in some way enhance their ability to use the airspace in this environment. They are found widely in the hills and mountains of southern Africa, ranging across the climatic spectrum from the moist, high-rainfall escarpment in the eastern parts to the arid, low-rainfall regions of the north-western Cape and southern Namibia. Their range does not extend north of about 21°S, where the very similar Augur Buzzard is found. Jackal Buzzards are common in many parts of their range, and especially in montane grassland. They are plentiful, for example, in the Natal Drakensberg, an area in which visitors can scarcely fail to see them.

Identification, at least of the adult birds, is easy. In flight they have a characteristic broad-winged silhouette and distinctive black-and-white underwing pattern, superficially similar to the underwing pattern of the Bateleur. Jackal Buzzards are slate-grey on the head and back with a richly contrasting rufous tail. In front they can be variably coloured. Most birds have a broad rufous chest band bordered above by a ragged white bar which leads into a dark grey throat. The lower chest and belly are usually barred black and white. There are individual variations, though, particularly in the extent of the white at the front: some have little or no visible white; others have a lot, and a few are almost as white-fronted as Augur Buzzards. There has, in fact, been some debate as to whether these birds are hybrid Jackal-Augur Buzzards or a 'white-fronted' colour-phase of the Jackal Buzzard.

Immature birds are streaked and mottled brown, and lack any of the distinctive plumage clues used to identify adults. They are best told apart from other brown buzzards by their large size and their broad, bulging wing shape when seen in flight. Females are about a third larger than males and can also be distinguished by their lower-pitched call.

The bird's call, a high-pitched 'kweeya', is reminiscent of, but not likely to be confused with, the barking sound of the Blackbacked Jackal and is obviously the origin of the species' name. They call frequently during the early part of the breeding cycle, and will also fly around, calling angrily, if any attempt is made to climb to their nest.

The nests are usually re-used each year, and may be built either in a tree or on a cliff-face ledge. Some pairs seem even to alternate annually between a tree and a cliff site. The nests are made of sticks and, on a ledge, are often well hidden among vegetation. The eggs – usually a clutch of two – are laid in late winter, and the parents share the incubation, with the female doing more. Occasionally both chicks are reared, but usually the second-hatched is eliminated as a result of sibling aggression. The surviving chick fledges when it is about 50 days old.

Jackal Buzzards prey on a variety of animals but especially favour rodents, lizards, young birds and insects. They also feed on carrion – such animals as springhares, mongooses and hares which become victims of night-time road traffic, and dead sheep. The latter source of food is fraught with danger, however, since some stock-farmers adopt the callous (and illegal) practice of lacing carcasses with poison in order to rid their lands of jackals and other scavenging animals. Two ringed Jackal Buzzards have been discovered dead as a result of this.

The ringing of Jackal Buzzards has provided an insight into their movements. Pairs are often found year after year at the same localities, which suggests that they are sedentary and occupy territories throughout the year. Established pairs very probably do, but two adult birds ringed in the Karoo were recovered 300 to 400 kilometres away within a year, and an immature bird was found to have moved 640 kilometres in just seven months.

BUZZARDS

The Jackal Buzzard is easily identified by its dark grey head and upperparts and its rufous chest and tail. Like most buzzard species, however, individual birds vary and an array of different front patterns occurs. While most birds have a broad rufous area across the chest, some have part or all of this replaced by a mottled black and white plumage.

Lizard Buzzard

Lizard Buzzards are squat, thick-set little hawks, somewhat larger than the Blackshouldered Kite, and they wear a 'monogram' on their throats from which their specific name, *monogrammicus*, is derived. This clear vertical black line on a white throat is one of their most distinctive plumage characteristics.

Despite their name, they are probably not buzzards at all and their final taxonomic resting place may be with the goshawks of the 'chanting hawk' clan. In earlier editions of Roberts' *Birds of South Africa* they resided (even less comfortably, one felt), among the eagles, cowering between the Crowned and the Brown Snake eagles. They share several physical and behavioural features with the chanting hawks: they are mainly grey-plumaged, they have conspicuous white rumps, two-tone fronts (grey breasts and barred bellies) and red legs and feet. They resemble the chanting hawks most of all in their calling behaviour. The call is a far-carrying, melodious whistle which starts with a drawn-out 'peeeeoo' followed by a series of sharper, lower pitched notes that accelerate and then fade away, a sound like 'wot-wot-wit-wit-wiet-wiet...'. This song or chant is uttered both by perched birds and by those soaring over their woodland habitat.

The birds are heard most frequently during August and September, at the start of the breeding season, calling from the nest and its vicinity. Once incubation is underway they become relatively silent. The chicks, however, solicit noisily for food, uttering a 'weeeeu' that can be heard a full kilometre away. The breeding cycle is similar to that of many other raptors. Male and female share in the construction of the nest, which is a solid little platform of dry sticks placed in the fork of a tree and lined with dry grass, leaves and pieces of lichen.

The entire incubation is undertaken by the female. The clutch normally comprises two eggs, white in colour and usually unmarked. These hatch after 33 days, and the chicks are initially covered in white down, their feathers emerging after two weeks. There is no evidence of cainism (the death of the younger as a result of sibling aggression) in this species, and both young are often reared. At about 40 days old, when they make their first flight, the chicks look very much like their parents, which is unusual among birds of prey. They have the same grey plumage as the adults, with barred bellies and black tails, crossed by a single white bar, but can be distinguished by their brown eyes (their parents' are red-brown) and by the buffy tipping to the body feathers.

Lizard Buzzards occur throughout the savanna belt of Africa, but are most common in tall, mature, broadleaved woodlands. In West Africa they are at their greatest density in this type of country, averaging one pair per 80 hectares, a density far in excess of that in any region of southern Africa. In many parts of the subcontinent, too, the resident birds are greatly outnumbered in winter by an influx of visitors, though the invasions vary in intensity with the years: 1979, for instance, was a 'good' Lizard Buzzard year, whereas in other years there is little or no sign of an influx. To date there have been no ringing recoveries to show where the visitors actually come from or go to. On the other hand there was one recovery which demonstrated the sedentary nature of some members of the species, for the bird was found (dead from electrocution) on the farm, near Nelspruit, where it had been ringed 10 years previously.

The seasonal movement, or nomadism, that apparently occurs among Lizard Buzzards is probably related to food availability, although there are other raptors which feed on the same prey and which do not move about. As their name suggests, they take lizards, and also rodents and insects (especially large grasshoppers). Snakes, too, are tackled, though sometimes too ambitiously, for there have been recorded cases of a snake getting the better of a Lizard Buzzard. Their hunting technique is rather unspectacular: they simply watch the ground from a perch, or occasionally from the telephone poles and wires that line the roads in bushed country.

More like a goshawk than a buzzard, and something of a taxonomic misfit, the Lizard Buzzard is nonetheless easily identified by its distinctive throat pattern. When it takes to the wing, it exhibits a broad white rump and, midway down its black tail, a single white bar. Occasional individuals have two tail bars instead of one. The sexes are alike in size and plumage, and young birds are very similar to the adults. Although common in many savanna areas, it is subject to local movements, the exact nature of which is not known.

BUZZARDS

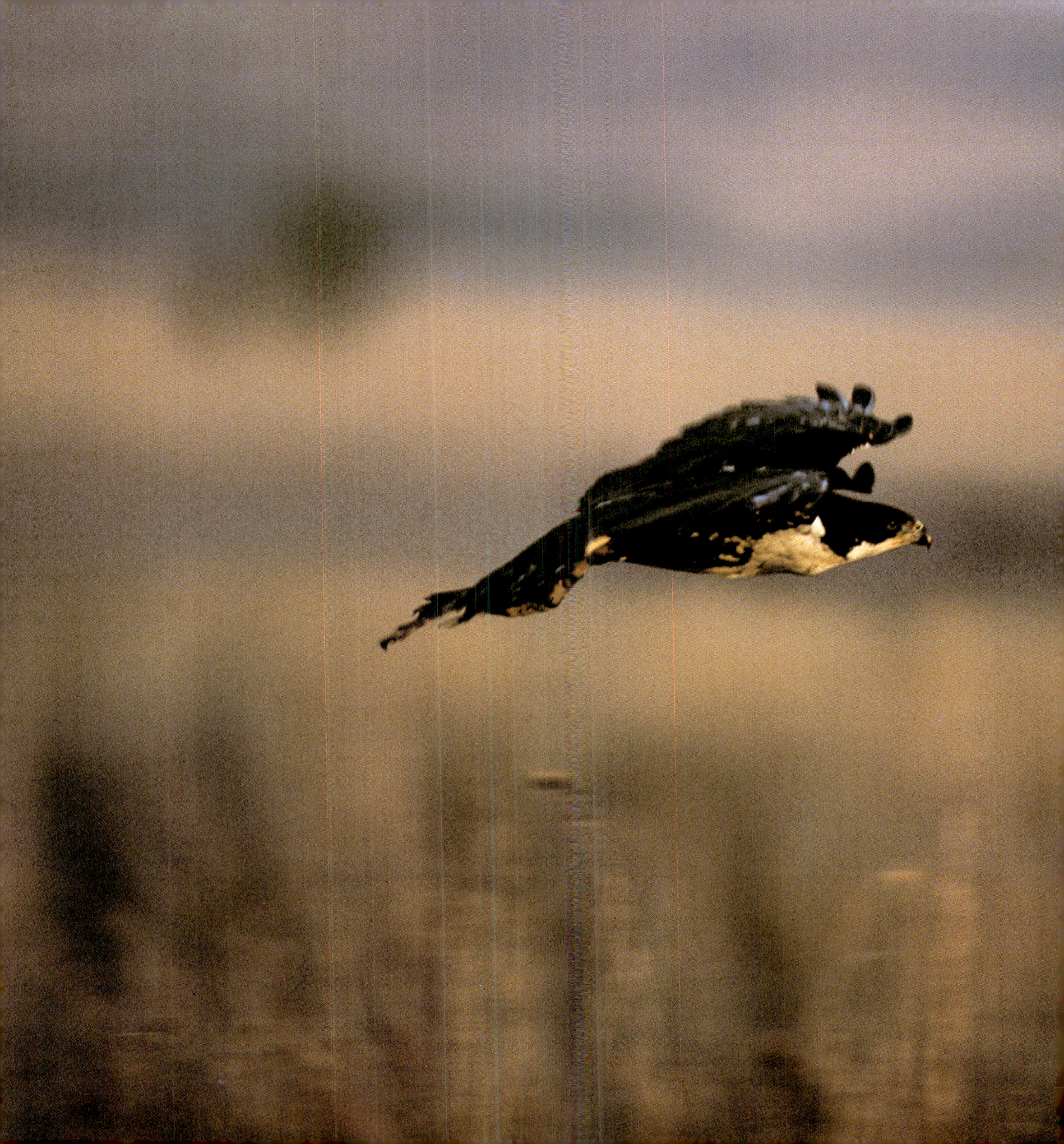

Sparrowhawks and Goshawks

Of the nine species in this group, six are members of the *Accipiter* genus and three belong to the somewhat different chanting goshawk group. The accipiters are known in falconry as 'shortwings' and are much sought after for this sport because of their rapaciousness. They have long legs and toes and needle-sharp talons, and their short, rounded wings and long tails give them great manoeuvrability in pursuing prey. Most hunt other birds, chasing and catching them on the wing. Accipiters are retiring and not easily observed. Females are much larger than males. By contrast, the chanting goshawks are not secretive and often perch conspicuously along roadsides. They have a similar build to the largest accipiters but are lethargic hunters, swooping on to rodents, small birds and reptiles on the ground.

(Left) A Black Sparrowhawk heads for cover with its quarry. The sparrowhawks are a rapacious group of avian predators and many of them hunt prey as large as, or larger than, themselves. (Above) The bloodied bill of the African Goshawk bears testimony to a recent meal.

Redbreasted Sparrowhawk

Until recently, authoritative books on southern African birds described the Redbreasted Sparrowhawk as a bird of the forests, but recent observations show that, while it needs trees for nesting and roosting, it hunts mostly in open country. Its preferred habitat is open grassland, low fynbos and open karroid vegetation, provided that there are copses of tall trees in the area.

The species occurs throughout Africa in a series of discontinuous populations, its distribution restricted to the so-called Afromontane belt. In southern Africa it ranges southwards from the montane areas of eastern Zimbabwe, through the eastern Transvaal highlands into Natal, Lesotho, Transkei and the eastern Cape and thence westwards to the Cape Peninsula. It can also be found in parts of the Karoo, which contrasts markedly in climate with the well-watered montane areas, but the open nature of this dry region suits its hunting techniques and, thanks to the introduction of trees around rural homesteads, its nesting and roosting needs are also fulfilled here.

Its expansion into the Karoo has occurred in relatively recent times. Today, these birds occur and breed in the two Karoo national parks, making use of the alien trees that grow in the areas, and they may be having a depressing effect on the small bird populations in the vicinity of the nests. If the trees were removed there is little doubt that the sparrowhawks would disappear, to the benefit of the parks' other avian species. On the other hand, although the Redbreasted Sparrowhawk is not listed as a Red Data species, it has the most restricted range of all southern Africa's accipiters and, moreover, has lost significant areas of suitable habitat to the massive afforestation of the escarpment grasslands.

The Redbreasted Sparrowhawk is closely related to the Ovambo Sparrowhawk, which is evident from the similarity between the Redbreasted's adult plumage and the plumages of some juvenile Ovambo Sparrowhawks. The two can be distinguished only with difficulty. Indeed, many earlier records of the species found outside the Afromontane region have since been re-identified as Ovambo juveniles, and it has been suggested that the Ovambo is the ancestral form from which the Redbreasted Sparrowhawk is a derivative – a condition known as 'neoteny', in which the derived form retains the immature plumage of the ancestor into adulthood. The Redbreasted Sparrowhawk is also similar in many respects to the European Sparrowhawk (which does not occur in southern Africa), to a degree that has prompted some authorities to list them as races of the same species. In recognition of the close relationship between the three they are grouped into a single 'superspecies'.

All three prey mainly on birds, which they catch by hot pursuit. The Redbreasted Sparrowhawk's prey includes larks, pipits, longclaws, canaries and other open-country birds up to the size of a dove. There are also some unexpected records, from the Drakensberg, of Alpine Swifts being taken.

The only place where one can expect to see Redbreasted Sparrowhawks is at their breeding sites. Here, in contrast to their otherwise unobtrusive lifestyle, they are relatively obvious, and if they become accustomed to people near the nest, as often happens around a farm, they will lose their shyness, becoming bold enough to attack someone attempting to climb to the nest. In early spring, when the eggs are laid, both sexes call frequently, and the fledged chicks, too, noisily solicit food. A few months later, when the breeding cycle is complete and the young are independent, quietness descends once again, and one is hardly aware that the birds are there.

A young Redbreasted Sparrowhawk. Diagnostic features at this age are its whitish eyebrow and throat, and dappled buff-coloured front. Initially the young bird has a grey eye but this changes to yellow when it is four months old.

SPARROWHAWKS AND GOSHAWKS

An immature Redbreasted Sparrowhawk peers suspiciously from its sheltered perch. Despite the secretive nature of this species and its habit of remaining in cover, it does most of its hunting over open ground, flying low and fast just above the contours, ready to snatch up any small bird. Its rounded wings and long tail enhance its manoeuvrability, while its long thin legs and toes with their needle-sharp claws are used to pluck the victim out of the air.

SPARROWHAWKS AND GOSHAWKS

A moment of indecision on the part of a Laughing Dove resulted in its falling victim to a hungry Ovambo Sparrowhawk. In the same mould as the Redbreasted Sparrowhawk, this species is an agile, rapacious, bird-hunting hawk. It can be distinguished from the other grey-coloured accipiters by its small 'beaky' head, its dark reddish brown eye and (not visible in the bird illustrated here) the pattern on its upper tail. The Ovambo Sparrowhawk hunts in a variety of ways: often by hot pursuit, sometimes by ambush from a perch, and occasionally by soaring high in the manner of a falcon and then diving down after birds passing below.

Ovambo Sparrowhawk

Identifying this species is an acquired skill, fraught with pitfalls for the newcomer. It is a smallish, greyish hawk in the sleek, short-winged, long-tailed and long-legged mould of the accipiters, and it looks like half a dozen other smallish, greyish raptors. Familiarity with their shape and jizz – the smallish head, 'beaky' face and proportionately rather long wings – enables easy identification, but to the uninitiated they can look like the Little Banded Goshawk, the Gabar Goshawk, the Little Sparrowhawk, the African Goshawk and, in juvenile plumage, the Red-breasted Sparrowhawk.

One of the difficulties with the identification of the accipiter group as a whole and with this species in particular is its unobtrusiveness and the fact that the birds seldom provide the opportunity for a leisurely, clear view. If one could systematically go through their diagnostic features, their identification would not pose a problem. Usually, however, one is left wondering if the tail was barred or the rump was white – and was the eye yellow or red? These are the features that need attention.

Ovambo Sparrowhawks do not have white rumps, which distinguishes them from Gabar Goshawks and Little Sparrowhawks; and they have wine-red eyes, quite distinctive from those of Little Sparrowhawks and African Goshawks. Above all they have a unique upper-tail pattern, and a clear view of this will immediately establish their true identity, be they adult, juvenile or melanistic. The upper tail is broadly barred with pale and dark grey. In the pale bars which cross the centre two tail feathers, the feather shafts are white, producing three clear elongated white flecks. Immature birds, which may be rufous or dull white streaked with brown, have a dark patch behind the eye and a prominent white eyebrow and are thus easily identifiable.

These are savanna birds that range northwards from Zululand through the eastern and northern Transvaal into Zimbabwe, northern Botswana and northern Namibia. They hunt over open ground. In pristine landscapes they probably occupied areas where woodland abutted on vleis, dambos and other open country. However, in the south-central Transvaal, where they have been studied most intensively, they occur commonly at the interface between the bushveld (savanna) and the highveld grassland. Here they nest in the copses of tall exotic trees that have been planted in the past 80 years or so, and hunt in the mosaic of bush and grassland on which has been superimposed a mosaic of farmland, both intensive and pastoral. Nesting pairs are resident in this region and, depending on the location of plantations, are usually spaced at intervals of about five kilometres. In early summer, when they start nesting, one is aware of their presence from their call in the nesting area – a sharp, repeated 'keep, keep, keep, keep...'. Later in the season the fledged young are also noisy, but once breeding is over the birds are among the quietest, least noticeable of hawks.

In this region of the Transvaal the favoured nesting tree is the grey poplar and the stick nest is built in a high fork, some more than 25 metres above the ground. Little Sparrowhawks sometimes share a plantation with Ovambos but if a Black Sparrowhawk takes occupation then the Ovambos move out. The nest is intermediate in size between those of a Little Sparrowhawk and a Black Sparrowhawk, and is built, by both sexes, of small dead branches collected from neighbouring trees. The eggs are laid in September or October, the clutch comprising three or four (rarely two or five). The female undertakes most or all of the incubation, and is fed by the male; in most aspects of the breeding cycle they are similar to other accipiters. They differ, however, in some respects in hunting habits. One of their special techniques is to soar and then stoop down on birds flying below in the manner of a falcon. They also hunt from perches in tall trees, watching the open country for passing birds.

Ovambo Sparrowhawks are exclusively bird-hunters, their prey comprising such species as pipits, bulbuls and weavers. Dove-sized birds are about the largest item they take. In common with other dimorphic accipiters the larger female probably takes bigger prey than the male. However, as most records of the sparrowhawk's feeding habits have been based on an identification of the feathers lying around plucking sites, it is not usually possible to determine the sex of the bird that made the kill.

Little Sparrowhawk

This species is second only to the Pygmy Falcon in being the smallest southern African bird of prey. The males weigh only 70 to 80 grams, and the slightly larger females about 100 grams.

How do such tiny hawks, smaller than doves, survive in the competitive world of predators when they themselves are potential prey for other bird-catching hawks? The answer, simply, is by stealth, for Little Sparrowhawks are among the most unobtrusive and difficult-to-find of the subcontinent's raptors. Not that they are scarce; on the contrary, in parts of their range they are commoner than any other bird of prey and, in suitably wooded habitat, nesting pairs may be found at intervals of as little as three to four kilometres. If their calls and the places they choose to nest in are known, they can be located without difficulty in early summer, which is the start of their nesting season. Visits to the nest during the following month will then reveal the incubating female, or, more usually, only the end of her tail protruding beyond the edge of the little stick nest placed high in a tree. If a visit coincides with the arrival of the male with food for his mate, there will be a brief spell of calling and she will slip off the nest to feed, and give the watcher a better view.

But these are special circumstances, for usually Little Sparrowhawks are spotted only by chance. A small hawk (or is it a cuckoo?) planes across the road while we are out on a game-viewing drive in Zimbabwe's Hwange or in one of the Zululand reserves. It settles in a tree and we are momentarily surprised at its tameness. We can see its bright yellow eye and eye-ring and the almost-black tail with its two conspicuous white spots. Then it is off and we glimpse its white rump. Although so small that one would think it unmistakable, it is easily confused with other small accipiters, since size is a poor field character.

Little Sparrowhawks prey largely on birds but other items, such as lizards and insects, also feature in the diet. One of its common hunting techniques is ambush. Waxbills, which are the size of bird it takes most frequently, have the habit of visiting waterpoints in the heat of the day to drink. The Little Sparrowhawk knows this and chooses a foliaged tree near the spot to wait. It is fascinating to watch it hunt, intensely alert, head bobbing, looking this way and that. When a brace of small birds has settled to drink, out it shoots, accelerating towards its chosen victim with rapid wingbeats. If unsuccessful (as more often than not it is), it veers off and goes back to a perch. One would think that, having had such a fright, the waxbills would go elsewhere to drink, but within minutes they are back again.

The breeding cycle of the Little Sparrowhawk is typically accipiter-like, the male assuming the role of hunter, the female that of nest-defender and incubator. However, both help build the nest, which is a small platform of twigs placed high in the fork of a tree, sometimes as much as 25 metres above the ground. Eucalypts, where they are available, are much favoured. The clutch consists of two eggs (rarely more or less than this), white and unmarked. They take about 32 days to hatch, which is much the same as the incubation period of other accipiters, and the chicks fledge after 26 days or so. They remain in the vicinity of the nest for a few weeks and are fed by the parents, before gradually moving farther afield, eventually to become wholly independent.

Little Sparrowhawks have an unusually broad habitat tolerance: they are found in moist evergreen forests, through a range of woodlands and savannas and into semi-arid areas, where they occur mainly along wooded drainage lines. They share the forest end of the spectrum with African Goshawks, the woodlands with Ovambo Sparrowhawks and Little Banded Goshawks and the semi-arid end with Gabar Goshawks. They range from the humid Zululand and Mozambique coastal plains across to the dry edges of the Kalahari and Namib Desert. Despite their wide distribution and relative abundance in some areas, there is no particular place that can be recommended in order to be absolutely sure of finding them.

The Little Sparrowhawk is one of southern Africa's smallest birds of prey but, gram for gram, is as rapacious a hawk as any of the larger accipiters. It preys mainly on birds and is capable of catching and killing species the same size as itself. The bird depicted, pausing while wolfing down a small bird, displays immature plumage and is distinguished from the adult by its spotted, rather than barred, front.

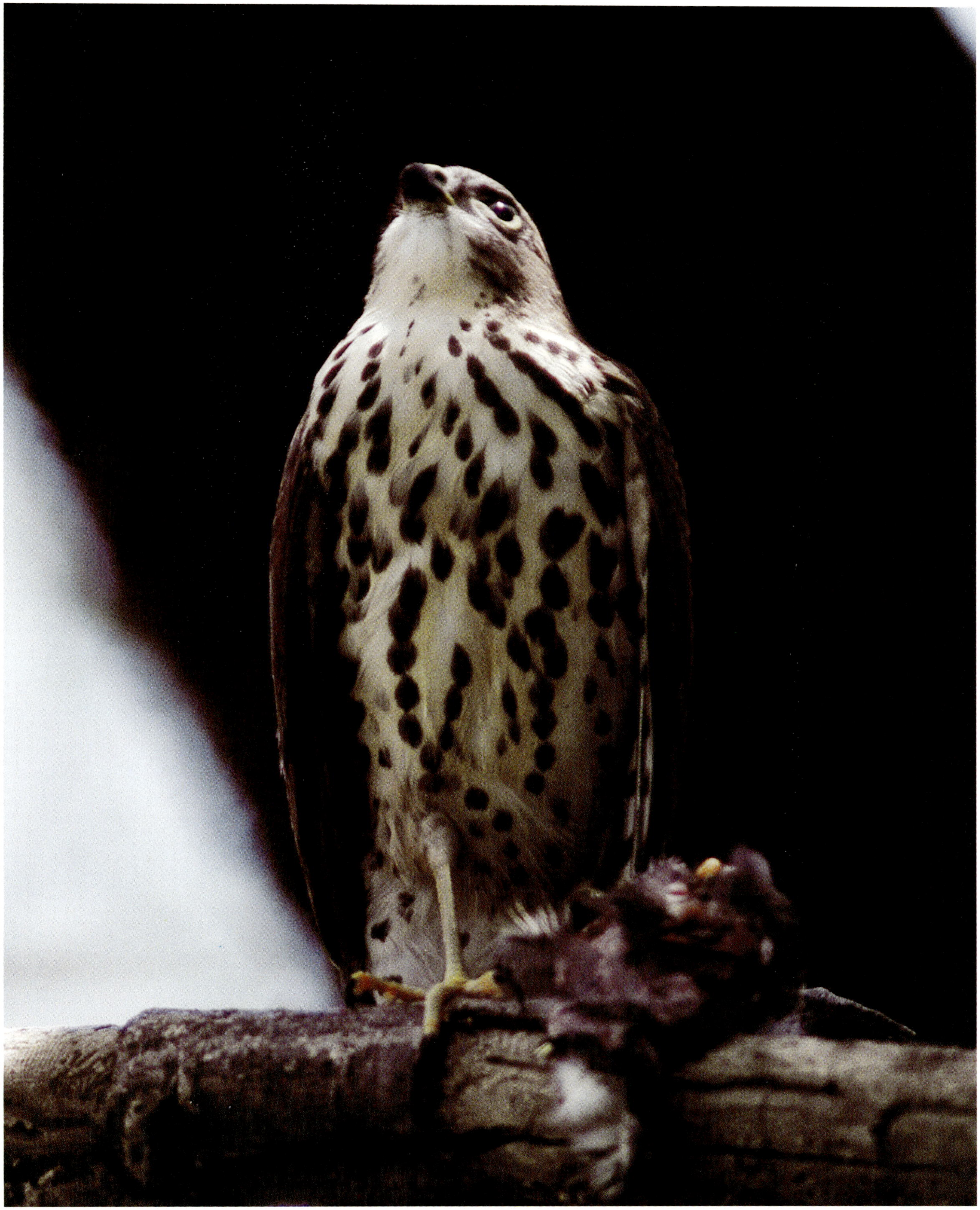

Black Sparrowhawk

Despite its size and bold black-and-white plumage, the Black Sparrowhawk is as unobtrusive as any accipiter. It is restricted to areas where there are tall trees and, ancestrally, was probably confined to the forested eastern parts of southern Africa and, elsewhere, to the kloofs and riverine galleries where large trees occurred. Now, with copses and plantations of exotic trees established over much wider areas, the species has extended its range dramatically. Pairs occupy many of the bigger clumps of eucalypts, poplars and pines planted, 50 or even 100 years ago, around farms, and it is almost certain that the species is much more widespread today than it was a century ago. Thus man's encroachment, which is threatening so much of our natural heritage, has in this instance had quite the contrary effect.

The Black Sparrowhawk's general lifestyle is typical of an accipiter, though there are some differences determined by its larger size. Pairs live throughout the year in their chosen areas and, in prime habitat, adjacent ones may nest just three or four kilometres apart. During the breeding season their activities focus on the nesting area; at other times of the year they range more widely and, because of their secretive nature, often go undetected. In contrast to most other accipiters they often re-use the same nest, which grows in size over the seasons until it can resemble a metre-thick eagle's nest. Some sites are known to have been occupied for over 20 years. Even a newly built structure is a substantial affair, much larger than that of any other southern African accipiter. Black Sparrowhawks have been known to take over the nests of Ovambo Sparrowhawks, Gymnogenes and Longcrested Eagles and, in turn, to have had their own nests hijacked by African Hawk Eagles, Giant Eagle Owls and Egyptian Geese.

While the other southern African accipiters lay eggs in summer, Black Sparrowhawks produce theirs in late winter, mostly during July and August. At this time of the year established pairs simply move in to the old nest, add to it and lay with minimum fuss, but males who have not bred before spend much more time calling from their prospective nesting areas. When a female responds, there is much chasing and calling before the serious business of nest-building gets under way. The result of these first attempts is often a solitary egg, in contrast to an experienced pair, which will usually produce a clutch of three or four. In the preceding weeks the female does not range far from the nest. She is fed by her mate during this time, and throughout the incubation and the early part of the nestling period. The eggs take 37 to 38 days to hatch, followed by a lengthy fledging period of about 45 days. As a result most broods fledge during October and November, a time when many smaller bird species are breeding and there are plenty of recently fledged chicks about for the inexperienced young hawks to hunt.

The male sparrowhawk weighs about 550 grams, the female 900 grams – a substantial size difference, which influences the type of prey taken. The former generally hunts dove-sized birds (and especially doves), the latter a higher proportion of francolins and even larger species such as the Helmeted Guineafowl which can weigh up to two kilograms. The Black Sparrowhawk is a formidable predator and for this reason it is a popular falconry bird.

The reasons for this size dimorphism, found among many raptors and exhibited so markedly in the Black Sparrowhawk, have been the subject of much debate. The contrast is greatest in species that prey on other birds and is minimal or non-existent in scavengers such as vultures. One theory holds that the size difference serves to expand the prey base for the species and to reduce male-female competition for food. Another is that females are larger so they can both force their mates to bring them food and prevent them from eating their chicks.

However that may be, any explanation has to account for both the variation in dimorphism found between raptor groups and the fact that it is the female that is invariably the bigger bird. Birds of prey with high dimorphism have strongly partitioned roles in the breeding cycle, a feature well illustrated by the Black Sparrowhawk. The male is the hunter and the female the incubator and nest-defender. It is thought that the size difference is related partly to this partitioning and partly to the nature of the prey being taken. Those species that hunt the most agile prey (birds) have the widest differential; those that

SPARROWHAWKS AND GOSHAWKS

From its striking black and white plumage one would expect the Black Sparrowhawk to be a conspicuous bird. It is, when it so wishes, such as when defending its nest from intruders or when in hot pursuit of a fast-flying dove across open country. At other times, however, it lives in typical sparrowhawk fashion, in a shroud of secrecy, coming and going unobtrusively, and perching high up in foliaged trees.

feed on the least agile prey (and there is nothing less agile than carrion!) are the least dimorphic. To carry the point further, agile prey is most successfully caught by equally agile predators, and smallness enhances this quality.

However, a conflicting requirement during the breeding period is the need to be able to store body fat to survive those times when hunting is poor; obviously a bird cannot be both agile *and* fat. One theory which accommodates this anomaly argues that the roles are partitioned so that, when necessary, both ends can be achieved: males do not store fat, remain agile and do all the hunting; females do not hunt during the breeding period but instead incubate and tend the young, and, being larger, have the enhanced ability to store fat – an ability which may play a role in other issues such as nest defence. In species which do not depend so much on agile prey for food, the dimorphism is less marked, and parental roles are often less clearly demarcated.

Immature Black Sparrowhawks have the same build and jizz as adults but are quite differently coloured. The rufous bird illustrated here is one of two juvenile colour forms, the other being white in front, streaked with dark brown. Young birds begin their slow moult into adult plumage from about a year old. Here, the first black feathers of adulthood can be seen on the bird's thighs.

Pale Chanting Goshawk

There are two sounds that epitomize the Kalahari. One is the barking geckoes clicking from the entrances of their holes at dusk; the other is the melodious 'song' of the Pale Chanting Goshawk, which carries across the silhouetted thornveld in the cold dawn. It is a series of piping notes which accelerates into a trill at the end: 'kleeu, kleeu-kleeu-klu-klu-klu-klu-klu…', finishing like a spinning plate coming to a standstill. It carries over a long distance and usually signifies that spring is in the air – for that particular pair of birds.

One cannot fail to see this species while visiting the Kalahari or any of the semi-arid westerly parts of southern Africa – Namaqualand, the Karoo, southern Namibia. It perches conspicuously (as often as not on a telephone pole alongside the road) and it is strikingly handsome and conspicuous with its long red legs and bold stance. The legs (and cere) are well set off against a pale grey plumage, finely barred on the belly and with a broad white rump and white secondaries in the wing. There is no noticeable size dimorphism between the sexes and no cases of melanism have been recorded in this species. It looks very much like its sister species, the Dark Chanting Goshawk, and in the few places where the two overlap one needs to look carefully to distinguish between them. Juvenile Pale Chanting Goshawks have the same bold look and jizz about them, but they are an overall mottled brown colour with yellow legs and cere and a less distinct white rump. Juveniles of the Pale and Dark Chanting Goshawks are even more alike than the adults and can only be distinguished by the plain white (not barred) rump of the Pale Chanting Goshawk.

Pale Chanting Goshawks penetrate as far as any raptor into such desert areas as the Namib and, in these arid or semi-arid conditions, they need to be opportunistic hunters. They take birds, snakes, lizards, rodents and insects unselectively, and feed on carrion when they find it, often scavenging on carcasses of small animals or birds killed on country roads. Most of their hunting is done from an exposed perch, and the goshawks may sit at the same spot for hours at a time, often in fierce sun, looking this way and that, watching the ground for movement. When a lizard or small mammal is spotted they glide slowly down and, if necessary, complete the chase on foot. The victim is then taken to a perch to be eaten. This low-intensity hunting style belies the fact that they are also formidable predators: when they put their minds to it they will determinedly pursue such large species as Black and Redcrested Korhaans over hundreds of metres, gradually gaining on them until the gap is closed and the tiring bird is snatched in one quick movement. Such large prey, too heavy to take into a tree, is simply devoured on the ground.

An interesting phenomenon that has been observed several times in the Kalahari is the association between Pale Chanting Goshawks and honey badgers, or ratels. One goshawk, or perhaps a pair, may come across a ratel foraging during the day and will follow at a safe distance for hours, sometimes standing on the ground nearby as the animal scratches away at rodent holes, and sometimes perched in a bush above it. If a gerbil or mouse is flushed out and escapes, the goshawk is on to it in a trice. The association may even have some benefit for the ratel, who could receive warning from the bird of an approaching predator.

Pale Chanting Goshawks live in pairs throughout the year, occupying permanent territories covering a few square kilometres. They sometimes hunt or perch together, but more usually they operate on their own. In very dry years they make no attempt to breed, but make up for this in wet seasons, when they occasionally attempt to raise two broods. The upper branches of a thorny tree are chosen for the nesting site, and the building work (they construct a typical hawk stick-nest, about 400 millimetres in diameter) is shared. In a few instances the same nest is re-used during the following season.

These birds have the odd habit of lining the nest with pieces of dung, rags, wool or other rubbish found on the ground nearby. The eggs – usually two, white and unmarked – are laid in late winter or early summer. However, more than one chick is seldom raised. The incubation, which lasts for about 37 days, is undertaken by the female, who is fed by her mate during this period of the breeding cycle. The chick fledges after seven to eight weeks.

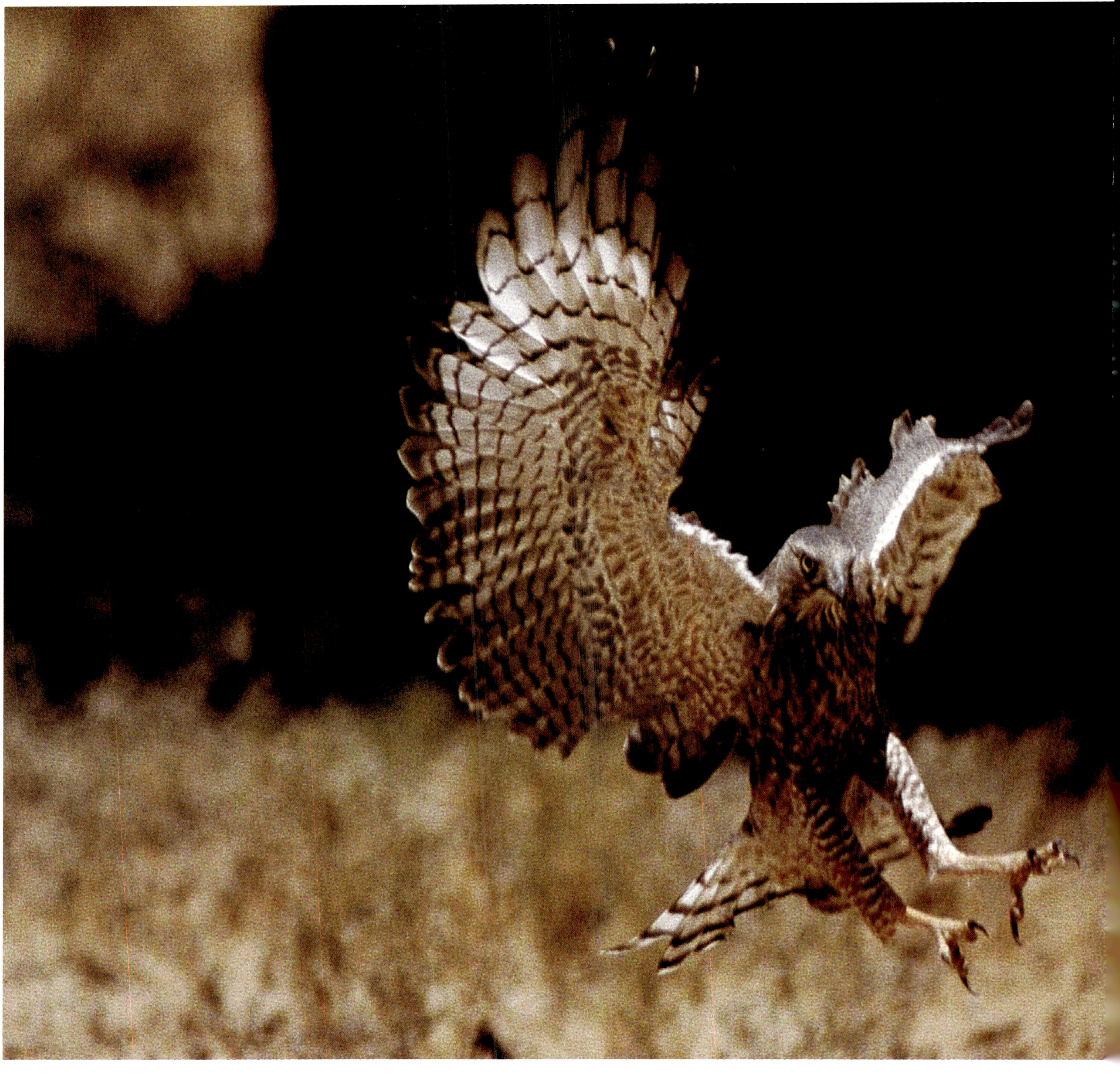

*T*he Pale Chanting Goshawk is common in the semi-arid areas of southern Africa. It is conspicuous, and easily identified from its habit of perching prominently on a tree, shrub or telephone pole. It hunts from such positions, scanning the surrounding ground for a lizard, rodent or unsuspecting bird. When prey is sighted it swoops down, talons extended, and snatches it up. Although most of its prey tends to be small, it is capable of catching gamebirds as large as korhaans, francolins and guineafowl. Carrion is also eaten when available: in the early morning these goshawks can be found scavenging off the carcasses of birds and mammals that were killed by traffic on the road during the night.

The Dark Chanting Goshawk's distribution begins more or less where that of the Pale Chanting Goshawk ends. A species of the moist savanna, it is a darker, somewhat smaller version of its arid savanna sister species. Like the Pale Chanting Goshawk it takes a wide range of prey – reptiles, mammals, birds and insects – and it hunts these from perches. It is not, however, nearly as conspicuous, perhaps because the woodland habitat it frequents makes it less likely to be seen from a distance.

Dark Chanting Goshawk

Dark Chanting Goshawks are little more than darker, slightly smaller versions of Pale Chanting Goshawks, and prefer to live in a more heavily wooded habitat. The behaviour, calls, hunting techniques and nesting habits of the two species are very similar. However, their ranges do not overlap to any great extent, the Dark Chanting Goshawk being essentially confined to the 'moist' savanna and its Pale sister species to the 'arid' savanna. In the few places where they do overlap it would be instructive to know whether they live side by side and simply ignore each other, whether they live apart by occupying slightly different habitats, or whether they are inter-specifically territorial.

Because they are so alike, one needs to look carefully to distinguish the two where they do occur together. Dark Chanting Goshawks are a uniformly darker grey and, in the two areas where Pale Chanting Goshawks are white – on the secondaries and the rump – the Dark Chanting is, respectively, plain grey and finely barred grey and white. The differences can be seen when the birds are in flight. The immatures of the two species are more of a problem, for they both have mottled brown colouring. Here too, though, the rump colour can distinguish them, as it is whitish in the Pale and greyish in the Dark.

Dark Chanting Goshawks extend from the eastern Transvaal lowveld and Mozambique, northwards into Zimbabwe and then westwards into northern Botswana and Namibia, in all of which regions they are fairly common. They live in tall-tree woodland or savanna. They share the Pale Chanting Goshawk's habit of perching on a prominent vantage point but, because of the denser nature of their surroundings, are not as conspicuous as the latter.

The biology and nesting habits of the Dark Chanting Goshawk have not been thoroughly studied but, again, indications are that they resemble the Pale Chanting Goshawk in these respects. They prey on snakes and lizards, birds, insects, and small mammals such as dwarf mongooses, squirrels and mice, and feed on carrion when the opportunity presents itself. Woodland species such as the Yellowbilled Hornbill and Laughing Dove have been recorded in their diet, the Helmeted Guineafowl being the largest bird known to have been taken. They have also been observed using ratels and foraging groups of Ground Hornbills as 'beaters', perching a little way ahead of the latter and catching the small animals and birds which the hornbills miss.

The breeding period is early summer, at which time the Dark Chanting Goshawk calls frequently, both from a perch and from the wing. According to reports, its song is faster and higher-pitched than that of the Pale Chanting Goshawk. Male and female share in the building of the nest, which is sited in the fork of a large tree. The clutch comprises two white, unmarked eggs.

The dark, not pale, secondaries help distinguish the Dark Chanting Goshawk from the Pale.

Little Banded Goshawk

Although the Little Banded Goshawk, or Shikra as it is more widely known outside southern Africa, is typical of the genus *Accipiter* – which includes the bird-catching hawks – it is not moulded in the tradition of this rapacious group. It is proportionately shorter winged, shorter tailed and shorter legged than other accipiters and, as one would expect with this morphology, it preys not so much on swift-flying birds as on small reptiles and large insects. It is also less stealthy than the typical accipiter and ventures out of cover, on occasion, to hunt from telephone poles in a very un-sparrowhawk like fashion. Consequently it is more frequently seen and more familiar to us than other accipiters.

The species frequents the savanna belt of Africa, and is found in similar habitats in India and Sri Lanka. When actively hunting, it moves from perch to perch through the bush, choosing a concealed branch in a tree from which to watch the ground below for movement. One of its favoured prey items is the Cape Rough-scaled Sand Lizard which is an abundant species in many savanna areas. Little Banded Goshawks can easily spot these conspicuous and lively little lizards, for the males are brightly coloured, and they catch them with a quick dive to the ground. Insects are taken in the same way, and small birds, such as waxbills and weavers, may also be caught while feeding on the ground. They snatch geckoes and cicada beetles from tree trunks, and, when presented with the opportunity, rob nests of their nestlings. In short, they are very generalized hunters, a factor which may well contribute to their abundance in much of their range.

These goshawks begin nesting in early summer, and it is during this period that they are most obvious. The chosen site is usually high up in the fork of a tree, the nest a small saucer-shaped platform made of twigs. Tall eucalypts are often selected for the security they offer from predators. Both the male and the female collect sticks for their nest, at intervals chasing each other or soaring over the nesting area and making their characteristic 'kli-vit' call. At this time, and throughout the incubation period, the female virtually ceases hunting and is fed by her mate. When she is not involved in building or courtship she perches quietly in the vicinity of the nest. At about the time she is ready to lay her eggs, usually a week or two after starting the nest, she begins to add a lining of bark chips, which she collects from the flaking trunks of neighbouring trees. None of the other accipiters use this material for a lining to the same extent as the Little Banded Goshawk and its nest can immediately be recognized by this characteristic, if inexplicable, feature.

The cycle from egg-laying to fledging takes about two months, during which time the parents play different and well-defined roles. The male provides the female – and later the young – with food. He is away for most of the day, visiting his mate at intervals to bring prey. At night, too, he sleeps away from the nest. The female never leaves the vicinity of the nest during the incubation period and thereafter until the young are at least half-grown. She spends about 90 per cent of the daylight hours and the entire night incubating the eggs, and broods the young when they are small. This changes in the later stages of the nestling period, when the chicks start growing feathers and she begins hunting again, helping her mate feed the hungry brood.

There are several other small hawks with which Little Banded Goshawks can be confused. The adults are grey-coloured with a finely barred front, and bear a superficial resemblance to the adults of the Ovambo and Little Sparrowhawks and to the African and Gabar Goshawks. One very distinctive feature, however, is the coral-red of the eye: none of the otherwise similar-looking birds have such brilliantly coloured eyes, and there are only a few other birds of prey (among them the Blackshouldered Kite) that have similar brilliant red eyes. It has been suggested that females can be distinguished from males by having orange eyes, but this does not stand up to examination – birds with orange (or yellow) eyes are usually also found to have traces of immature plumage on them and when they reach full maturity their eye-colour changes accordingly.

Immature Little Banded Goshawks are essentially streaked and barred, brown birds, distinguishable from immatures of some of the other species only by careful scrutiny.

SPARROWHAWKS AND GOSHAWKS

*L*ittle Banded Goshawks are small, grey accipiters with coral-red eyes (in adult birds) and a distinctive whistling callnote. They live in bushveld country and do not venture into forests or grassland and scrub vegetation. This species breeds in early summer, constructing a small stick nest high up in the fork of a tall tree. Two or three young are raised, fledging after about four to five weeks in the nest.

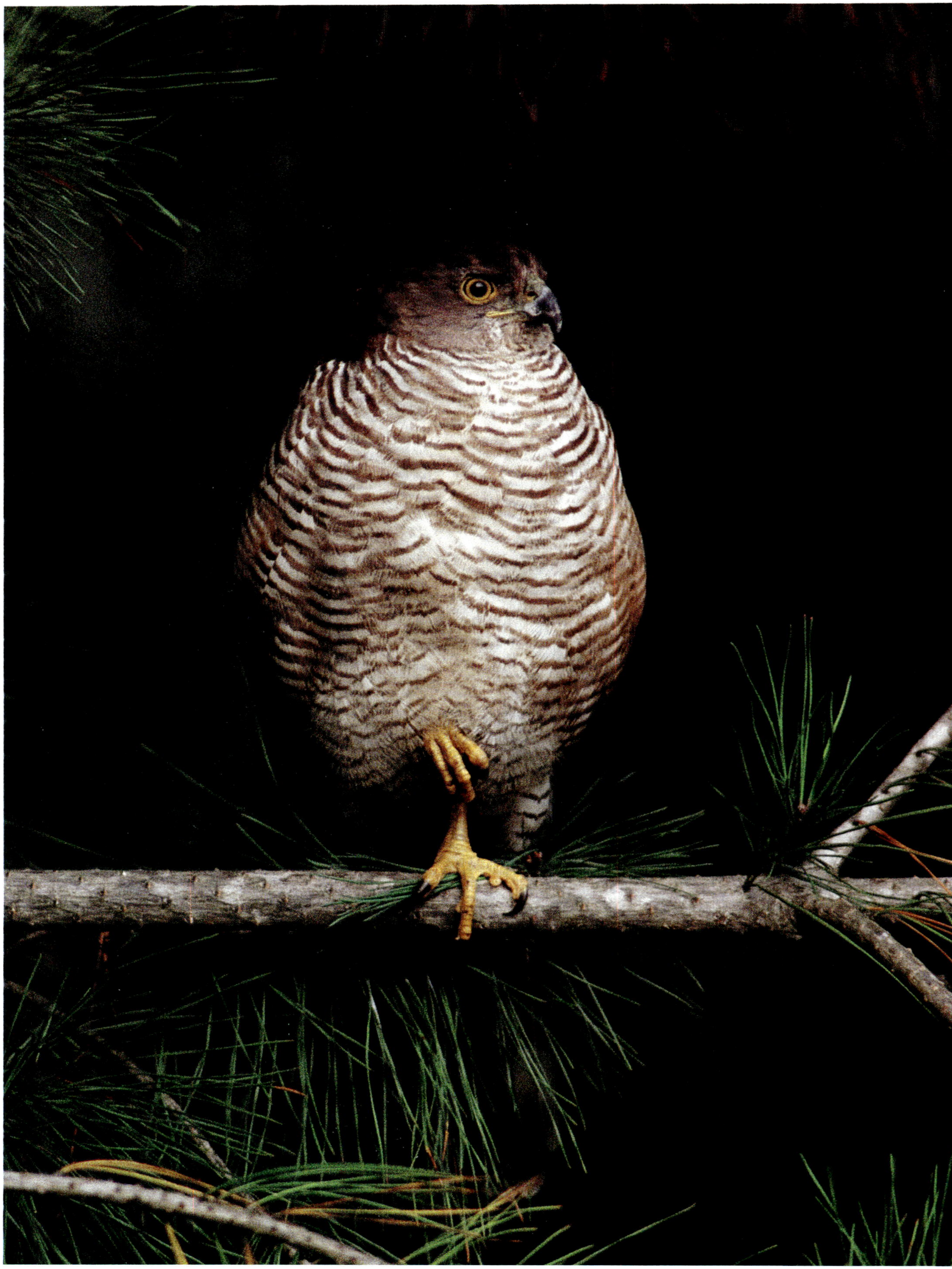

AFRICAN GOSHAWK

Negotiating the track through the forest after a rainstorm is always tricky, with the puddles of water sometimes concealing deep ruts. Jolting around the next corner, we are suddenly confronted with the spectacle of a very wet, pigeon-sized bird sitting in a pool of water. Looking embarrassed at being caught in the bath, so to speak, it takes off and soggily flies to a low branch just off the road, where it stays as we pull up alongside it. At close range we can see its piercing yellow eye, accentuated by a yellow eye-ring, its yellow legs and feet, the hooded effect created by its dark cap, its uniform bluish-grey back and its barred front washed at the flanks with rufous. It is clearly an accipiter, and the forest habitat, as well as the distinctive physical features, tells us we are looking at an African Goshawk. Then it drops off its perch and with a few quick wingbeats is lost in the tangle of the forest.

African Goshawks are *the* hawks of the forest, built for manoeuvring at speed through the confusion of branches and vines. Encountering them in their environment is a matter of sheer luck, although Squaretailed Drongos seem to find them easily enough and, when they do, they pester the goshawks relentlessly, giving a shrill alarm call and clicking at them from a safe distance. A sign that an African Goshawk is about is the sound of the same clicking note that the drongo imitates so well, sometimes coming from the depths of the forest, but more usually from high in the sky above the forest.

If one lives within the range of a pair of these goshawks, then their call, and their early morning display flight, will be a familiar and almost daily event. Throughout the year, but most frequently in the months from late winter through to early summer, one or sometimes both birds soar over their territory in the early morning, alternately gliding and flapping, every few seconds uttering a far-carrying clicking note – a 'krit... krit... krit...' – which sounds much like the opening note of a Blackeyed Bulbul's call. The birds' morning flight can last from a few minutes to half an hour or more, and when it is over the goshawks once again become invisible.

The sexes are so dissimilar that one could be excused for thinking that they belong to two different species. The female is nearly twice as large as the male and is much browner in colour. She has brown upper parts (in contrast to the male's bluish-grey) and her front is barred with brown (the male's is rufous-barred). The juvenile birds have a quite different, and distinctive, plumage. They are brown above, with some buff tipping to the feathers, clean white below, and they display bold, pear-shaped spots all down the front. The size difference between males and females is already evident in nestlings.

African Goshawks are opportunistic hunters, for the most part taking birds but also such non-avian items as chameleons, lizards, frogs, small rodents, forest squirrels and occasionally insects, including moths. A wide variety of birds has been recorded in the goshawks' diet, most of them in the size range between bulbul and dove. One of the most spectacular prey species documented is the Narina Trogon. There is evidence to suggest that the male hunts smaller birds than the female, which is to be expected when taking into account the marked size dimorphism between the sexes.

The African Goshawk's breeding cycle is typical of an accipiter but, because the bird is so secretive, has not often been studied. The nest is well hidden in creepers or parasitic plants growing high in a forest tree, and the birds arrive and depart unobtrusively. The degree to which the nest is re-used annually varies, some being occupied only once, others up to eight times. The male and female share in the nest construction, and keep the structure lined with fresh green leaves throughout the breeding cycle. The clutch of two or three white, unmarked eggs is laid in early summer and hatches about 30 days later. The young fledge about 35 days afterwards, but return to be fed for some time after they learn to fly. They remain in the vicinity of the nest for two to three months, during which period they become increasingly proficient hunters, and decreasingly dependent on the adults. Thereafter they disperse and, like their parents, become shadows in the forest.

The male and female African Goshawk differ dramatically both in size and plumage. The female (shown opposite) is uniform brown above, and white finely barred with brown below. The male is bluish grey above and barred with rufous below. In both sexes, however, the eye and eye-ring are yellow. This is the only southern African accipiter to have a grey-coloured cere.

GABAR GOSHAWK

In summer thousands of visitors to Skukuza, in the Kruger National Park, are entertained by the activity and bustle in the large weaver colonies in the trees in front of the restaurant. Spottedbacked and Lesser Masked Weavers share the branches of the large fig trees overhanging the river, building their suspended kidney-shaped nests at the very tips of the branches. They are probably safe here from most of their enemies, but there is one villain by which they are always threatened. This is the Gabar Goshawk, a small grey-coloured bird built on the lines of an accipiter, with broad, short wings, a long tail and long legs and toes. And, like accipiters, it preys largely on a variety of other birds, but specializes in the robbing of weaver nests.

A shrill clamour in the weaver colony signals its arrival. It has probably been perched quietly out of view, watching from a distance, noting which nests are being attended by females, and, having completed its homework, it flies in, ignoring the scolding weavers. In a flash it is hanging under the nest and tearing a hole through the wall. One of the chicks inside, nearly ready to fly, jumps out in a desperate attempt to escape, but the goshawk quickly snatches it up and carries it, struggling, to a branch.

Gabar Goshawks prey on a great variety of birds, hunting mainly by hot pursuit, first flushing out the victims and then chasing them down with considerable speed and agility. Most prey fall within the sparrow- to thrush-sized category, with doves at the upper limit. On one occasion, however, a Crested Francolin, weighing 238 grams, was taken by a Gabar weighing 207 grams. Gabars are more opportunistic than most accipiters, including in their diet small mammals, reptiles and even insects.

Although these little hawks look so similar to some *Accipiter* species that their identification can be difficult at times, it is thought that they are most closely related to the Chanting Goshawks and Lizard Buzzard, collectively associated in what could be called the 'chanting hawk' clan. In this group adults are essentially grey-plumaged with two-tone fronts (plain grey chest and throat and barred lower parts), a prominent white rump and/or barred tail, and orange or red cere and legs. However, while the other members have melodious whistling calls, the Gabar makes a rather feeble piping sound.

Gabar Goshawks occur throughout southern Africa in areas of thornveld, scrub or open savanna, and they are probably most common in the more arid western part of the subcontinent. In suitable habitat one encounters them singly or, less often, in pairs, usually perched in the upper branches of a tree. A small proportion of the birds are melanistic, which means that instead of the normal grey plumage, they are entirely black. These melanistic birds lack the conspicuous white rump that characterizes adults with normal plumage.

Gabar Goshawks begin breeding in early summer and, like many other birds of prey, are then vocally active for a short period. They have one very unusual habit, which is not shared by any other southern African bird of prey, of adding a particular species of spider's web to their nest. The spiders rapidly spread their nest over the goshawk's, so that by the time the chicks fledge the entire structure is festooned with cobwebs. This provides a degree of camouflage, for it looks just like a monstrous spider's nest, though whether it fools any potential predators, and thus makes for a higher survival rate, is uncertain.

In other respects the breeding cycle is not very different from those of other similar-sized hawks. Two to four eggs are laid; they hatch after 33 to 35 days, and the young make their first flight 35 days later. The female incubates and broods the chicks and the male hunts to provide food for the family.

Melanism is unusual in birds of prey except in the case of the Gabar Goshawk, where up to 10 per cent of the population consists of entirely black individuals. These birds have a red cere and legs, as do normal-plumaged birds, but they lack the species' characteristic white rump.

SPARROWHAWKS AND GOSHAWKS

The Gabar Goshawk is a small bird, typically accipiter-shaped with its short, broad wings, long tail, and long legs and toes. It occurs mainly in semi-arid thornveld, where it hunts opportunistically, taking diverse prey, including many species of birds, as well as lizards, rodents and insects. It varies its hunting methods and uses either hot pursuit, still-hunting or nest-robbing; when indulging in the latter method, the Gabar's most frequent victims are weavers.

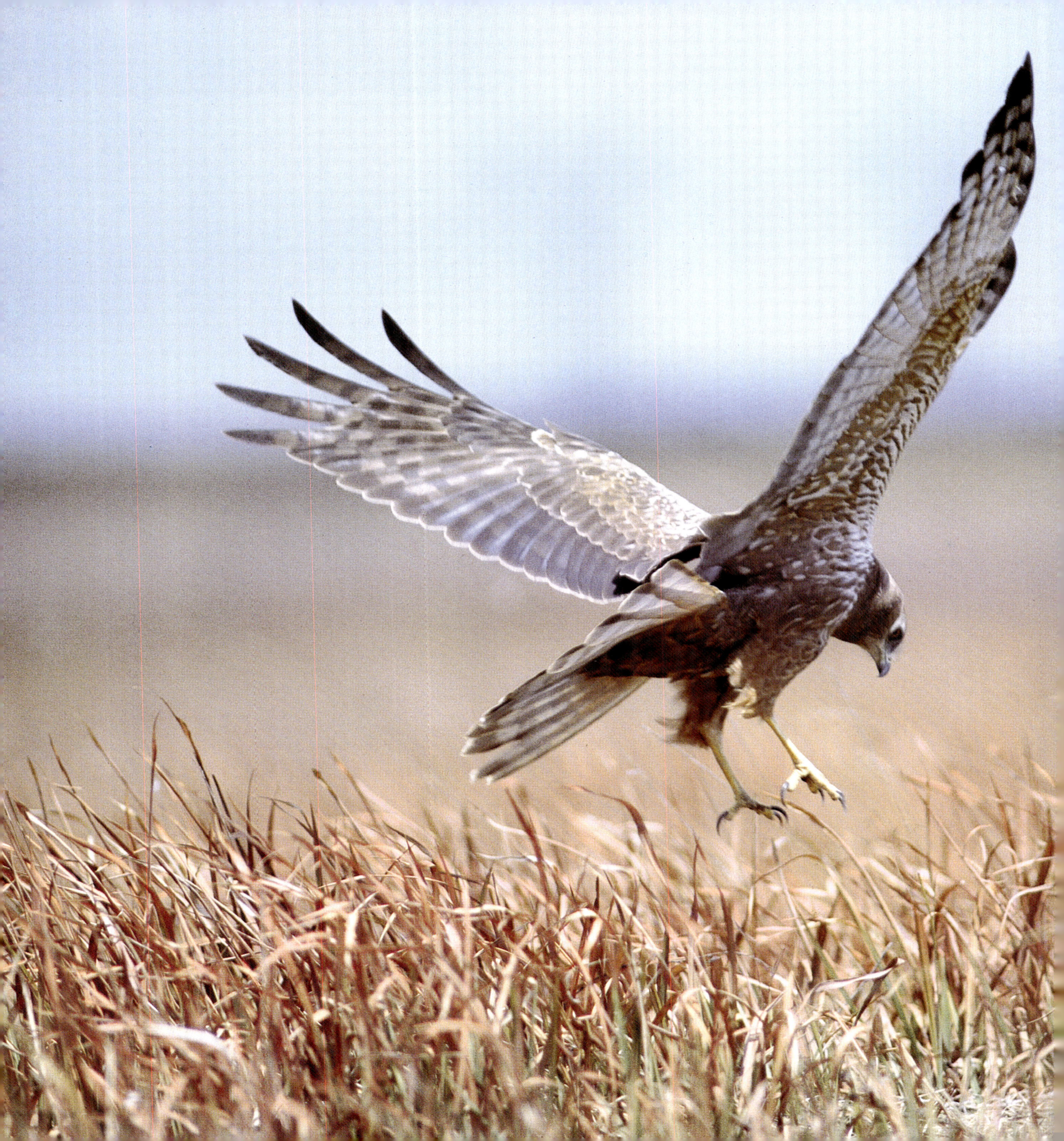

HARRIERS AND ALLIED SPECIES

The harriers are a distinctive group, characterized by having long, thin bodies, wings and tails, cowled faces and a preference for open, treeless habitats. Five species occur in southern Africa. They share the same distinctive flight and hunting technique – that of flying slowly, head facing down, with alternate bouts of flapping and gliding, when they hold their long wings in a shallow, raised V. Usually seen close to the ground, they may soar to considerable heights on occasions. They prey mostly on rodents, small birds and small reptiles. All build their nests on the ground and the Black and African Marsh Harriers conceal these in reedbeds, sedges or shrubby vegetation. Included in this group is the peculiar Gymnogene, formerly named the Banded Harrier Hawk. It bears some similarities to the harriers and is lumped with them for want of a better place.

(Left) Open grasslands and beds of sedge provide typical habitat for most harrier species. Here an African Marsh Harrier hovers momentarily before dropping into the vegetation. (Above) A fine male Montagu's Harrier perches at ground level.

European Marsh Harrier

The naturalist Thomas Ayres collected, near Potchefstroom in the Transvaal, the one and only southern African specimen of this harrier species, and wrote about it in the *Ibis* journal in 1871. A century passed before the next one was observed (in Zimbabwe). Despite the existence of Ayres' specimen, which was sent to the Norfolk Museum, the record had slipped off the books to become one of the 'list of doubtful species' for which there were 'no authentic records' in the 1970 revision of Roberts' *Birds of South Africa*. The 1972 sighting vindicated Ayres' record, and was the first of a number of sightings of European Marsh Harriers in southern Africa.

This phenomenon – of a 'new' bird being seen in a region for the first time, to be quickly followed by a spate of further recordings – is a surprisingly common one. Does it mean that the bird has changed its range, or that it has simply been overlooked or misidentified in the past? Once the new bird's identity has been established, however, the information disseminates rapidly through the bird-watching fraternity. Misindentification is probably the reason for the mystery of the European Marsh Harrier. It has the same general appearance as the resident African Marsh Harrier, and it frequents the same areas. African Marsh Harriers are variable in their plumage, a fact which has not been adequately illustrated or described in local field guides. An added source of confusion has been the practice, in some books, of treating the two species as one.

However, if one knows what to look for, European Marsh Harriers are not difficult to recognize. They are substantially larger than the African species and if the two are seen in flight in the same area this difference will be obvious. Most of the 'Euros' reaching southern Africa are juvenile birds or females, which are similar to each other but quite different from the adult male. They are an overall chocolate-brown in colour with a strongly contrasting pale creamy-white cap on the head. The extent of this cap is variable, sometimes almost absent (in juveniles) or, at the other extreme, extending on to the throat. Adult females also have a similarly coloured leading edge to the top of the wing, which is an obvious feature when the bird is in flight. Juvenile African Marsh Harriers are also often chocolate-brown but the colouring tends to be smudged and streaked with buff feathers, particularly around the chest, where they have a pale gorget, and on the nape. If one can see the tail and wing feathers clearly this should ensure identification, as these are barred in the African species but not in the European. Male European Marsh Harriers are striking birds: they have rufous-brown bodies and wing coverts, and pale grey heads, tails and secondaries and primaries, the latter tipped with black.

European Marsh Harriers breed in the Palearctic, and are common birds there in many of the wetland areas. The southern European populations tend to be resident while those from the colder northern latitudes migrate south into Africa during the northern winter. They regularly reach the large wetlands of Zambia, but it is probably only the occasional straggler that ranges as far as South Africa.

The European Marsh Harrier is a very rare non-breeding visitor to southern Africa. This species was virtually unknown in southern Africa a decade ago but in the last few years has been recorded at several places.

HARRIERS AND ALLIED SPECIES

Unlike the closely related African Marsh Harrier, the sexes of the European Marsh Harrier look quite different from one another. The female (above) is chocolate-brown except for a creamy white crown (and sometimes throat and shoulder patches), while the male (opposite) has a rufous-coloured body, straw-coloured head, and mainly pale grey wings and tail.

HARRIERS AND ALLIED SPECIES

The African Marsh Harrier builds its nest at ground level, usually hidden in reeds or sedges above wet ground. Here a female broods her young on such a nest. The main breeding period for this species is during winter and spring when the chance of the nest being flooded by rising water is slight. The female does most of the nest construction and virtually all the incubation, while the male hunts and provides her, and later the chicks, with food.

African Marsh Harrier

The South African highveld presents a bleak landscape in winter. The veld is golden-brown, the mealie-lands that have been harvested are trampled down by the cattle and every breeze launches dozens of broad, crackly, dry leaves into the air. Down along the river the reedbeds are brown and their fluffy tops are almost spent. Groups of streaky-brown, winter-plumaged bishops and widows are flying back and forth from the reeds to the dry branches of the gnarled willow trees, to the stubbled mealie-lands and back. All at once they burst from the reeds and fly, calling shrilly, up into the trees. A harrier is quartering the reedbed: flap, flap, flap … glide, with wings held stiffly angled a little above the horizontal and head looking down. More leisurely flapping, and then the bird executes a sudden somersault and head-first dive into the vegetation. It is lost to view for perhaps a minute and then out it comes carrying a fat, short-tailed brown rodent in its claws. The bird climbs steadily and then heads off towards the large reedbeds at the bulge in the river. As it approaches it starts calling and soon a second bird rises from the reeds and in a smooth, well-rehearsed aerobatic movement, takes the prey and drops back out of sight.

What was that all about? If we venture into the reeds we will find the answer. Sitting low on her nest, the female is surrounded by a wall of reeds broken only by the window of sky above and the seemingly lifeless, still water half a metre below her. She and her mate started building the nest six weeks ago, collecting dry stems of weed and reeds and even some of the dry mealie leaves being scattered by the wind, and when the base was firm and secure she added a lining of dry grass and laid four white eggs. Now she listens for the sound of her mate. Away on the hill she hears the distant voices of farm labourers and the noise of a vehicle starting and moving off. Close by in the forest of reed-stems an African Sedge Warbler chucks quietly, but keeps out of view. On the left an aircraft drones in the distance. Then she hears the chattering note of her mate. She calls in reply, a plaintive 'kjeeeeuuk', waits for his approach, then rises from the eggs and launches into the air to meet him for the food-pass.

African Marsh Harriers are breeding residents in southern Africa and, as their name implies, are birds of the marshlands, preferring the permanent vleis of reedbeds and sedges to those that are seasonally flooded. In suitable vleis pairs occupy territories throughout the year, and the nests may be spaced at intervals of just a few hundred metres. Territory occupants advertise their presence by soaring above the reeds, calling 'wiee, wiee…', and express their displeasure at intruders by flying with their talons down. They do all their hunting on the wing, slowly quartering the ground, listening for prey rather than looking for it. They have cowled, rather owl-like facial features, which may enhance their ability to detect the squeaks and rustles coming from below. Rodents, like the Vlei Rat, are often taken, as are frogs and birds, but almost anything that they are capable of overpowering is a potential prey item. At times they may even feed on carrion – dead fish that have been beached, for instance, or dead birds. They occasionally catch ducks but these are probably at the upper limit of what the harrier can handle.

Breeding may take place at any time of the year but it occurs most frequently in early summer. Like so many other raptors the parental roles are divided: females incubate and tend the young, males hunt and provide the food. As many as six eggs may be laid although the usual clutch size is three to four. The incubation, which lasts about 35 days, starts when the first egg is laid and so the hatching process is staggered. The consequent size disparity often results in the starvation of the youngest of the brood. The chicks are covered in buff-coloured down from the time they hatch, start to sprout feathers when about nine days old, and are capable of making their first flight after about 38 days.

Wetlands are among southern Africa's most threatened habitats, and the African Marsh Harrier is often one of the first victims when these areas are polluted or drained, dammed or interfered with in some other way. There is evidence that the birds are far less plentiful now than they once were and, although they are not listed in the South African Red Data Book of Birds, their status and continued welfare needs careful monitoring.

BLACK HARRIER

The southern Cape and Karoo are renowned for their endemic plant species, but it is perhaps less well known that these regions are also home to a number of localized breeding birds.

One of the most striking of these and, to the raptorphile, the most interesting, is the Black Harrier. It holds a worthy place in the mountain fynbos and wheatlands landscape, a conspicuous black and white bird cut in the classic harrier mould, flying slowly, head down, flapping and gliding, scrutinizing the ground for prey, holding a position briefly to investigate a sound, with heavy wingbeats and tail fanned, then continuing its methodical quartering of the land. From a distance it appears an essentially black bird with a bold white rump, and these features, and the harrier-like flight, are sure pointers to its identity. At closer range the other pale areas in its plumage can be seen. The tail is barred black and white and the underwing has an extensive whitish area between the leading and trailing edges. As it comes closer still, its rich yellow legs, eye and cere and its typical harrier-like 'cowled' face are revealed.

Until recently the Cape Province could claim the honour of supporting the only breeding population of Black Harriers, but recently a pair was found nesting near Oliviershoek Pass in Natal. However, the southern Cape is unquestionably the species' main breeding area, stretching eastwards from Langebaan and the west coast 'strandveld' through the southern Karoo as far as Cathcart and Grahamstown. During the breeding period (July to December) they are seldom seen outside this range, but in the non-breeding months (January to June) there is a weak movement of birds northwards. It is during this period that odd individuals are encountered in the highveld grasslands of the Transvaal and Orange Free State, and in Natal, the northern Cape and, occasionally, in Namibia and Botswana.

The first Black Harrier recorded in the Transvaal was observed in 1961, but in recent times half a dozen or more birds are regularly found each year, at scattered localities in the region, suggesting that there has been a significant change in the status of the species.

Although Black Harriers occur alongside African Marsh Harriers in places, they are not restricted to wet locations for nesting purposes, and generally frequent much drier habitats, often far from water – especially mountain fynbos, karoo scrub, renosterbos, wheatfields and pastures, and open grasslands.

In marked contrast to the African Marsh Harriers, there is a feeling that they have become more numerous in recent decades and are extending their breeding range (as indicated by the recent Natal record). If this is indeed the trend it requires monitoring, particularly as it was only 40 years ago that they were thought, though probably erroneously, to be on the verge of extinction. Their expansion, if such it is, may even be linked to the much-publicized encroachment of the Karoo semi-desert into the eastern Cape and Orange Free State. At any rate the Black Harrier, though scarce and restricted in range, is certainly not threatened now.

Black Harriers breed in early summer and lay their eggs principally during the months of August and September. Before this they often soar and call in the nesting area, and then select a site on the ground, one that is hidden in fynbos or sedges, sometimes on a hill slope. The male and female share in the nest-building, bringing in sticks and then adding a lining of dry grass, which the female supplements during the incubation period. She lays three or four white eggs, and undertakes all the incubation, while her mate brings her food at intervals during the day. He spends much of his time hunting and the remainder perched on a favourite vantage point, not far from the nest, from which he can quickly alert the female to approaching danger or chase off predators. The eggs hatch after about 34 days, and once the chicks start feathering the female spends more time helping to hunt. In this and other respects the nesting cycle is similar to that of the African Marsh Harrier. The young Black Harriers make their first flight after about 36 days, gradually become more independent of their parents, and then disperse.

The wheatlands of the south-western Cape provide a classic backdrop for one of southern Africa's few endemic birds of prey, the Black Harrier. Its striking black and white plumage and warm yellow legs and cere enable easy identification. When nesting, it is virtually restricted to the southern Cape but out of the breeding season birds wander northwards, reaching the Transvaal, northern Cape and southern Namibia.

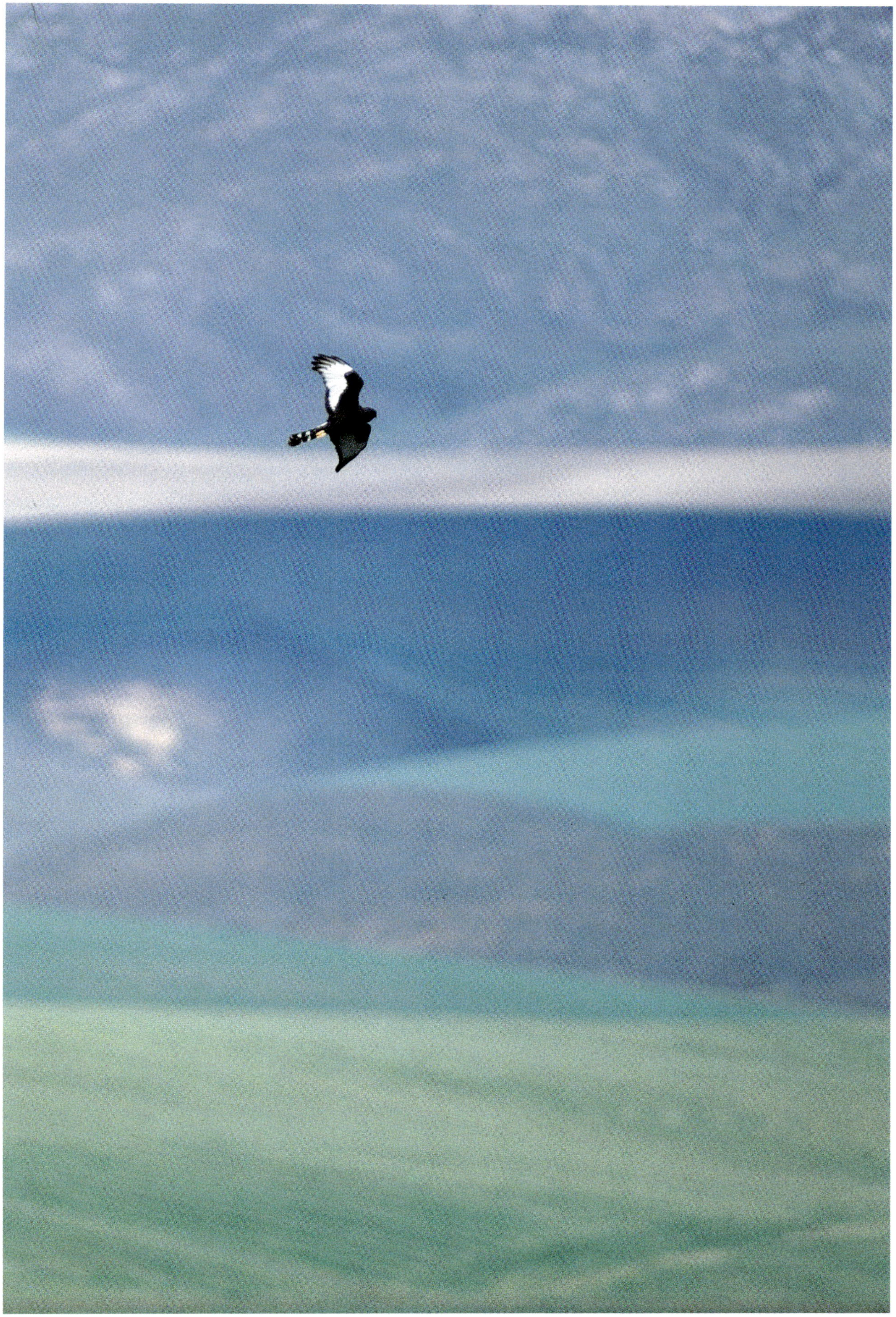

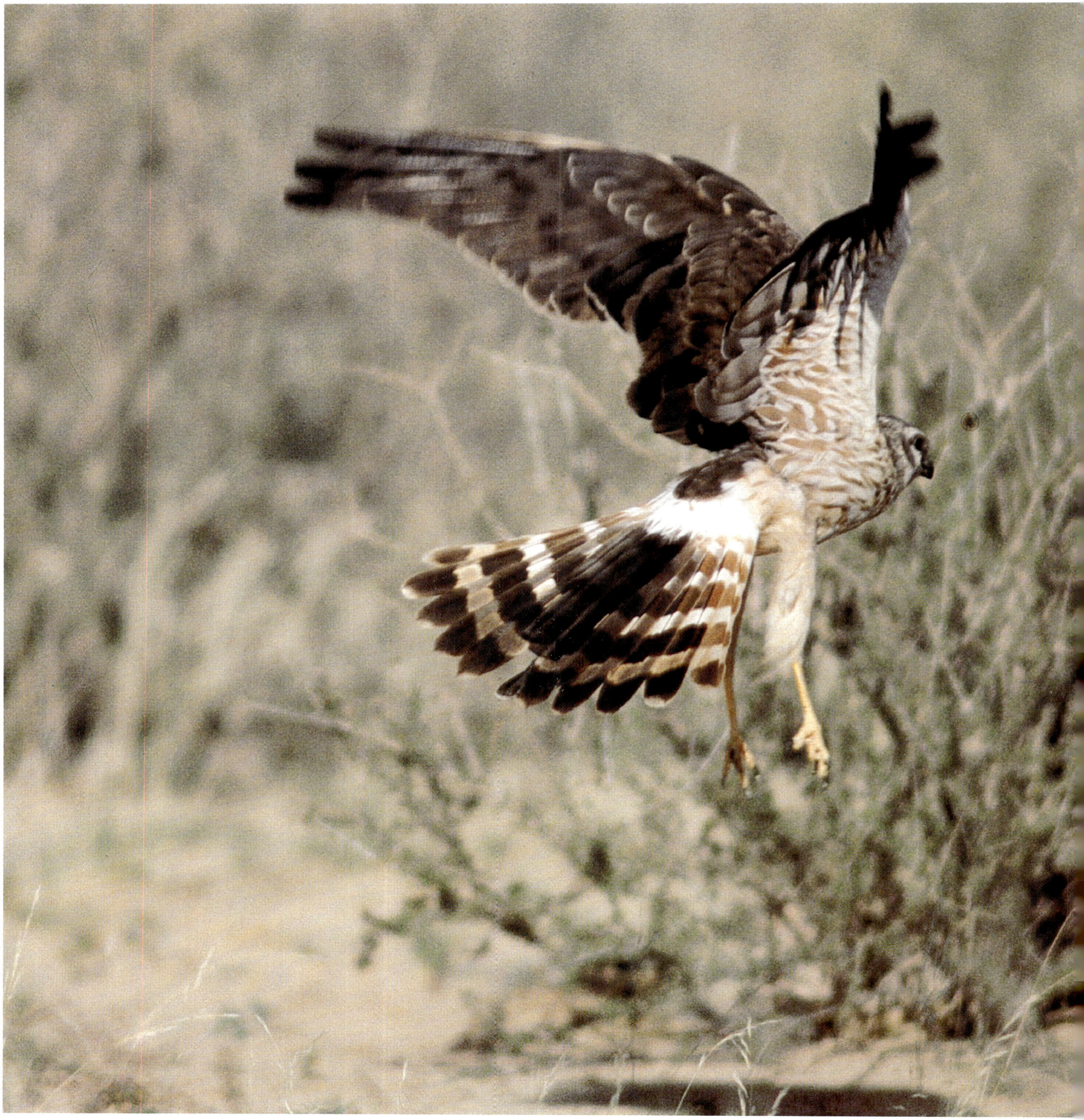

*T*he immature Black Harrier (above) is chocolate brown above, with buff edges to its wing feathers. Its yellow iris is a distinctive character – in other young harriers the iris is brown. (Left) A young 'ringtail' harrier beginning its moult into adult plumage. Its poorly defined collar and the barring just visible on the newly emerged secondary feathers suggest that the bird is a Montagu's and not a Pallid Harrier.

HARRIERS AND ALLIED SPECIES

The Montagu's Harrier is an uncommon non-breeding visitor to southern Africa. Once much commoner on the subcontinent, its numbers have greatly decreased in recent years. The male, illustrated above, is dove-grey, with white underparts lightly streaked with brown. Females and immatures are streaky brown-coloured birds with whitish rumps, similar in appearance to female and young Pallid Harriers; these are often collectively referred to as 'ringtails'.

Montagu's Harrier

Like other harriers, the Montagu's is all wing and tail. It has a small, slim body and long, narrow wings, and its low wing loading enables it to fly at very slow speeds, which it does with a characteristic alternating flapping and gliding flight.

Montagu's Harriers are non-breeding visitors to Africa. They breed during the northern summer in western and eastern Europe and then move southwards, those from western Europe coming into Africa and those from farther east migrating to India for the winter. The species' stronghold in the western regions is Spain, where an estimated 3 000 pairs breed in the fields of wheat and other cereal crops, in the heaths and in the moorland. They nest during May to July; the female incubates her clutch of four or five white eggs while the male hunts and brings her food. As can be expected, nests in wheatlands are often destroyed during harvesting and this no doubt contributes in a small measure to the species' steady decline in numbers. This decline is apparent in southern Africa too and Montagu's Harriers, once a regular sight in suitable areas in summer, are now seldom seen on the subcontinent.

Montagu's Harriers spend their winter months throughout the savanna belt of Africa, extending as far south as the eastern Cape. Nestlings ringed in Holland and Scandinavia have been recovered in several West African countries. It is interesting to note that, whereas such other migrating raptors as buzzards and eagles are reluctant to fly across the Mediterranean and instead funnel through the Straits of Gibraltar or go around its eastern edge, many harriers apparently fly straight over the sea. This is perhaps because they are not designed for soaring flight.

In their winter quarters these harriers usually remain solitary. On the other hand, when they are migrating they are often to be seen in small parties: during March as many as a dozen birds may wing their way northwards. In southern Africa females and immatures, in their nondescript brown plumage, greatly outnumber males and, together with the very similar-looking immatures and females of the Pallid Harrier, are collectively known as 'ringtails'.

In the northern hemisphere there is a third 'grey' harrier species which is known as the Hen Harrier in Europe and as the Northern Harrier or Marsh Hawk in North America. It is not a long-distance migrant in Europe: the birds from the northern areas simply fly south into the Mediterranean countries. Across the Atlantic, however, they move to South America for the winter. Surprisingly, a male of this species was reported recently from Namibia, and if this is confirmed it represents not only the first documentation of the bird on the subcontinent but in the whole of sub-Saharan Africa, so it is certainly something to look out for. Hen Harrier males can be easily distinguished from males of the Pallid and Montagu's Harriers by their white rumps, but females and immatures look much like their 'ringtail' counterparts in the two latter species.

The male Montagu's and Pallid harriers can be differentiated in flight: whereas the Pallid has uniform grey wings with black tips, the Montagu's Harrier (below) has a narrow black line along the centre of the wing where the coverts meet the secondaries.

Pallid Harrier

This species is a rare, non-breeding migrant to southern Africa. Its breeding grounds are largely on the steppes of the Soviet Union (hence its German name, 'Steppe Harrier'). In these dry grasslands scattered pairs nest during the brief summer, from May to July, and then move southwards, funnelling into Africa during September and October and then streaming down the Nile River and Rift Valley into their winter quarters. Many overwinter in the open country lying north of the Equator in West and East Africa, but some continue southwards to the tip of the continent.

Pallid Harriers were much more widespread in their winter quarters as late as the 1950s. There has been speculation about the decline, though a contributory factor is almost certainly the loss of breeding habitat as a result of large-scale agricultural development. Another is the accumulation of pesticides on the land, in both their breeding areas and their winter quarters.

Males are almost gull-like in appearance, pale grey above from head to tail, with long, grey wings that are black-tipped, and wholly white below. At first glance they could be mistaken for the male Montagu's Harrier, but their clean, unmarked lines distinguish them. Females and immatures are different, however, being generally streaked brownish birds (females are streaked below) except for the broad white rump. They too are very similar to the female and young of the Montagu's Harrier, and the two species are often simply referred to as 'ringtails'. They can, however, be distinguished providing one gets a good look at the facial markings: the Pallids have a more distinctly marked cowl.

Like other harriers, Pallids hunt over open ground, especially open grassland and cultivated fields. They hunt in typical harrier mode, alternately flapping and gliding. They take a variety of prey, including rodents, small birds such as larks, pipits, queleas and quails and their eggs and nestlings, grasshoppers, crickets, beetles and other insects, and lizards and other small reptiles. In southern Africa they are nomadic, and move about the subcontinent in response to changing weather conditions.

The Pallid Harrier leaves the steppe region of the Soviet Union at the end of its breeding cycle and migrates to Africa and India. Once a fairly common visitor to southern Africa, it is now seldom seen. Like all harriers, it frequents open country and hunts by quartering the ground with a slow, deliberate flight.

Gymnogene

At first glance the Gymnogene has a gangly, unco-ordinated look about it – disproportionately long wings and tail, an undersized head and pinched little face, and strong tarsi which terminate in ineffectual-looking feet. It looks, and is, an unusual bird, but very effectively designed for its speciality, which is to seek out helpless or inactive prey.

The Gymnogene's long, broad wings and little body give it an exceptionally low wing loading and the ability to cruise along the edges of hillsides and ravines at close to stalling speed, so it can watch for prey. It is particularly adept at finding and robbing birds' nests, using the increasingly anxious mobbing behaviour of the parents to home in on its target. It steals eggs and nestlings from colonies of weavers and swifts, and from breeding herons and egrets. It also clambers about on tree trunks, hopping along branches, and probing into the crevices with its bill or feet. Its intertarsal or 'knee' joint can bend backwards as well as forwards, enabling it to reach into deep holes, such as those of woodpeckers and barbets, to extract the contents. For prey that would otherwise prove inaccessible, the Gymnogene hangs on to the underside of a branch, or to the side of a cliff, flapping to keep its balance. Just about anything that it comes across – sleeping dormice or bats, mice, lizards, nestling birds – is taken. Curiously, in the areas of West Africa where oil palms grow, the fruits provide Gymnogenes with the bulk of their food, whereas in southern Africa fruit is apparently excluded from the diet.

Another curiosity is the Gymnogene's 'blushing' behaviour. It has an unusual unfeathered face (its name, in fact, means 'bare cheeks'), a feature which, it is thought, facilitates probing into holes. The bare skin is normally pale yellow in colour, but in certain contexts it can flush, almost instantly, to deep red. Unexpected disturbances, like a branch snapping near the bird, can trigger a blush, though it most often happens during interactions between the pair, suggesting an increased level of excitement. In male-female exchanges the phenomenon is believed to represent an appeasement signal made by the individual who assumes the submissive role. The bare face may also have a thermoregulatory function.

Gymnogenes occur widely in southern Africa, living in a variety of landscapes. Most characteristically, though, they are found either in the galleries of tall trees fringing the larger rivers, or in hilly country where there are deeply incised ravines and steep hillsides. Pairs are territorial throughout the year, and in hilly habitats range over areas of five to 10 square kilometres. In early summer they can be seen soaring together in display flight, making their plaintive, drawn-out whistle, a kind of 'pu-eeeeee-oo'. Pairs usually have one or two regularly used breeding sites in the territory. A favourite nesting site is in a tall tree at the head of a ravine and overhanging a waterfall, or in the base of a rock fig growing out of a cliff, but they may use a wide variety of sites ranging from rock ledges to eucalypt plantations.

Their clutch of two eggs appears in September or October. Richly blotched with dark red-brown, they are among the most striking of all raptor eggs. Throughout the incubation and nestling periods the nest is kept thickly lined with green leaves. Both the parents help gather these, and both incubate the eggs, although the female's share of work is the larger. She is provided with some of her food by the male, but she also leaves the nest to hunt, at which times the male takes over the incubation. After about 36 days the eggs hatch and the younger chick, which emerges a few days after its elder sibling, is disadvantaged by its smaller size and usually starves. From this point on the male does all the hunting. The mother looks after the youngster until it is about three weeks old, after which she starts helping to bring in prey. The chick fledges after about 52 days and soon begins ranging away from the nest and learning how to catch insects and other easy prey.

Adult Gymnogenes, with their smoky grey plumage, barred bellies and very distinctive flight pattern, are easy to identify. The sexes can also be distinguished: the female is larger and has more black spots on the wing coverts than the male. By contrast, immature birds can be very confusing as they come in a range of buff, brown and ginger colour forms. They do, however, have the same gangly look as the adult, and their habit of flopping about on tree trunks is a sure aid to their identification.

HARRIERS AND ALLIED SPECIES

The Gymnogene, one of southern Africa's more unusual birds of prey, hunts by scrambling about among tree trunks and rocky cliffs looking for insects, lizards, mice and nestling birds. With its unique double-jointed 'knees', it can insert its feet deep into holes and cracks. It is also known for its habit of pulling open weaver nests to get at the chicks. Its large, broad wings enable it to sail very slowly above the ground, scanning for potential prey.

HARRIERS AND ALLIED SPECIES

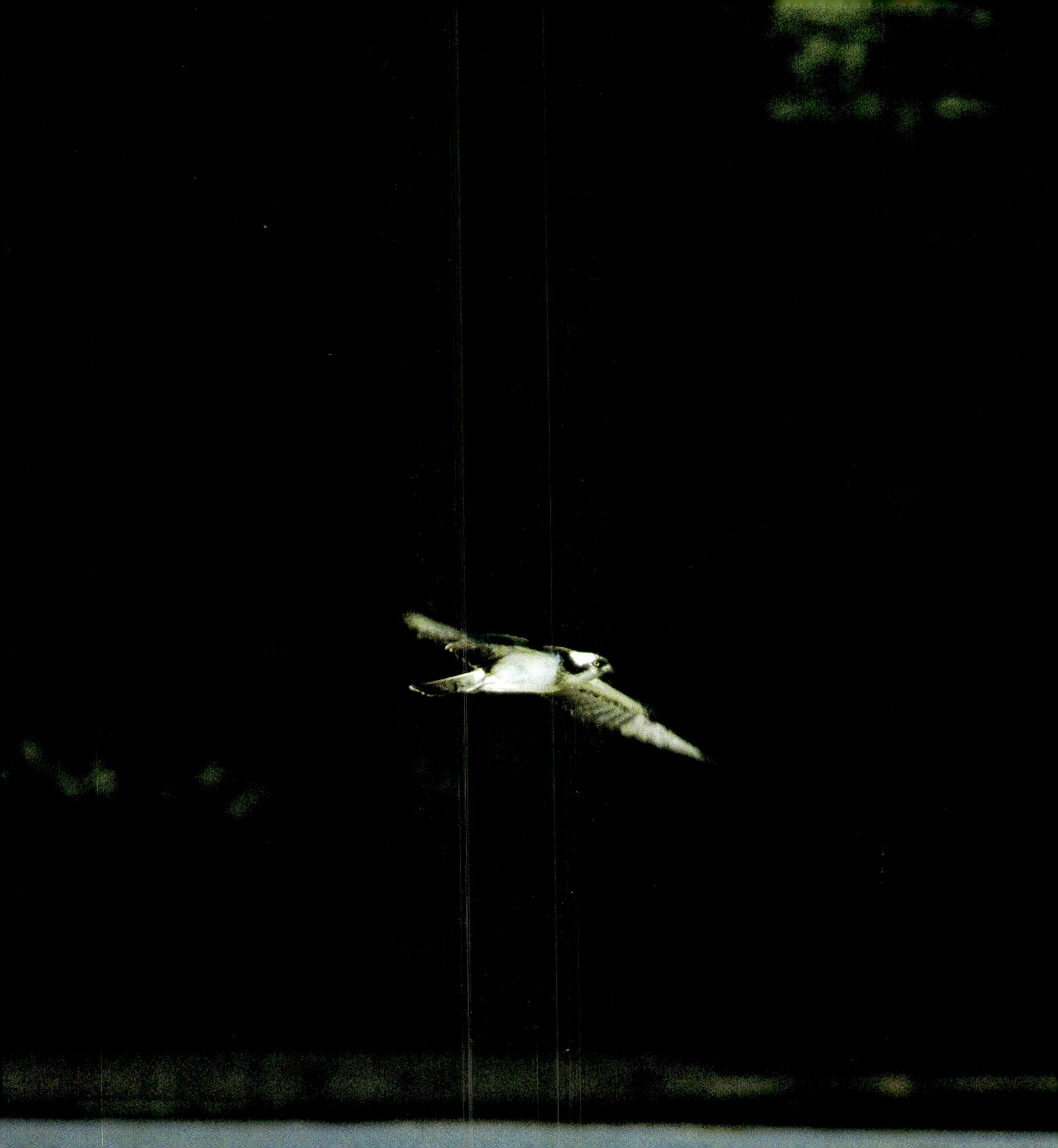

OSPREY

A single cosmopolitan species, the Osprey, comprises this family. It is a fish-eating specialist and the adaptations it has in this respect make it substantially different from other birds of prey. Its head is small and narrow, it lacks the jutting eyebrows of most other raptors and it has a dense, oily plumage. It has large powerful feet with long curved claws, a reversible outer toe and spiny soles, which enhance its ability to handle fish.

Renowned fish-catching hawks, Ospreys occur almost worldwide. They breed in North America, Europe, Asia, Australasia and around the Red Sea and Persian Gulf, and are non-breeding visitors to the rest of Africa and to South America. Everywhere they are closely tied to aquatic habitats – estuaries and rocky shores along the coasts and inland to the larger lakes, lochs, dams and rivers. In parts of their range, for example along the eastern seaboard of North America and on the Scandinavian lakes, they are a common sight to most of the local residents.

An Osprey on the hunt. Easily identified in its preferred habitat alongside water, it is the only bird of prey in southern Africa that is mainly white below and brown above, and that has a broad black mask through the eye.

The habits and behaviour of Ospreys have been well studied in many parts of their range, and they surely rank as one of the best-known birds of prey; one of the conservation world's real success stories is the return of the Ospreys to Britain to breed after an absence of nearly half a century. Ospreys bred widely in Scotland during the last century, but their numbers were gradually reduced to the extent that, by 1917, they had become extinct in Britain. Then, in 1955, the first pair re-established itself and, with strict protection – including round-the-clock guards at some nests during the whole nesting period – its numbers have crept upwards again. In 1986 a record 42 pairs attempted to breed in Scotland. It is extraordinary that even in that year, despite nest guards and widespread publicity for the project, several clutches were stolen from nests by egg thieves.

In southern Africa, as in most other parts of the continent, Ospreys are mainly non-breeding visitors, present (usually) from October to May. Ringing has shown that these birds are migrants from Europe. A few individuals, thought to be immature birds, stay over in southern Africa during June to September, which is the breeding season in Europe, and the occasional pair has attempted to breed in these southern regions. Several other Palearctic species, notably the Black Stork, Booted Eagle and European Bee-eater, have established breeding populations in southern Africa, and it is somewhat puzzling that the Osprey has not been more successful. Certainly habitat, nest-sites and food are not limiting factors.

Ospreys are unquestionably scarce in southern Africa and are localized in their occurrence on the subcontinent. Vagrants may appear briefly from time to time at almost any waterbody but it is only at the larger lakes, dams and river estuaries that the birds stay for more than a few days. They are regularly present, year after year, at a few such sites, and at some, occasional birds remain year-round. Ospreys are eagle-sized raptors with a wingspan of 1,6 metres and a mass of about 1,5 kilograms. They have long, narrow wings which, in flight, are distinctly angled backwards from the elbow. They are off-white below and brown above, with a white head cut by a broad black stripe through the eye, a mottled brown band across the chest, a barred tail and conspicuous black carpal patches. It is not easy to distinguish between immatures and adults, as they are much alike in plumage (though the former are a little less clearly marked). Neither do the males and females differ to any great degree. Females, however, are between 10 and 15 per cent larger.

The birds like to sit on vantage points above the water, especially on dead trees and poles, and use the same perches day after day, even returning to them in successive seasons. They hunt by watching the surface, somewhat like a huge kingfisher, or else they soar and, at times, hover slowly at a height of between 20 and 50 metres. They catch their fish prey by gliding down towards the target and then plunging feet-first into the water, sometimes submerging completely. A moment later they emerge, give a vigorous shake of the wing and, if successful, head off to a perch to eat. The whole hunting operation is skilled and well co-ordinated, and the birds are generally successful predators irrespective of weather conditions. Occasionally, however, mishaps do occur: the fish may be too large and the Osprey will get its claws caught in the bones, cannot escape, and will drown. Others are often robbed of their spoils by African Fish Eagles.

A study made of the species' feeding habits on the lakes of the southern Cape coast revealed that for the most part they took fish around the 200-gram mark, mullets being the favoured meal. Elsewhere in the world they have been observed catching prey with a mass of up to three kilograms. One or two average-sized fish will fulfil their day's needs – a target often easily attainable after half-an-hour's hunting.

Because they are wholly dependent on fish for food, Ospreys are especially sensitive to the effects of environmental pollution, and are therefore prime indicators of just how contaminated waterbodies have become. In many parts of the world, and particularly in North America, pollution has drastically reduced the species' numbers. It is hoped that a similar pattern will never develop in southern Africa.

Ospreys live almost exclusively on fish, which they catch by diving feet-first into the water. Where they are available, perches overlooking water are used day after day. In the absence of suitable lookout points, Ospreys have to resort to the energy-costly technique of hunting by hovering.

OSPREY

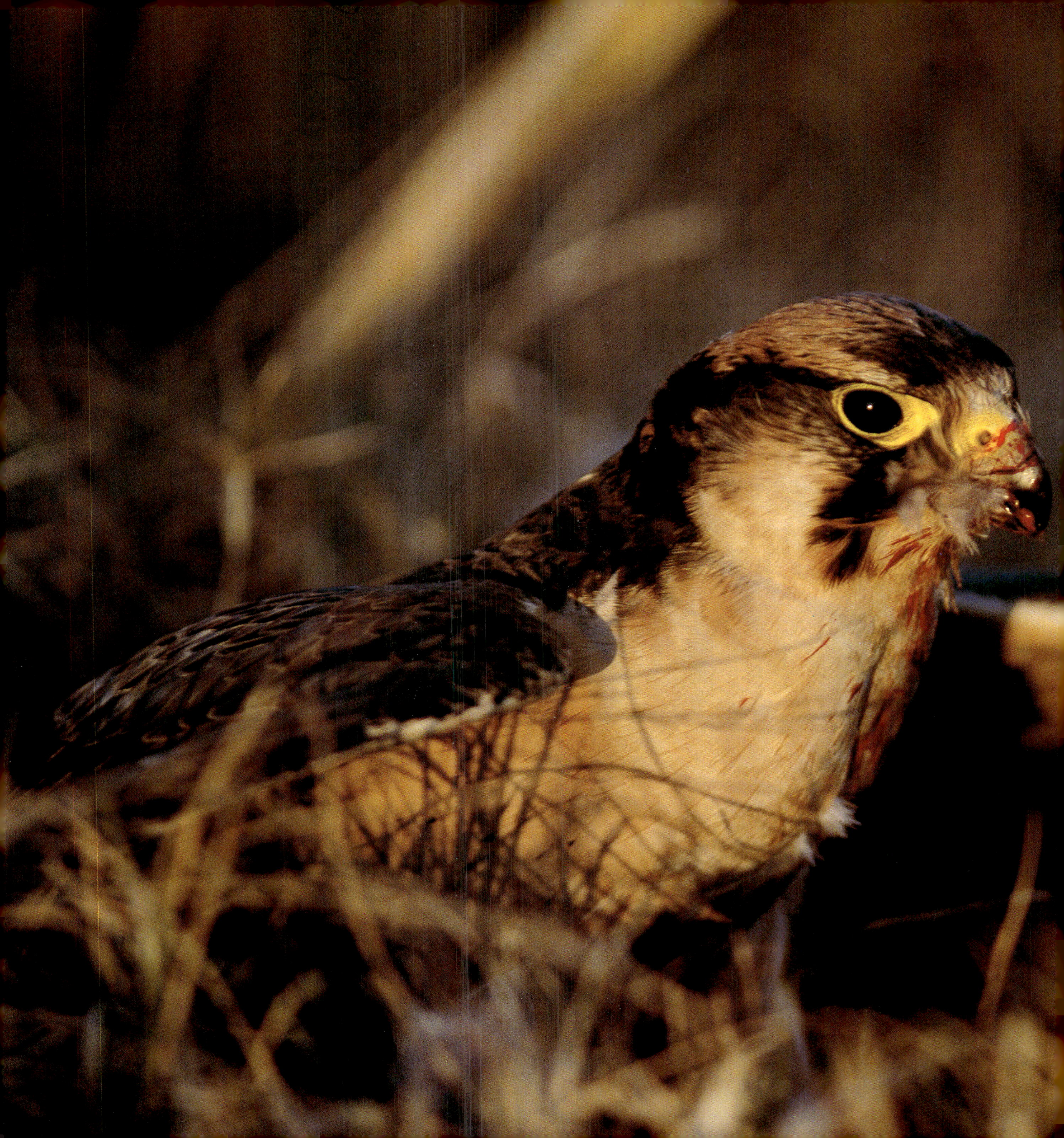

FALCONS AND KESTRELS

The sixteen southern African species in this group are part of a large, well-defined family called the Falconidae. Small to medium-sized, diurnal, long-winged hawks, they are sufficiently different from the other diurnal birds of prey to be regarded by some authorities as belonging to an entirely different order, possibly being more closely related to owls. One of their distinctive features is their toothed bill which has a cutting projection on the upper mandible corresponding with a notch in the lower beak. Another, which suggests a link with the owls, is that they do not build their own nests. They lay their eggs either on a cliff ledge or in a pothole, in a hole in a tree or in the old stick nest of another bird. Falcons prey mainly on birds which they catch in the air, while hobbies and kestrels eat mainly insects which are caught by hawking on the wing or picked up on the ground.

(Left) An adult Lanner Falcon, easily identified by its almost unmarked buff-coloured front and rufous crown, mantles over its prey. Such mantling behaviour is common in birds of prey. (Above) A Greater Kestrel sweeps in to land on its perch.

Peregrine Falcon

The Peregrine has an almost worldwide distribution, ranging across every continent except Antarctica and found on many oceanic islands such as the Falklands and Cape Verdes. No less than 23 races are recognized, the largest being the subspecies known as Peale's Peregrine, found on the islands in the north-east Pacific. The race found in Africa is the smallest; it is named *Peregrinus falco minor* and it has a mass about half that of the Peale's subspecies.

It is certainly among the most celebrated of all birds, being a dazzling flier and a much prized falconry bird, but above all it has come to symbolize the unreconciled conflict between nature and man, or, more specifically, between environmental conservation and the use of agricultural pesticides.

In the late 1950s Peregrine Falcon populations showed a rapid decline across the northern hemisphere. It was the concern at what was happening to them that led to an understanding of the deleterious side-effects arising from the use of agricultural pesticides. In Britain, for example, the Peregrine population dropped dramatically from some 800 pairs in the mid-1950s to only 68 in 1962. Worse, in the eastern half of North America an entire subspecies, *Falco peregrinus anatum*, became extinct during the same period. Gradually the chain linking the bird's disappearance to the use of organochloride insecticides, especially DDT, in agriculture, was unravelled. Doves and pigeons were picking up these poisons while feeding in cultivated areas, and the falcons, in turn, by feeding on them were continuously accumulating toxins in their own bodies. Some poisons such as Dieldrin often killed the falcons outright, but DDT and its metabolic products simply accumulated in the bird's fatty tissues, leading to chronic illness and to a phenomenon known as eggshell thinning. This syndrome caused females, through some metabolic disorder, to lay thinner-shelled eggs than normal and because of this many breakages occurred and breeding success was lowered. Thus the eggshell thickness index is often used as a measure of the level of contamination by these pesticides in bird of prey populations.

Once the problem had been identified, many countries banned or restricted the use of organochlorides. The effect of this on the Peregrine population in Britain has been a steady recovery. In the eastern United States of America, where no birds remained to re-establish themselves after these pollutants had been withdrawn, a captive-breeding and release programme was launched, using a mixed gene pool of birds brought in from Europe, Alaska and elsewhere. Millions of dollars later, genetically different, wild Peregrines are back spreading panic among the pigeons in Massachusetts and elsewhere.

In addition to the *minor* Peregrine found in southern Africa (where it is a scarce, resident species), a second race, which breeds in the Arctic regions of Scandinavia and the Soviet Union, visits during the summer months as a non-breeding migrant.

African Peregrines are closely associated with high cliffs and invariably nest on these. No nest is made beyond scraping out a shallow cup on the shelf to hold the eggs. Such sites are often re-used season after season, and pairs tend to frequent the nesting area for much of the year. They breed in early summer, the female laying her clutch of three well-marked reddish brown eggs during August or September. The sexes share the incubation duties, with the female usually doing the most. The eggs take about 30 days to hatch and the nestlings fledge in 35 to 42 days. At the time of hatching the chicks are covered in dense white down but this is soon replaced by the brownish feathers of the juvenile plumage.

A brood of three Peregrine Falcon chicks explore the ledges around the cliffs that form their nest site, awaiting the return of the parent bird (opposite) with food. These dashing falcons breed on cliffs in southern Africa, laying their eggs on inaccessible ledges in early summer. They prey exclusively on birds, especially doves and pigeons. These they catch in the air in spectacular fashion, stooping on them from above.

FALCONS AND KESTRELS

LANNER FALCON

This species, usually referred to simply as the Lanner, is a large Peregrine-sized falcon that is found right across Africa and throughout the southern subcontinent. In some places it lives alongside its more illustrious cousin the Peregrine Falcon, but almost everywhere outnumbers it tenfold: whereas pairs of Peregrines are confined to limited areas of suitable mountainous or gorge habitat, Lanners extend across southern Africa, from the flat gravel plains of the Namib Desert to the precipitous escarpments of the Drakensberg.

At a distance the two species look alike, and it takes an experienced eye to distinguish the longer-winged, longer-tailed silhouette of the Lanner from that of the shorter, sharper-winged and more compact Peregrine. A clear view of the colour of the bird's crown or its front will establish its identity. The Lanner's crown is rufous (in both adult and immature birds) and the Peregrine's (again, among both age groups) is black, giving the species its well-known 'hangman's hood' look. Adult Lanners and Peregrines also differ in the coloration of and markings on their fronts. The entire front of a Lanner is pinkish buff and virtually, or sometimes completely, free of markings, while Peregrines have white fronts which are finely barred with black on the belly and vent. The light chest and dark belly give them a two-toned appearance. The immatures of both species are alike in having heavily streaked fronts.

Lanners are widely distributed and have a broad habitat tolerance, partly because they are not restricted to cliffs for breeding purposes and partly because they are versatile hunters. Cliff nest-sites are chosen when available, but away from hills and gorges they resort to breeding on the old stick nests of storks, crows and birds of prey. In many parts of the highveld grassland, where Pied and Black Crows often nest on electricity pylons, the Lanners have followed suit, and on some lines pairs may be found at intervals of five to 10 kilometres, having commandeered the best crow's nest available in the area. Because these are in exposed positions they do not last long, and Lanners often have to change nests. By contrast, those nesting on cliffs may well re-use the same ledge or pothole year after year.

The nesting area is defended by the Lanner pair from well before the eggs are laid. Other birds of prey – and the displaced crows – are chased away when they venture near the nest. Occasionally, on a cliff with limited space, Lanners will nest alongside a pair of Black Eagles which, being a few months ahead in their breeding cycle, will have laid before the Lanners move in. The Lanners harass the eagles endlessly, diving and screaming shrilly at every arrival and departure. The less agile eagles have little option but to put up with the indignity.

Lanners lay during July and August. The clutch usually comprises four eggs, and occasionally five, and the sexes share the incubation, though the female assumes the larger role. Incubation lasts some 32 days, and the young take to the wing when they are about 42 days old.

Lanners are much prized for falconry. When flown to the fist they easily catch francolin, but in their natural state hunt smaller-sized prey, the upper limit being a bird the size of a sandgrouse. A wide variety of bird species is taken, pigeons heading the list in most areas. In desert regions the species often hunts at waterholes, preying on birds coming to drink. Quelea flocks are especially vulnerable, and when such large prey concentrations are available 10 or more Lanners may aggregate, patrolling overhead, diving into the massed birds to snatch victims. Lanners are also bold chicken thieves in some areas. Where poultry is left to free-range in the dust around a kraal the falcon will sweep through, quickly taking a half-grown chick and disappearing long before the alarm has been raised. Rodents, lizards and insects also feature in the bird's diet.

It is puzzling why the Lanner is common and widespread whereas the similar-sized and -shaped Peregrine is rare and localized. Obviously the two species are not identical and the subtle differences in shape and wing loading confer different advantages and constraints on each when hunting. Peregrines hunt birds exclusively, catching them from spectacular stoops. The Lanner is a less impressive but much more diversified hunter, and this generalist strategy and the greater opportunities it offers may be the reason for this species being more common.

At close quarters there is no likelihood of the Lanner Falcon being confused with the similar-sized Peregrine: the absence of barring on the front and the rufous crown are diagnostic. On the other hand, when a falcon is seen soaring high overhead and silhouetted against the sky, distinguishing these two species can be impossible. Lanner Falcons have a more diverse diet than Peregrines and range across a much wider spectrum of habitats. As a consequence they are by far the more numerous of the two.

European Hobby

It is dusk and a great mass of swallows wheels about in the air above a reedbed, swirling this way and that, with a steady stream of birds dropping out and diving into the safety of the reeds. Suddenly among them appears a larger, long-winged, dark bird flying with rapid wingbeats, gliding briefly with stiff, slightly downbent wings, flapping again, briefly jinking, then climbing away out of the swallow cloud, soaring up, banking leisurely and starting to accelerate with a burst of wingbeats back into the milling swallows. It sweeps out of the flock carrying a fluttering victim in its talons and makes for a tree across the river, where it settles and starts tearing off the feathers of its still struggling prey.

The predator is clearly long-winged, fast and agile. The chances are that the bird is a European Hobby, though the scenario described could apply equally to an African Hobby, a Lanner Falcon or perhaps even to a Bat Hawk. To be sure of its identity one needs a good view of the bird's underparts as it skims by. If its front is white, heavily streaked with black, and if it has chestnut undertail coverts, then it is definitely a European Hobby.

As the name implies, these birds breed in Europe (and also in Asia across to China and northern Japan) and are non-breeding visitors to southern Africa. At the end of their breeding season, in September, they start to move southwards, funnelling through the Mediterranean crossings at Gibraltar and the Bosphorus and on into Africa, reaching their final winter quarters in southern Africa in late October and November. In March and early April they begin their movement back through Africa to the northern hemisphere. Although there are no ringing results to confirm their origin, southern African birds probably come from regions stretching right across Europe, the largest breeding populations being located in France, Scandinavia and Poland.

In southern Africa, European Hobbies are found mostly in the moister eastern half of the subcontinent, extending southwards as far as the eastern Cape. They tend to wander in search of the most favourable conditions, sometimes aggregating but usually occurring singly. Nowhere is their presence predictable, although they do favour certain habitats, especially riverine woodland and larger waterbodies in which there are standing dead trees. They are elegant fliers and catch virtually all their meals on the wing. Always opportunistic, they take a variety of aerial prey ranging from the gregarious European Swallows to other small birds like larks and pipits, the occasional bat, and such insects as dragonflies and hover-moths. When hunting these they are less dashing and more graceful in flight than in their pursuit of larger prey. They do not take the insect to a perch to eat, but simply bring the foot that holds it up to their beak and consume it in flight.

Now and again one may see a European Hobby perched, usually high up on a branch of a dead tree, where it sits with a characteristic vertical pose, head hunched into shoulders, tail pointing straight down, one foot grasping the branch and the other clasped into a ball and almost hidden in the belly feathers. This inactivity may be interrupted periodically when the bird lifts its balled foot, leans forward and scratches the back of its neck, and it is at these times that one can clearly discern the black hood, the moustachial stripes and the vividly contrasting yellow rings which surround its dark eyes.

Several other falcon species – notably the immatures of the Lanner, Peregrine and Sooty Falcons and that of the Eastern Redfooted Kestrel – bear some resemblance to the European Hobby. They too have dark backs and white chests, heavily streaked with black. The adult European Hobby has rufous undertail coverts and thighs, which distinguishes it from the others, but the immature of the species lacks this characteristic and can best be recognized by its slim build (Peregrines and Lanners are bulkier birds); by its black cap (Eastern Redfooted Kestrels have pale heads), or by its dark brown back (Sooty Falcons are greyer at all ages).

The European Hobby nests during May and June throughout its wide European and Asian breeding range. Like all falcons, it does not build a nest of its own but usually commandeers an old nest of a crow, favouring one placed high in a tall tree and offering a sweeping view. The female does most or all of the incubation and the male plays the role of provider to her and later to the young.

FALCONS AND KESTRELS

The dark, slender European Hobby visits southern Africa in the summer months from its Palearctic breeding grounds. It is usually seen only at dusk, hunting by flying back and forth with rapid wingbeats, pausing now and again to glide with stiffly held wings. In poor light, when its markings are not easily discernible, it is the bird's shape that distinguishes it as a hobby. In better conditions, its black hood and moustache, heavily streaked front, and rufous thighs and undertail coverts (the latter obvious in adult birds) are diagnostic.

African Hobby

The best time to observe an African Hobby is in the last half hour of daylight, at dusk, but before it becomes too dark to make out the bird's rufous front. It is essential to see this feature, for the bird would otherwise be indistinguishable from the European Hobby, which is also out and about just before the sun goes down, and is so similar that in the past the two have been treated as races of the same species. The time of day is important, as this is when African Hobbies are at their most active, hunting insects and perhaps bats and small birds, speed-flying back and forth above the tree-tops, skimming down along the river now and then, dipping out of sight, re-emerging seconds later and heading off in another direction. The to-and-fro dusk flight is rewarded at intervals with a prey item, perhaps only a winged termite or a hover-moth in which case it will be torn up and swallowed on the wing.

The subcontinent is clearly right at the southern end of this tropical species' range and its status here is uncertain: it appears to be a migrant from the north, though elsewhere in Africa it is reported to be a resident species. It occurs mainly on the northern fringes of the subcontinent and one's best chance of seeing it is probably along the Zambezi or Kavango Rivers in Zimbabwe or Namibia. Occasionally one is seen quite far south: the type specimen in fact comes from the eastern Cape, at Groot Kei River, but the species has never again been recorded in this area during the intervening 150 years. Much farther north in Africa it is reported to be locally common. In the Ivory Coast in West Africa, for example, it is locally abundant, with pairs breeding at densities of one per 200 hectares; and in Kampala, Uganda, they often nest in old crows' nests in the tall eucalypts that grow in the town.

For the birdwatcher who is especially intent on seeing this bird, the choice lies between a 150-year wait in the eastern Cape, perhaps a week on the Kavango River, or two minutes in the Ivory Coast...

Very similar to the European Hobby, the African Hobby is distinguished by having a warm rufous chest and belly. Young birds, like the one illustrated, have a browner wash in front overlaid with dark brown streaks. This species is a fast-flying aerial hunter.

TAITA FALCON

The discovery of Taita Falcons in southern Africa dates back to the memorable first Pan-African Ornithological Congress held in Livingstone, Zambia, in 1957. Many leading experts of the time attended, and the late Leslie Brown, renowned for his study of and writings on birds of prey, announced the presence of the species in one of the gorges below the Victoria Falls. Since then these gorges have become notable as virtually the only place in southern Africa where one has a reasonable chance of seeing this rare tropical falcon, and every year many birdwatchers search intently among the myriad swifts for a slightly larger, heavier, longer-winged bird that is also rufous in front.

Several pairs of Taita Falcons are known to be resident in the Falls gorges, and both they and the Peregrines, also resident there, probably obtain all their food by hunting the swifts and other birds that share the terrain – incautious Redwinged Starlings flying from one side to the other, bulbuls making the hazardous crossing to reach a fruiting tree, and so on.

Watching Taita Falcons stooping for prey in the confined space of the gorge is breathtaking. One moment the bird is high above the lip, soaring among the milling swifts, the next it is accelerating downwards, wings fanning rapidly at first, then folding back to give it a crescent-like shape, plunging downwards, until soon it is so small that it is lost, even in the binocular view, against the thundering darkness of the Zambezi far below. Some minutes later, if one closely scans the opposite wall of cliff, one sees a tiny bird perched on a ledge, holding something down with its feet and rapidly pulling off feathers and discarding them with an upward flick of the head. The chase has been successful.

Apart from the Victoria Falls, there are only one or two areas in southern Africa where the Taita Falcon is known to nest. At the Falls it chooses a deep pothole in the basalt walls, often using the same site year after year, laying its clutch of three to four brown eggs in September. During the breeding season it becomes aggressive towards crows, ravens and birds of prey (and even towards Peregrine Falcons) that pass near the nest. The pair share the incubation, though the female takes on the larger quota, and both sexes brood and feed the young.

Little is known about the Taita Falcon's life history away from the nest; and just why it is such a rare species, not just in southern Africa but throughout its range, also needs to be investigated.

Cruising past a backdrop of steep basaltic cliffs, a stockily built Taita Falcon shows its distinctive rufous nape patches. This is one of southern Africa's rarest and most exciting falcons and is eagerly sought after by birdwatchers in the Victoria Falls' gorges.

REDNECKED FALCON

Originally described on a specimen collected in India and named *Falco chicquera* after the Hindi word for a hunter (shikari), the Rednecked Falcon is a widely occurring but very unevenly distributed little bird of prey which ranges patchily through East and West Africa and extends into southern Africa.

Two widely separated and discrete populations occur on the subcontinent. They are racially distinct and their respective habitats are quite dissimilar. One is the northern race, *ruficollis*, which is found across central and West Africa and just in southern Africa, in northern and central Mozambique, with occasional vagrants reaching the Kruger National Park. This bird is locally common farther north. The southern African race, *horsbrughi*, is a bird of arid country: it is found in the Kalahari and Namib deserts where it lives among the larger thorn trees. Physically, the races are much alike and differ only in size, the desert birds being the larger of the two.

Rednecked Falcons prey mainly on birds, employing a sparrowhawk-like perch-and-chase hunting technique. They sit and watch for a passing victim from the interior of a shady tree, and then launch out on a high-speed chase. This is quite different from the vertical stoop method used by some other falcon species, but similar in that success depends on speed – and, in level flight, Rednecked Falcons are very fast indeed. They often perch on the edge of a dry pan, the few hundred metres of open ground enabling them to outfly and catch even such fast-flying birds as doves. The latter are in fact at the upper limit of their capabilities, and most of the prey comprises such smaller passerines as the flocks of larks and finches that collect to drink at waterholes. Many of the desert larks and other prey species are nomadic, sometimes occurring abundantly in a particular area and at other times being scarce, so the falcons of the arid regions are probably far less sedentary than their Zambian counterparts, at times extending and even breeding well beyond their normal range.

The Zambian birds appear to live year-round in the same territory, in which a large *Borassus* palm is the focus of activity and provides the nest-site in summer. In ideal habitat – open palm savanna – birds may be found at two-kilometre intervals, disclosing their presence by their high-pitched 'yak, yak, yak…' rasping call.

Rednecked Falcons breed in early summer, usually laying their eggs during August and September. Like other members of the family they do not build their own nests, but instead take over the abandoned structures of other birds, most notably those of crows. In palm trees old fronds often provide a suitable nest platform. The roles of the sexes in the breeding cycle are sharply partitioned, the male hunting and the female incubating and brooding the young. In good years in the Namib the former performs his role with remarkable efficiency and it is not unusual to find an incubating female surrounded by a pile of dead Stark's Larks in far larger quantity than she is capable of eating at one sitting. The clutch consists of three to four eggs, which take about 33 days to hatch. The nestling period is 34 to 37 days.

The young birds differ from the adults in their colouring: they have brown rather than rufous heads and they lack the fine grey and white barring on the underparts. They may breed while still in this immature plumage, which has caused some confusion in the past: a pair of immatures, collected while breeding outside Pretoria, were mistakenly classified as a separate species and, for a time, went under the name of Horsbrugh's Falcon.

The Rednecked Falcon is a swift-flying, capable hunter, taking mainly birds by pursuit. The dark brown crown and rufous-washed underparts of the birds shown here indicate that they are not yet adult.

FALCONS AND KESTRELS

ELEONORA'S FALCON

This species is a very rare vagrant to southern Africa, recorded only once or twice in the past decade. It is a bird with an interesting and unusual life history, reminiscent of that of the Sooty Falcon.

The world population of Eleonora's Falcons is estimated to be around 2 500 pairs, of which 70 per cent breed on the islands off Greece, the remainder occupying other barren, uninhabited islands that lie between Cyprus and the Canaries. The birds breed in colonies, nesting in potholes in cliffs overlooking the sea, timing their breeding to coincide with the autumn migration from Europe to Africa of the small birds which form their main prey. They lay their eggs in July and August, and at the end of October depart for their winter quarters south of the Equator. A few occur in East Africa each year but most go to Madagascar and the nearby islands, where they sometimes consort with Sooty Falcons, who follow the same migratory pattern. Those Eleonora's Falcons that occasionally venture as far south as the subcontinent are perhaps East African birds that overshoot their destination.

Very few authentic records exist of the Eleonora's Falcon in southern Africa. It breeds around the Mediterranean Sea and, outside the breeding season, migrates annually to Madagascar. It has been seen in Maputo (Mozambique) and in northern Zululand; the one illustrated here was photographed in captivity in Durban.

SOOTY FALCON

The Sooty Falcon is one of the more recent species to have been discovered in southern Africa. The first record came from Tongaat, in Natal, in 1961 and the specimen lay for six years in a museum drawer, incorrectly identified as an immature European Hobby. Then, in March 1967, a second specimen was sent in from the Durban area, and the identity of the two was confirmed by the British Museum. As so often happens once the ice is broken, birdwatchers became aware of the species and it has since been observed all along the Natal coast, in Mozambique, in the eastern Transvaal Lowveld and as far south as the eastern Cape. Although it is not a common bird there are some localities, such as in Zululand, at which one can be fairly certain of sighting it if visited at the right time of the year.

Relatively little is known about Sooty Falcons except that they spend their non-breeding season (November to May) on Madagascar and along the south-eastern seaboard of Africa, moving on to breed (during June to October) in one of the world's least hospitable desert areas: that stretching from Libya in the west through Egypt, northern Ethiopia and the Red Sea into the Sinai Peninsula and Negev Desert. The contrast between their summer and winter environments could not be more marked.

Their breeding is timed to coincide with the migration of the many small birds which leave Europe for Africa and have to cross the great desert belt which separates the Palearctic from the Afrotropical region. Here tired bee-eaters, rollers, crakes, hoopoes, warblers, swallows, pipits, wagtails and others fall easy prey to the Sooty Falcons. The species normally nests in the desert, on ledges or in potholes on cliffs, and lays its clutch of two or three eggs in late July or August. The nestling and post-nestling periods coincide with the peak migration of the prey species. Thus the eggs hatch after about 30 days, in September, and the chicks fledge 32 days later.

For the rest, these birds resemble other falcons in their breeding biology. Most or all of the incubation is undertaken by the female, and the male's role is to hunt and provide his mate, and later the chicks, with food. Sooty Falcons are aerial hunters, catching virtually all their prey on the wing. Although in southern Africa they do take birds, it seems that the bulk of their diet on the subcontinent comprises insects.

Adult Sooty Falcons are a slate-grey colour from head to tail, but with dark wing-tips and dark malar stripes. Only the bright yellow eye-ring, cere, legs and feet relieve the monochrome impression. They could be mistaken for the one other uniform grey falcon found in southern Africa, the Grey Kestrel, but are distinguishable by their longer, slimmer build, their dark malar stripes and, when perched, by the extension of the wings beyond the tail. Immatures most closely resemble the immature European Hobby. They can be recognized, however, by their greyish rather than dark-brown head and back, and by their paler, more mottled underparts.

The occurrence of the Sooty Falcon in southern Africa is a relatively recent discovery, the species having been seen each summer at various places along the Natal and Zululand coastal belt.

GREY KESTREL

This species is a stockily built, swift-flying little falcon, rather inappropriately called a kestrel. It is all-grey except for its yellow cere, eye-ring, legs and toes. The male, female and immature birds are virtually indistinguishable. Rare and little-known in southern Africa, it is found on the subcontinent at the southernmost edge of its range – in northern Namibia, and especially in Ovamboland. It has not yet been ascertained whether it nests in these areas, and most of our information comes from observations made in East and West Africa.

In the tropical regions of Africa it is a bird of the open savanna, forest clearings and cultivated ground, hunting (not by hovering, but from perches and by pursuit) from tall trees overlooking clearings or watercourses. In West Africa it is common along the roadside, using telephone and electricity lines as hunting perches. It preys on lizards, rodents, small birds and such insects as grasshoppers and termites, and is consequently attracted to bush fires. One of the interesting aspects of its life history is its seemingly exclusive use of Hamerkop nests for breeding. Dickinson's Kestrels also breed in these, but employ more flexibility in their choice and more often make use of natural holes in trees.

The only other southern African bird of prey with which the Grey Kestrel is likely to be confused is the Sooty Falcon. Both birds are wholly grey and have a yellow cere, eye-ring, legs and feet. They are best distinguished by the differences in their shape and jizz. The Sooty Falcon is larger, proportionately slimmer and, when perched, its wingtips reach the end of the tail whereas those of the Grey Kestrel stop well short of the tail. The rarity of both species in the region minimizes the chance of having to test one's identification skills.

The Grey Kestrel is a species of West and tropical Africa and is rarely seen in southern Africa, the southern extremity of its range. It is a thickset bird which perches quietly on a vantage point for long spells on the lookout for prey. One of three grey-plumaged falcons found on the subcontinent, care is needed in distinguishing it from the Sooty Falcon and Dickinson's Kestrel.

Western Redfooted Kestrel

The males of this species are remarkably similar in appearance to those of the Eastern Redfooted Kestrel, though the females are quite different. The two are regarded by some authorities as being conspecific but, because of the marked disparity between the females, they are usually treated as two species. Nowhere do their respective breeding ranges overlap. They are obviously closely related, having similar breeding patterns, hunting methods and prey choice, and in Africa (where they spend their non-breeding season), mixed groups are often found.

Western Redfooted Kestrels are gregarious, living in flocks throughout the year. In their breeding grounds in eastern Europe (most notably in Hungary) and Russia, they nest colonially, often taking over the tall-tree nests of Rooks. They also migrate in flocks, and in their winter grounds they forage and roost collectively. They reach southern Africa in November and stay until mid-March, but are far less numerous than the two other gregarious migrant kestrels (Eastern Redfooted and Lesser). They also tend towards the western areas of the subcontinent, and especially Botswana and Namibia, in contrast to their two sister species, who are concentrated in the eastern half of the region.

All three species are almost exclusively insectivorous, hunting by hovering gently, 20 to 30 metres up, watching the ground and swiftly dropping down the moment a prey item is sighted. In this fashion the birds catch grasshoppers, locusts, crickets, caterpillars and other insects, which they either eat on the ground or, more usually, take to a perch.

The Western Redfooted Kestrel is sometimes found in mixed flocks of Eastern Redfooted and Lesser Kestrels. The males of the two redfooted kestrel species can be distinguished in flight, when the all-grey underwing of the Western species (top) is visible. Females (above) differ markedly from their mates.

FALCONS AND KESTRELS

In flight the male Eastern Redfooted Kestrel shows its white underwing coverts which serve to distinguish it from the Western species. A common non-breeding migrant to southern Africa, it reaches the subcontinent after a spectacular trans-oceanic migration. In summer it is a common sight in agricultural areas in the east, occurring in flocks and often mixing with Lesser Kestrels. It is entirely insectivorous, hunting grasshoppers and other insects from perches or by hovering above the ground.

Eastern Redfooted Kestrel

Eastern Redfooted Kestrels are common, and even locally abundant, non-breeding visitors to the eastern half of southern Africa, arriving in November and leaving in March. They are habitually found in groups or flocks and, at night, thousands may gather to sleep at communal roosts. These are in tall trees, usually eucalypts, and in places within their winter range the same trees have been used year after year for decades. The roosts are often shared with Lesser Kestrels, and sometimes with the rarer Western Redfooted Kestrel, and because all three of these species have their own male, female and immature plumages, as many as nine different-looking kestrels can be seen together.

Eastern Redfooted Kestrels hunt in open country, often over cultivated lands, searching the ground for insects either from perches (using telephone or electricity lines wherever available) or while hovering. When prey is spotted the bird drops down, alights briefly and, in many instances, often takes its prey, perhaps a grasshopper or cricket, to a perch to eat. It is a gentle way of hunting, and though many textbooks refer to these birds as Redfooted Falcons, their behaviour in this respect indicates that they are properly called kestrels.

The males are handsome birds, characterized by their two-tone slate grey plumage (darker behind than in front), rufous thighs and vent and contrasting red eye-ring, cere, legs and feet. Only in flight can the obvious difference between the male of this species and that of the Western Redfooted Kestrel be seen: Easterns have a contrasting white and grey underwing in which the front half (the coverts) is white; Westerns have an all-grey underwing. In its markings, the female is quite different from the male, most closely resembling the European Hobby, a species for which it is sometimes mistaken. It is white in front, boldly streaked and blotched with black and, like the European Hobby, has a rufous undertail. Above, it is barred dark grey. The head pattern, however, immediately distinguishes it from the Hobby: the latter has an all-black head; the Eastern Redfooted Kestrel female has a greyish crown, a white forehead and cheek and a black mask through the eye which leads into a moustachial stripe. Its legs, feet, cere and eye-ring are orange-red, in contrast to the yellow of the Hobby. Its gregariousness is also a distinguishing factor, as the European Hobby is usually a solitary bird.

Eastern Redfooted Kestrels undergo a spectacular annual migration, the precise route of which is not known. Their breeding grounds lie in eastern Siberia, Manchuria and northern China, and to reach southern Africa they have to cross the Himalayas, India and 3 000 kilometres of ocean before arriving at the east coast of Africa. Like most long-distance migrants they lay down a store of sustaining fat before embarking on their immensely long journey.

The female Eastern Redfooted Kestrel bears no resemblance to the male of the same species. It is grey above and white below, streaked and blotched with black, with a greyish hood and moustache, and superficially resembles a European Hobby.

ROCK KESTREL

When the term 'kestrel' is used it is this species that provides the model. In Britain the same bird (though a different race) is known simply as the Kestrel, and elsewhere it is referred to as the Common Kestrel. The name 'Rock Kestrel' has become entrenched in southern Africa, and it is an appropriate one here as it conveys the bird's preferred habitat. In a wider context, however, 'Common Kestrel' is the name with the greatest currency.

It is a widely occurring species, represented by numerous races and found throughout the Palearctic, in Asia and throughout Africa. The Rock Kestrel is one of the races, confined to the southern third of Africa and distinguished from those elsewhere by the female's plumage. There is marked dimorphism between the sexes in other regions, where the females are paler and duller and have brown rather than bluish-grey heads. Among Rock Kestrels, however, the difference between the male and female is slight and both sexes have a grey head.

Kestrels are a distinctive group within the falcon family. They hunt mostly by hovering – hanging virtually motionless in the air except for gently fanning wings, with tail spread, head down and body inclined forward. The Rock Kestrel is unsurpassed in its mastery of stationary flight, holding a position for a short while, then turning and letting the wind take it, pulling up again into the wind and hovering over another spot. They catch and eat insects, especially grasshoppers (as do the Lesser and the Eastern and Western Redfooted Kestrels) but also take larger prey, notably lizards, small rodents and birds. To do so they parachute down from their hover, making a final rapid plunge to the ground.

Rock Kestrels occur patchily throughout southern Africa, and are at their most common in the hilly or mountainous country where cliffs provide nest-sites and montane grassland provides hunting terrain. Ranges of hills such as the Magaliesberg, north of Johannesburg, support many pairs. In the absence of cliffs the birds may breed on disused crows' nests in trees or on man-made structures like bridges and tall buildings. Although they breed now and again in southern Africa's towns, they have not taken to city life to the same extent as their European counterparts, a difference reflected in that race's German name, 'Turmvalke' (turret or spire hawk). It could be that the subcontinent's urban centres have too few suitable open spaces in which to hunt.

Rock Kestrels are generally sedentary, resident in the vicinity of their breeding sites, although in winter there is a movement of birds into the highveld grassland areas. These perhaps come from the high-lying Malutis, which may be snowbound for periods during winter. Common Kestrels from northern Europe and Russia migrate to Africa and are often gregarious in their non-breeding grounds north of the Equator. None of these, however, reach southern Africa.

Like other members of the family, Rock Kestrels do not build their own nests. Sometimes they take over a crow's disused nest placed high in a tree or on a pylon but more usually they find a safe, inaccessible pothole or crevice in a cliff-face. The pair is closely tied to the nesting area at this time of the year and, while the female is incubating, the male remains in the vicinity, either perched on a nearby vantage point or on the wing searching for food. The pair maintain contact with their shrill 'kee-kee-kee...' call and, should an intruder approach the nest this changes pitch to a harsher, scolding 'kik-kik-kik...' alarm note. Another more melodious trilling call is made by the female when she sees the male approaching with food and it is this note, one presumes, that has given rise to the bird's scientific name *tinnunculus* (meaning 'little bell').

The clutch of three or four buffy-brown eggs is laid during September or October. These are incubated by the female, who is fed during this period by the male. The eggs take about 30 days to hatch and this is followed by a 34-day nestling period. As the chicks approach fledging age, they venture to the edge of the nest hole to await their parents' arrival with food and it is not long after that the boldest makes its first flight.

When perched, the Rock Kestrel appears to be a brick-red bird with a grey tail and head. However, when it takes to the wing, the white underwings become visible, creating the impression of a pale-coloured bird. This species is resident in southern Africa and, although its numbers are swamped in summer by the arrival of the three migrant kestrel species, it is common and widespread. It is likely to occur anywhere, but is most numerous in hilly and mountainous areas.

FALCONS AND KESTRELS

LESSER KESTREL

This is probably the commonest of the three migratory kestrels that overwinter in southern Africa. It has the widest breeding range of the three, extending from Spain through the Mediterranean countries, eastwards into Asia Minor and China.

The birds are gregarious throughout the year and many of the time-worn village churches in Spain, and elsewhere, support little colonies of 10 or perhaps 20 pairs in the crevices and holes in their walls, some of the colonies perhaps almost as old as the churches themselves. The southward migration to Africa begins at the end of the breeding season, and the following ringing recovery attests to the magnitude of this journey: on 18 September 1975 an adult male Lesser Kestrel was ringed by an unnamed ornithologist in central Russia (on longitude 70°E). Just over two months later, on 24 November, it was recovered in the eastern Cape, having died during a night-time storm. The straight-line distance between the two points was 8 785 kilometres; a maximum of 66 days had elapsed from start to finish.

During the day Lesser Kestrels forage in flocks; at night they roost in even larger groups – as many as 5 000 birds – and a high proportion of these roosts are of long standing. Towns in the highveld grassland region of South Africa, such as Standerton, Senekal, Ladysmith and Christiana, all have groves of tall, old trees which see the arrival of the kestrels each summer. In 1970 a countrywide survey was conducted in an attempt to estimate, by calculating the numbers of birds using each known roost, how many Lesser Kestrels spent the summer in South Africa. The estimated figure was 154 000. Today, nearly 20 years later, it would be useful to repeat the exercise, if only to support a widespread suspicion that the population has declined. Lesser Kestrels are still a common sight, however, and in the areas where they occur the telephone wires along the roads are often dotted with them.

Males are trimly turned out in grey (head and tail), warm rufous (back) and buff (front, spotted with brown on the flanks). Their primaries are black and the tail has a broad black terminal bar, tipped with white. They cannot easily be mistaken. Females, on the other hand, are quite nondescript: they have a sandy front streaked with brown, and a brownish, barred back, and they may be confused with the Greater Kestrel or a young Rock Kestrel. They are considerably smaller, though, than Greater Kestrels and have brown rather than cream-coloured eyes, and are less rufous and more streaked than young Rock Kestrels.

Flocks of Lesser Kestrels arrive from Europe in late October and stay until March. This species is a common sight, especially in grain-growing areas, and sometimes in the evenings thousands can be seen heading for large tree clumps to roost.

GREATER KESTREL

The landscape most favoured by Greater Kestrels is one that is flat, dotted with thorn trees and covered with a sparse grass layer, so that there is bare ground visible between the tufts. If the terrain is too hilly, the tree cover too thick or too thin, or the grass layer too dense or too sparse, then these birds are not interested. Their kind of country is typical of much of the dry western parts of southern Africa, and indeed from their sandy-brown colouring alone one would guess that the species is at home in semi-arid environments. Their breeding range in the subcontinent extends from the gravel plains of the Namib Desert, eastwards to the western parts of Zimbabwe and the Transvaal, just touching on the thornveld of northern Natal where, one imagines, they feel uneasy in years of good rainfall.

As its name implies, the Greater Kestrel is the largest of the seven kestrel species found in southern Africa. It is also the least colourful and least flamboyantly marked, being an overall buffy brown to pale rufous, strongly barred above and streaked below with black. It has a grey tail, also barred with black, and a white eye which distinguishes it from all other kestrels. In flight it displays silvery white underwings with contrasting black tips and a boldly barred undertail. The sexes are alike in plumage and can only be told apart if seen together, when the slightly larger size of the female becomes apparent. The young Greater Kestrel differs from the adult in having brown eyes, a brown tail and streaked rather than barred flanks. It gradually acquires adult plumage over a period of two years.

Greater Kestrels have been studied in detail near Pretoria and Johannesburg. Although what happens in this fairly high (600 to 700 millimetres) rainfall area may not be representative of the species in the Namib Desert, it does show how the birds behave in a relatively stable environment. Once they become adult they live in pairs, each pair occupying an area of between 500 and 600 hectares. This is their territory, from which they exclude other Greater Kestrels. Its boundaries may outlive the occupants, as the death of one partner usually makes way for a replacement, and the newcomer inherits the real estate as well as the mate. Presumably the size of the territory is somehow related to its food yield, for Greater Kestrel pairs do not attempt to exclude conspecifics from a larger area than necessary.

Food apart, the pair need a suitable nest-site. Like all other falcons they do not build; Greater Kestrels take over – at the end of winter, which is the beginning of their breeding season – the nest of a crow, kite or sometimes of a Secretarybird or other large raptor. A suitable site is crucial to a territory and when the nest falls apart and is not replaced by a new one, the territory is likely to be abandoned. It often happens that the kestrels' territory overlaps with that of a pair of crows, leading to a tandem arrangement in which the kestrels take over the crows' most recent nest, prompting the crows to build a new nest which, in the following year, may be used by the kestrels, and so on. Electricity pylons are favourite crow nest-sites and one will often see, not far away, a pair of nesting Greater Kestrels.

The kestrels start prospecting their nest options in winter and then, for a few months before laying, perch close to the chosen site. The three to five eggs are usually laid during August to October. Although the sexes are almost indistinguishable in size and plumage, the male and female do have clearly partitioned roles in the nesting cycle: the female incubates and the male provisions. When he brings in the food and she leaves the nest to feed, he may take her place for a brief shift, but his role in the incubation is minor. The incubation period is about 32 days, and when the chicks are about a week old the female begins helping her mate to hunt, mostly from the vicinity of the nest.

Greater Kestrels are mainly insectivorous. During a single day one of the females observed in the Pretoria study brought her brood of chicks no less than 110 grasshoppers. The females, though, have the habit of caching larger uneaten food items, taking them down to the ground and hiding them under a grass tuft, to be retrieved and eaten a few hours later. In unstable environments, where the contrast between good and poor years may be profound, the kestrels may have to be nomadic to survive, flourishing in the desert in the good seasons and moving elsewhere when conditions deteriorate.

FALCONS AND KESTRELS

The Greater Kestrel is the largest kestrel in the region. It is a resident species with a mainly western distribution. It does not flock like the migratory species, existing instead in pairs which tend to be sedentary in some areas and nomadic in others. The sexes are alike, being sandy brown, barred with black. Unlike other kestrel species, they have creamy white eyes. They often hunt by hovering.

FALCONS AND KESTRELS

DICKINSON'S KESTREL

This is one of relatively few birds of prey in southern Africa that is named for a person rather than a distinguishing feature or the region in which it occurs. The discoverer of the species was the missionary, Dr Dickinson, a member of David Livingstone's expedition to the Shire River in Malawi where, in the early 1860s, he found the first specimen.

Within South Africa Dickinson's Kestrels are regarded as scarce or uncommon birds, confined to low-lying areas and to places where tall baobab trees are well represented. In Zambia, however, the situation is different, for they are common on the Kafue Flats and associated there with tall palm trees. In both cases the trees provide the birds with their preferred nest-sites: on the Kafue Flats they nest in the hollow tops of dead, broken-off palm stumps and elsewhere they most often use natural holes high up in the limbs of baobabs, both being inaccessible. On occasions Hamerkop nests are occupied, a notable example of which is the well-known pair that for several years used a Hamerkop nest close to the Punda Maria rest-camp and overhanging one of the tourist roads in the northern Kruger National Park. Tree holes last much longer than Hamerkop nests, however, and some trees sites are probably used not just for years on end but for decades. One such nest, again in the northern Kruger Park, was occupied in 1972 and was still in use in 1983.

Probably because of the inaccessibility of the sites and the scarcity of the birds, relatively little is known of their nesting behaviour. They lay a clutch of three or four well-marked brownish eggs during early summer and parental roles seem partitioned, with the female attending the nest and male hunting.

One usually sees the Dickinson's Kestrel solitarily or in pairs, perched on a high vantage point: a slim, greyish bird with a rigid pose and a squared-off top to its head. Its two-tone colouring is the clue to its identity – the grey body contrasts sharply with the paler, ash-coloured head, and when it takes to the wing it flies off strongly and purposefully, displaying its second diagnostic feature – a pale grey rump which contrasts, again, with the darker body. These two characteristic markings distinguish it immediately from the other grey-coloured falcons, the Grey Kestrel and Sooty Falcon. There is a small size difference in the sexes (females are larger), but otherwise male and female Dickinson's are alike.

The species is as poor a candidate for the name 'kestrel', as is the Grey Kestrel, since it does not hover in the family tradition but, instead, hunts mostly from elevated perches, diving from these to the ground to catch prey. The birds are attracted to bush fires, hawking above the flames for insects and small animals that are flushed. Included in their diet are lizards, frogs and small birds.

The Dickinson's Kestrel, a shy, often solitary species, is usually encountered perched on a dead tree or other high vantage point where it sits motionless for long periods. It is a tropical African species which extends as far south as the north-eastern Transvaal.

FALCONS AND KESTRELS

*W*hen seen perched, the Dickinson's Kestrel is a grey-coloured bird; only when it takes to the wing can the extensive barring of its wing and tail feathers be seen. It is not evenly grey, as are the other grey-plumaged falcons, but has a light ash-coloured head and rump which contrast strongly with its darker grey body. Its legs, cere and eye-ring are bright yellow. Non-adult birds resemble their parents but have duller yellow bare parts.

Pygmy Falcon

One's first impression of this tiny hawk is that it is a shrike of some sort. It perches and hunts like a member of that family and its plumage is reminiscent of a shrike. But it is certainly a bird of prey, and a typical falcon in most respects. Both sexes have a white front, which makes them rather shrike-like, and both are dove-grey above, the female immediately distinguishable by her russet back. Their tails add a touch of flamboyance: they are black with white guineafowl-like spots. Both sexes have yellow ceres, eye-rings, legs and toes.

Pygmy Falcons occur in two discrete, widely separated populations in Africa. Each lives in semi-arid country, the one in the south-western part of the continent and the other in the north-east, in the Sudan, Ethiopia, Somalia and Kenya. Relatively little is known of the habits of the north-eastern race but the Kalahari birds have been studied in some detail, alongside their obligate hosts, the Sociable Weavers. Their range in fact mirrors exactly that of the Sociable Weaver, even to the point of stopping short of what sometimes appears to be perfectly suitable savanna habitat, though devoid of these weaver nests.

The latter are one of the more remarkable sights to be seen in the southern Kalahari: huge haystacks, built into trees and sometimes on to windmills and telephone poles, on the underside of which are the nest chambers of the weavers with up to 50 active nests in a colony. Each chamber is enclosed within the nest mass and is reached from below through a narrow vertical tunnel. The huge nest provides each weaver pair with a weather-proof, winter-warm, summer-cool, almost predator-proof environment for breeding. The Pygmy Falcons are small enough to enter the chambers to sleep in at night and to nest in during summer. They do not, apparently, molest the weavers beyond evicting one or two pairs from their nests, and perhaps eating the contents while doing so. Once established, they live in relative harmony with their hosts. The weavers continue adding to and maintaining the huge structure and, while they may alarm at the falcons' every arrrival and departure, they continue with their occupation.

The falcons derive all the benefits of the weavers' labours while the weavers, it is suspected (but not proven), gain a pair of bodyguards better able than they to repel the nest-marauding cobras that visit the colonies and can reach into the chambers. At any rate, if it is not technically a symbiotic relationship it is at least a stable one. According to observations, about one in four Sociable Weaver colonies in the Kalahari is occupied by Pygmy Falcons.

Insects and lizards form the bulk of the Pygmy Falcon's diet. The bird watches the ground intently for movement, looking this way and that, perhaps bobbing its head when prey is sighted. Then it executes a quick dive to the ground to snatch the victim up in its talons. Once dispatched, the lizard or cricket is taken back to a perch to be eaten at leisure. Like other hawks, one or two pellets which contain the hard, indigestible fragments of the day's takings are regurgitated daily. The species breeds in summer, when this kind of prey is most abundant. The nest-hole chosen for breeding soon becomes signposted with a white rim of excreta. The eggs – normally a clutch of three – are laid at any time during summer, but predominantly during October and November. They are pure white, which is unusual for falcons but consistent with many hole-nesting bird species. Both parents undertake the incubation, though the female's share is the larger. The male also provides her, and later the chicks, with food, and for a month or two after fledging the young remain with their parents, after which they disperse.

The pair remain together after breeding, and the regularly spaced nature of their occurrence suggests that pairs are territorial. They usually continue roosting in the nest colony (though some pairs may move locally to sleep in neighbouring colonies) until the time comes to breed again.

At first glance, the tiny Pygmy Falcon looks more like a shrike than a falcon, but a closer look will reveal its powerful little claws and deeply hooked falcon's beak. This is a characteristic bird of the Kalahari and arid western parts of southern Africa and its distribution follows that of the Sociable Weaver whose huge nests it uses for roosting and nesting purposes.

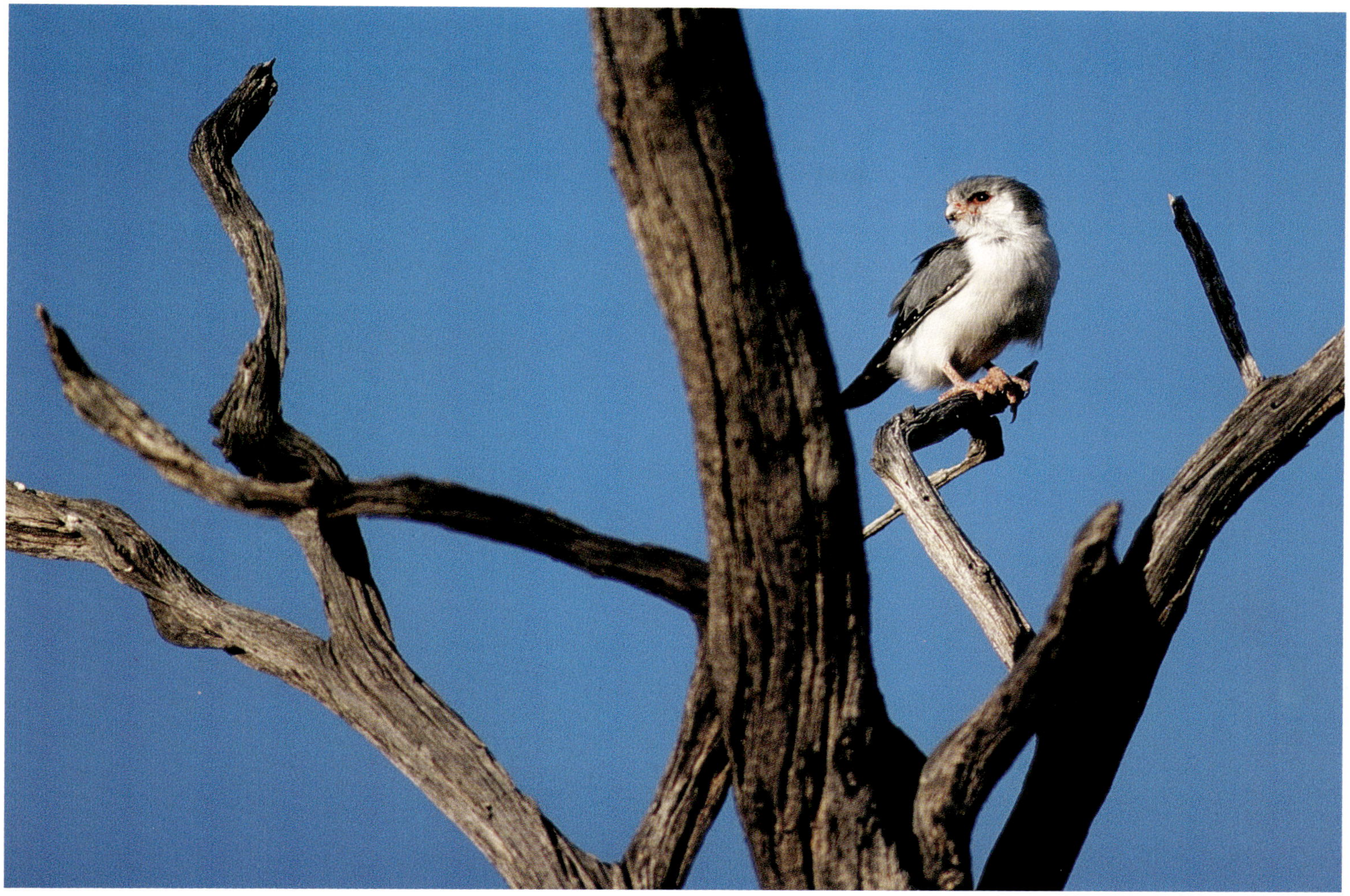

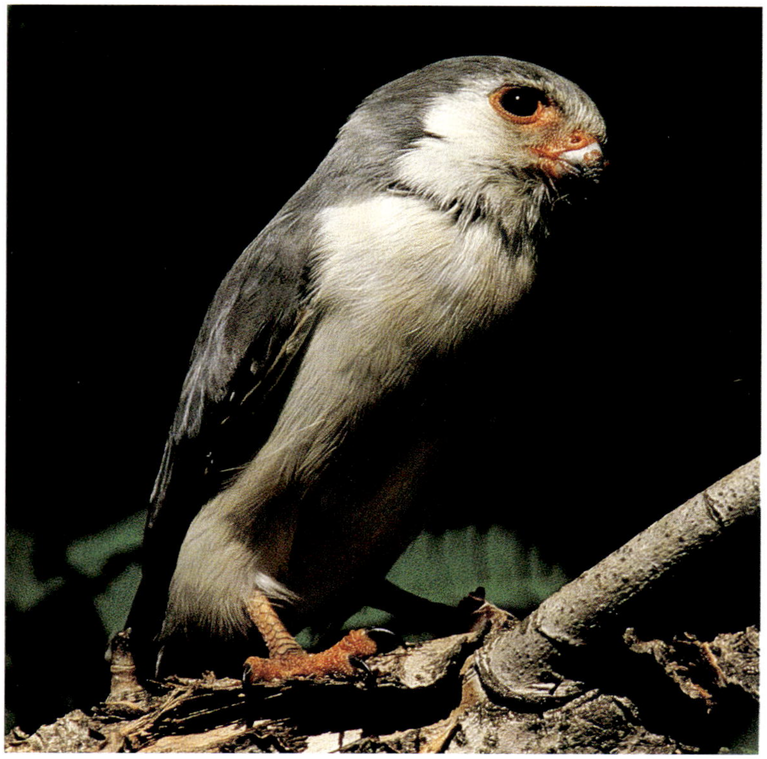

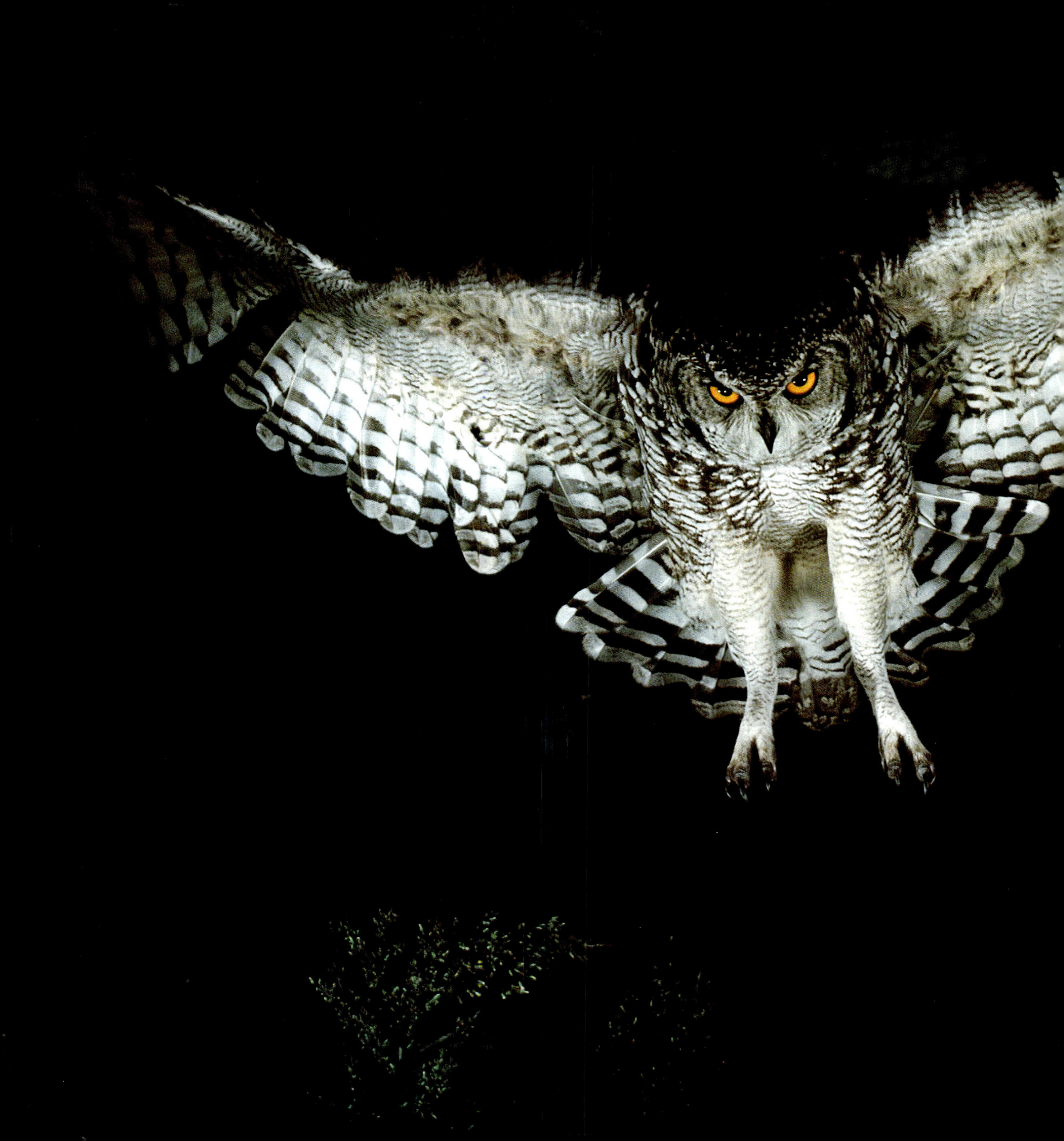

OWLS

The twelve owl species found in southern Africa range enormously in size from the smallest, 20 centimetres long, to the largest which stands 60 centimetres tall. They are the nocturnal counterparts of the Falconiformes and form the separate, unrelated order of birds known as the Strigiformes. They have excellent night vision and acute hearing. Their soft plumage and the fluffy edges to the flight feathers enables them to fly in virtual silence. Owls have distinct faces with forward-looking large eyes, giving them an almost human quality. All are brown, grey or black in colour which aids their sitting undetected during the day and when nesting. They are vocal at night, and most of the species utter a loud, distinctive hooting or whistling call. They do not build their own nests, apart from the rudimentary cups of grass made by the ground-nesting species, and they all lay white, unmarked eggs.

(Left) Talons extended, a Spotted Eagle Owl approaches a perch. Modified flight feathers ensure that its flight is silent: the only sound heard will be the soft thud as it alights. (Above) The rare Cape Eagle Owl can be distinguished by its orange eyes.

Barn Owl

Anyone who has shared a home with Barn Owls and had them huffing and puffing in the chimney, tap-dancing on the roof or whitewashing the veranda furniture will appreciate that these birds settle for barns only when firm measures are taken to discourage their liking for houses. By day they lie low, and – except for last night's mess, which has to be cleared up – one remains unaware of them. But at night they come out to groom, court, and ablute where it pleases them, and to utter their eerie, screeching call throughout the long hours.

Barn Owls occur on every continent except Antarctica and are found virtually throughout southern Africa, from the arid fringes of the Namib Desert to the highest rainfall regions of the eastern escarpment. By preference they are birds of open country, needing nothing more than a sheltered roosting and breeding site in an area where prey is to be found. These sites can be anything from houses and other buildings, to caves, mine-shafts, holes in quarry-faces or cliffs, and holes in trees. The large cavity nests of the Hamerkop are much favoured.

The location of the roosting or nesting sites is often revealed by the presence of pellets below them – compacted, egg-shaped wads of animal fur and bones about 50 millimetres long and half as wide. These are veritable mines of information about the food habits of the bird, reflecting as they do the nature of its previous night's meal. Through most of their range Barn Owls prey mainly on small rodents, and the skulls of these come out remarkably preserved in the pellets, are easily identifiable, and can even be aged by the wear on their teeth. In fact one desert mole species first became known to science on the basis of skull found in a Barn Owl's pellet.

An examination of pellets from different areas, or from different times of the year in one area, will reveal much. Although almost every small nocturnal rodent species has been recorded as prey, in many parts of their range the Multimammate Mouse forms the bird's staple diet. This rodent, in common with several others, undergoes cyclic or erratic population explosions, which greatly affect the Barn Owl's breeding schedule and productivity. In average years the birds tend to breed at the end of the wet season – during March to May in most of the subcontinent, but in August to December in the southern Cape. The number of eggs comprising the clutch is the first variable influenced by the availability of prey. They range between two and 12, the large clutches recorded during rodent plagues. On average, though, about six eggs are laid, often at two- to three-day intervals. Thus, hatching is unsynchronized and may even produce a brood varying in age from the just-born to the fully grown.

Food availability also determines how many chicks survive since, in times of shortage, the oldest and strongest eat at the expense of the youngest. In those years when rodents are super-abundant, Barn Owls not only raise large broods but lay successive clutches even before the last offspring has left the nest. During years when rodent numbers ebb, the owls often fail to breed at all and perhaps even disappear from the areas they previously frequented. So the species is mobile: one specimen was ringed in West Africa, for instance, and recovered 1 000 kilometres away. This ability to disperse has, undoubtedly, contributed to the Barn Owl's success story.

Although some baby owls are delightful creatures, the young of the Barn Owl are unlikely to win any beauty competitions. In this species it is not unusual to find broods of six or more, all of different sizes as a result of the eggs being laid at spaced intervals and hatching asynchronously.

OWLS

Barn Owls are masters of silent flight. They are strictly nocturnal, leaving their daytime roosts to begin their patrol when the last light has faded, flying between often-used perches like white ghosts, and punctuating their passage with a shrill, screeching call. Even on moonless, overcast nights, in inky blackness, they are active, pinpointing and catching their prey by sound rather than sight.

The Grass Owl is very similar to the Barn Owl in looks, and were it not for their completely different choice of habitats, the two species would probably often be confused with each other. The Grass Owl has the same size, shape and moon face as the Barn Owl, but is a darker bird with dark brown upperparts and a beige wash to its spotted front. Like the Barn Owl, it is strictly nocturnal, emerging well after dark from its roost-site hidden in the long grass to fly back and forth in search of prey. It utters a frog-like clicking call.

GRASS OWL

As its name suggests, this species lives in grassland, one of only two southern African owls to do so. In looks it is most like the Barn Owl, and belongs to the same genus (*Tyto*). The two are best distinguished by the colour of their backs: that of the Grass Owl is dark brown, while the Barn Owl's is a buffy colour. There is little chance of confusing the two, though, since they frequent different habitats, and if one of them is flushed from a grassland roost during the day it will certainly be a Grass Owl.

More likely to be confused, perhaps, are the Grass Owl and its sister species of the grassland, the Marsh Owl. These are often found alongside one another, and may even nest a few dozen metres apart. In appearance, however (and providing one gets a clear view), they are quite different. The Grass Owl has a large, white, heart-shaped face and strongly contrasting dark upperparts and pale underparts, whereas the Marsh Owl has a much less distinct facial disc, a brown 'beaky'-shaped head and less contrasting under- and upperparts. Nevertheless, when they are flushed from the grass one usually sees only their backs and the glimpse is often all too brief. In these instances one needs to observe behavioural differences in order to distinguish them. Here, the Grass Owl flies away without looking back and with a rather shallow wingbeat, whereas the Marsh Owl often does look back and has a deeper, more purposeful wingbeat. Moreover, the former is among the most nocturnal of owls and is seldom if ever seen flying about when it is still light (unless disturbed from its roost, of course). It emerges long after sunset to hunt. By contrast, the Marsh Owl often hunts before sunset and after sunrise.

Until recently, nothing was known of the Grass Owl's main call-note. It has long been known that in some situations it emits a shrill screech, much like that made by the Barn Owl, but it is now known that its most frequently used call is a remarkably frog-like clicking, a 'tick, tick, tick, tick...'. It is uttered in bursts lasting perhaps 10 seconds and is repeated frequently during the time that the bird is hunting. If a pair is hunting together they often call in this way, presumably in order to maintain contact. If one sits quietly after dark at the edge of a vlei in which there are Grass Owls, they will almost certainly be heard making this unusual sound, and from it one can follow their movements to and fro.

The Grass Owl is also more specific in its choice of habitat, and may well be absent from areas occupied by the Marsh Owl. It favours rank grass, often on the margins of wet ground rather than in the vlei itself. When vleis are heavily grazed by cattle and the grass cover is greatly reduced, Grass Owls move away, whereas Marsh Owls are much less sensitive to this degradation of their habitat and often remain. Many vleis become heavily grazed, especially in years of drought, and are rendered unsuitable for Grass Owls, which may account for the bird's scarcity. It is currently one of the species listed in the South African Red Data Book of Birds.

Like the Barn Owl, it preys heavily on small rodents, especially the Vlei Rat, and apparently hunts these by sound rather than sight, gliding on silent wings above the ground and dropping on to its victim from above. But it also takes a variety of bird species up to the size of a snipe, insects such as beetles and grasshoppers, and, rarely, frogs. The pellets are cast by the parent birds at their daytime roosts.

These roosts – often tunnel-like affairs – are sited in long grass, the birds lying up in them during the day and leaving them only if they are disturbed. The male and female usually spend the daylight hours in separate roosts, not far from each other. When breeding gets underway (it can start at any time of the year but usually occurs during February to May), the birds build a rudimentary nest comprising a saucer of grass and sedge blades on the ground at the end of one of the roost tunnels. The clutch consists of three to five white eggs (neither the eggs nor the nest are readily distinguishable from those of the Marsh Owl), and the female undertakes most or all of the incubation, which lasts about 32 days. During this period she is fed by the male. The chicks hatch within a day or two of each other and are initially covered with a thick coat of whitish down which gives way to feathers when they are five to six weeks old. At about this age they start wandering away from the nest on foot, and, when seven weeks old, they make their first tentative flights.

OWLS

WOOD OWL

The Wood Owl is so-called, one suspects, more by accident than design. The first specimen was collected at Knysna in 1834 and named by Andrew Smith, then curator of the South African Museum, in honour of a Colonel Woodford. For more than a century it was known as Woodford's Owl (and its scientific name, *Strix woodfordii*, attests to this) but popular usage has shortened it to Wood Owl. The Wood Owl is, coincidentally, a woodland species.

As the Knysna type locality indicates, these owls are denizens of the forests and are likely to be found in reasonably sized forest patches anywhere in southern Africa, ranging from the Cape Peninsula eastwards through the southern and eastern Cape into Natal, Zululand, Swaziland, eastern Transvaal, Mozambique, Zimbabwe, northern Botswana and Namibia. They are as much at home in the colder, high-lying Afromontane forests as they are in the warm coastal regions of Zululand and the narrow forest galleries along some east-flowing rivers.

Being strictly nocturnal birds, their daytime presence would almost certainly remain undetected unless one knew exactly where they roosted. At night, though, and at any time of the year, one would certainly hear their cheery, energetic call ('whu-hu, whu-uh-uh-uh') coming from one or other quarter of the forest. Males and females often duet, or their calls overlap, and during these times the higher-pitched notes of the female can be distinguished from those of her mate. These sounds are generally understood to be associated with territory advertisement.

Adult birds live together in pairs and remain in a well-defined territory (of perhaps 50 hectares in extent) throughout the year, roosting in it during the day, hunting in it by night and breeding in it at the start of summer. Interesting research being conducted along the Levubu River in the northern Kruger National Park has shown that pairs occur at half-kilometre intervals, and many of the territory-holding birds are individually recognizable by the slight variations in their voices.

Over the years such pairs must become intimately familiar with every tree and branch, every clearing and every ambush point within their domain. They have at least one favourite roost site, invariably inside a tree or bush draped with densely tangled creeper, and they return to these day after day. The same nesting hole is often re-used annually. It is usually located in the main trunk, where a branch has broken off and a cavity has formed. Some nest-sites are within a metre or two of the ground although they are normally much higher up than this. In indigenous forest, where every second tree has a hollow trunk or a broken-off limb, suitable nest-sites occur in excess, but in some habitats (such as plantations) the birds have to make do with nesting in less satisfactory positions – in open forks of trees where they may be flooded during heavy rain, on old Sparrowhawk nests, or even, occasionally, on the ground.

The female lays her clutch of two white eggs (on occasion one more or less) from July onwards, but most often during September and October, and she undertakes most or all of the incubation, being fed at intervals during the night by her mate. The bulk of the prey is taken on the ground by swooping from a perch, and the diet is very varied, comprising many insect species, including beetles, crickets, grasshoppers and so on, small rodents and some small birds, which are probably seized from their perches while asleep. The largest recorded prey of the owl (which weighs about 300 grams) was a Rock Pigeon, which has a mass of about 350 grams. Incubation lasts about 31 days. Newly hatched chicks are covered with white down and from about 10 days of age feathers emerge, gradually replacing the down so that at the age of four weeks they are virtually fully feathered. At this age they often emerge from their nest hole – though not yet flying – and hop out along a nearby branch, waiting to be fed. They fly for the first time between 30 and 37 days old and thereafter they live with their parents for a few months before dispersing and seeking their own forest patch.

Although the Wood Owl has a restricted range in southern Africa, being confined to forested areas and riverine woodland, it is a common bird where it occurs. After dark, its cheerful 'whu-uh, whu-uh-uh-uh' often betrays its presence. This medium-sized brown owl, which lacks ear-tufts, has deep brown eyes set in a round, whitish face.

MARSH OWL

If you are prepared to tramp about in vleis, Marsh Owls are easy birds to see as they readily fly up from their roosting sites in the grass. The sighting will be brief, though, for they soon drop back into cover. In fact, for a good view one should simply watch quietly from a vantage point overlooking a vlei in the late afternoon or early morning. Marsh Owls often emerge at this time of the day, well before sunset and often long after sunrise, to quarter the ground in search of food. They course back and forth a few metres above the grass cover, deep wingbeats interspersed with glides, peering intently at the ground below, turning their brown little faces this way and that, at times so preoccupied that they pass surprisingly close to you. Every now and again they plunge abruptly down into the grass, out of view, to emerge moments later and continue the search. Occasionally such an attempt is rewarded and the bird reappears with a small rodent in its talons.

In autumn, when rodent numbers are at a peak, the grass in the vleis is high and rank, and the risk of a sudden downpour and the flooding of the marsh is slight, Marsh Owls begin nesting. The male is spurred on to hunt by the sound of his mate who, at intervals, utters a short rasping call – a 'gggk' sound, rather like a piece of cloth being torn – from her concealed nest in the grass. This is when she is incubating the clutch of four white eggs, in the nest she has made at the end of a short grass tunnel on the ground. Unlike most owl species, which simply occupy a suitable site without any attempt at nest construction, Marsh Owls pull together pieces of grass and sedge and often build up quite a respectable platform, keeping the eggs well above the damp ground.

The male pauses every now and again during his hunt, perching on an old stump. He also calls, making a similar but more sustained croaking note: a difficult sound to describe, but something like 'gggg, ggk, ggk, gk'. He then takes to the wing and, in due course, one of his plunges into the grass is rewarded. He carries his trophy towards the nest, calling, and his mate flies up to take it from him.

Marsh Owls are common, widely distributed birds, likely to be found wherever there are suitable vleis and marshy areas. They favour terrain that is damp or wet underfoot (but not too wet), lie up during the day, and nest in the sedges and rank grass associated with the habitat. They do not, however, occur in reedbeds. Outside the breeding season the birds may roost in close proximity to each other during the day (as many as 50 have been observed at such communal roosts). The reason for this sociability is not fully understood, but it may simply be a consequence of the seasonal shortage of suitable areas of cover. Certainly much of the Marsh Owl's preferred habitat undergoes radical transformations during the year, drying out, being burnt, trampled by cattle and so heavily grazed that it finally resembles a tattered carpet.

To cope with such changes the birds, like their sister species of the marshlands, the Grass Owl, need to be mobile. They obviously do move about, as the communal roosting habit indicates, but they also appear to be more flexible in their selection of habitat and more diverse in their choice of prey than Grass Owls. Insects, especially beetles, form a large proportion of their diet, but a range of small birds, rodents, small reptiles and amphibians are also taken.

During winter, the Marsh Owl often emerges during the day and it is not uncommon to see it patrolling a marshland in the late afternoon sun.

The Marsh Owl is a medium-sized brown owl that resembles the Wood Owl. The similarity is coincidental as the two species are not closely related at all, nor do they share the same habitat. The Marsh Owl is, however, close kin to the Short-eared Owl, found in Europe, which is also a ground-living bird that frequents marshes. In southern Africa, Marsh Owls often occur alongside the scarcer Grass Owl.

Cape Eagle Owl

In the quiet of a chilly autumn night, the deep three-noted hoot of the male Cape Eagle Owl, its first note emphatic, its second and third softer back-ups, is a strong, far-carrying sound that leaves no doubt that it belongs to an owl of sorts. The call is often the only evidence of its presence in an area, for during the day, when it lies up in rocky outcrops, it is difficult if not impossible to locate.

The Cape Eagle Owl is a species of montane grasslands, its range following the Afromontane belt from the southern Cape through the forest-grassland mosaics found in the eastern Cape, Natal, eastern Transvaal and eastern Zimbabwe. It also occurs in the mountainous areas in the western Karoo, in southern Namibia, and in the granite hills of the Matobo of Zimbabwe. The latter birds belong to the northern race, locally called Mackinder's Eagle Owl.

Cape Eagle Owls are large, fine birds which stand half a metre tall and weigh one to 1,5 kilograms, making them one of the largest of African owls, and considerably bigger than the Spotted Eagle Owl for which they are sometimes mistaken. They have a typical eagle owl profile – thick-set body with wide neck, square head, and prominent eartufts. Their eyes are a glowing orange. In front they are boldly blotched with dark brown and chestnut, and just one of these distinctively marked breast feathers, if found, is sufficient to identify the bird.

Rocks, in the form of outcrops, shallow bluffs, cliffs or scarps, are essential to the species. Provided they have recourse during the day to such hideaways, the birds can live in otherwise treeless, featureless open grassland. But it is usually the mountainous, or at least the hilly, landscapes that provide the rocky cover. At night they range into the grassland to hunt and can sometimes be seen doing so, perched on fences or telephone poles alongside roads. By day they retire to a sheltered ledge or scree in a rocky gorge or cliff, and one can easily walk past such a roosting bird without realising it is there. During much of the year they are silent, but towards the end of summer, as the winter breeding season approaches, males can be heard calling during the night from the vicinity of their future nest-sites in these rocky retreats.

The favourite spot chosen for a nest is on a ledge or shelf that is inaccessible from below and overhung above, and sites that meet these requirements are used year after year. Although the owls do not make a nest as such, one can immediately detect a long-used site because of the accumulation of bone fragments in it. Some contain literally hundreds of bones, collected in what are termed 'ossuaries'. They simply mark the place where several successive nests have been located and where the surviving bone fragments from decomposed pellets have accumulated. These are useful in identifying the kind of prey taken by the pair. In Zimbabwe's Matobo region nearly 1 000 prey remains were gathered from them, and it was found that for the most part the birds were hunting dassies and scrub hares and, especially, rock hares. Ninety-nine per cent of the sample comprised these and other mammals, and the bird's ability to overpower prey of this size (one to three kilograms), puts the species in the 'big eagle' bracket of predators. By contrast, in parts of South Africa Cape Eagle Owls show a more diverse and often more modest choice of prey, taking rodents, birds, crabs, frogs and insects in addition to the larger items.

These birds breed in mid-winter, laying their two or three white eggs during May to July. The female does most or all of the incubation. During the day she sits tight and does not easily give her position away. At night the male brings food, and she leaves the nest to eat and to groom. During the nesting cycle the surrounding rocks become 'whitewashed' with round, chalky blobs, often the only visible sign of the nest-site. Incubation lasts about 34 to 36 days and, as the chicks grow, so they become more comical-looking and endearing. It is not surprising, but very unfortunate, that many people take owl chicks from nests for pets – unfortunate, because a high proportion of the birds are incorrectly fed and become crippled, fit only for a zoo- or cage-bound life.

The powerful feet are one of the distinctive features of the large, tawny-coloured Cape Eagle Owl. This species takes a diversity of prey, and is one of the few owls capable of catching and killing hares and dassies, both considerably heavier than itself. Its large size, orange eyes and heavily blotched black, chestnut and buff chest distinguish it from the superficially similar Spotted Eagle Owl.

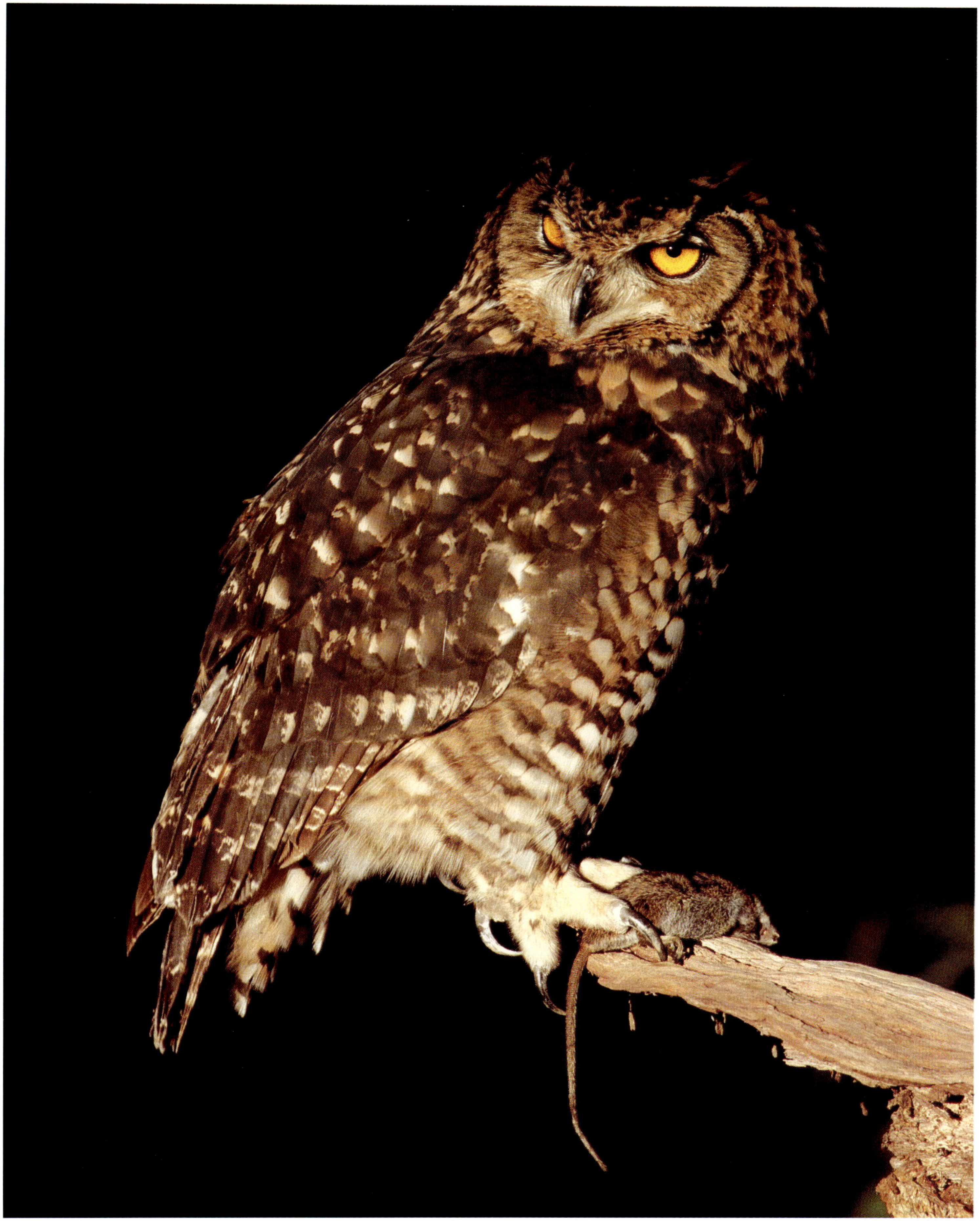

OWLS

The Spotted Eagle Owl is the commonest representative of the genus Bubo (Latin for 'horned owl') in southern Africa, and its quiet hooting can be heard at night in most parts of the subcontinent. It lives among rocks, in trees, in wooded suburban gardens, and in dongas. It has diverse food habits, preying on whatever is available, but especially insects and small rodents. The grey-plumaged bird illustrated here is typical of the species, but occasional tawny-coloured individuals are found and these can easily be mistaken for the larger Cape Eagle Owl.

Spotted Eagle Owl

Unless one happens to know where they roost or nest, Spotted Eagle Owls are unlikely to be seen during the day, except by chance. After dark, however, they become one of southern Africa's most commonly encountered night birds. With their rectangular chunky bodies, upright ear-tufts and the way they go 'who-whoo' in the night, they precisely match the public's image of an owl. And indeed they are fairly familiar to the general public for they often live within the precincts of towns and cities, where shady trees provide day roosts, and where hollow trunks, and window ledges or boxes serve as suitable nest-sites. They are equally at home in rural areas, of course, and a drive along a country road at night will often reveal a Spotted Eagle Owl perched on a telephone or fence pole, or standing like a little policeman in the road itself. Spotted Eagle Owls are widely distributed, both in southern Africa and across the African continent, and they exist in a variety of habitats ranging from those in the arid west to the mesic ones in the east. They appear equally at home in desert, karoo scrub, grassland and savanna, provided there are rocky outcrops or trees to give them shelter during the day.

Spotted Eagle Owls pair for life, living year-round in territories of a few square kilometres. During the breeding season their activities centre around their nest-site, which may be on the ground among an outcrop of rocks, in a donga, in a cavity or bole of a large tree, on top of a Hamerkop or Sociable Weaver's nest, or sometimes in a safe niche of a building. In places where they are not molested they often use the same site year after year. Breeding takes place in early summer and the male's two-note hooting call is frequently heard in the evening during the last weeks of winter. He and his mate prepare one or more nest scrapes, visiting these together in the weeks preceding egg-laying. At these times they cluck softly and display to each other. The female often replies to the male's call in duet with a soft three-noted 'ho-hu, hooo'. When hooting, the birds' throats are briefly inflated, revealing a white puff of feathers.

In common with other owls the eggs are plain white and are laid mostly during August to October. There are usually just two eggs, but larger clutches, of up to four, have been recorded. The female starts incubating after laying the first egg. She sits tight, and her mottled brown, grey and black plumage blends in with her surroundings so that she is difficult to discern. This cryptic effect is enhanced when she narrows her eyelids to slits and raises her ear tufts. At night the male emerges from his roost nearby and hunts for both of them, bringing her prey at intervals. She leaves the nest briefly during these visits in order to feed and groom.

Pairs that are not disturbed become very confiding and the incubating bird can even be stroked by hand. Some, however, become aggressive and will swoop at visitors to their nest. They are capable of inflicting nasty head wounds with their talons: more attacks on people have probably been made by nesting Spotted Eagle Owls than any other raptor.

The eggs take a little more than a month to hatch and the white chicks emerge at intervals of a day or two. They start out in life as featureless white lumps of down, but in a few weeks turn into delightful grey fluffy creatures with large yellow eyes and woolly legs and feet, standing up and snapping their bills when the nest is inspected. When about a month old, and if the nest is on the ground, they begin to wander away, even though they are unable to fly. Their first flight occurs after about seven weeks. Once they are able to take to the wing they range farther afield, but still depend on their parents for food for another month or two.

Spotted Eagle Owls take as wide an array of prey as any owl species, the items ranging in size from a termite to a large gamebird. Generally speaking, though, insects such as grasshoppers, crickets and beetles are most common in their diet, followed by rodents and small birds. Reptiles, frogs, fish and crabs are also taken. Occasionally unusual prey, such as a Lanner Falcon, is recorded.

The owl's dependence on insects is probably why it is so often encountered on country roads. Here they are able to see and ambush anything that leaves the verges to cross the open road. There are risks as well as advantages attached to this, and thousands of Spotted Eagle Owls are struck, and either killed or injured, by vehicles each year.

OWLS

A trick of light has imbued these Giant Eagle Owls' normally dark brown eyes with a brilliant red glow. This species is often found in pairs, roosting in tall, leafy trees during the day and becoming active at night. At the onset of the breeding season, their unusual grunting call can be heard in the evenings and early mornings, one bird uttering a deep 'uh-uh-uh-uh' and the other answering with a still deeper 'uh-uh'.

Giant Eagle Owl

As its name implies, the Giant Eagle Owl is a large member of the family – not the largest in the world, a distinction that belongs to the Eurasian Eagle Owl, but certainly the biggest in sub-Saharan Africa. It has the typical eagle owl salt-cellar-with-eartufts profile. Two unusual features are its dark brown eyes (these are usually yellow or orange in eagle owls) and its striking pink eyelids, which add a colourful touch to an otherwise grey bird. Its large size and overall grey plumage, from which its scientific name *Bubo lacteus* is derived, distinguish it from the other two southern African eagle owls.

This is the eagle owl of the savanna regions of southern Africa, found widely where there are tall trees in thornveld, mopane, marula-knobthorn, or other savanna-type habitats. It is commonly encountered, for example, in the tall camelthorns of the Kalahari Gemsbok National Park and in the baobab country of northern Botswana. Now and again pairs may turn up and even nest in unexpected places, such as in a Johannesburg park or at De Hoop on the southern tip of Africa.

In the typical bushveld country of the central Transvaal, pairs are spaced at intervals of four or five kilometres. They like to roost high up in tall, leafy trees, male and female often sitting close together but sometimes perching a short distance apart from each other. Disturbing a roosting Giant Eagle Owl during the day is among the worst things one can do to the bird. In no time it will have a mob of angry Grey Louries, drongos, perhaps crows and even other birds of prey dive-bombing it, confronting their natural enemy when it is at a disadvantage.

Pairs of Giant Eagle Owls often roost in the vicinity of the nest-site that they have ear-marked for use in the winter, which is their breeding season. They invariably nest in trees, usually choosing the stick nest of an eagle or a hawk. Because Wahlberg's are generally the commonest of the savanna eagles and their nests are a suitable size, these are the ones most frequently taken over, but virtually any large stick nest will serve the owl's purposes. Sometimes they will even lay their eggs atop a Sociable Weaver's nest, or on the roof of that of a Hamerkop. Indeed, there have been occasions when a pair of Giant Eagle Owls has nested on top of a Hamerkop's nest while the Hamerkops themselves were breeding inside.

Giant Eagle Owls are often heard calling after dark in the month or two preceding egg-laying. They have an unusual call, a series of three or more deep grunts that are audible from a long way off and which, for someone who is unfamiliar with the species, sounds more akin to that of an animal than a bird. At times the pair call in duet, occasionally beginning before sunset. This belies the belief that the species is strictly nocturnal.

Another, even less owl-like call is the wail uttered by the female before and during incubation to solicit food. This is an unearthly sound when heard at close quarters, and is often a signal that breeding is about to begin. The female lays her clutch of two large white eggs during June to August and it is she who does most of the incubation, with the male playing the role of provider. She sits on the nest during the day, but her eared, cat-like head usually breaks the smooth outline of the nest's rim and so reveals her presence. If she is flushed off the eggs she sometimes gives a curiously limp wing-flapping display, at the same time making a loud 'waaa, waaa, waaa...' wailing call.

Almost invariably, although two eggs are produced, only one young is reared. Just why the second chick dies is uncertain: is it a victim of sibling aggression (as occurs among eagles), or does it simply starve because it is at a size disadvantage? The chick fledges when a little more than two months old.

Giant Eagle Owls prey on virtually anything they can overpower, evidence of the varied diet accumulating below the trees in the vicinity of the nest. They are significant predators of such other members of the family as Barn, Marsh, Grass and Spotted Eagle Owls, and they take a wide variety of other birds, including chickens stolen from neighbouring kraals, and many small mammals. One of the least expected prey items, but a very common one, is the hedgehog. The Giant Eagle Owl is one of the few birds of prey that is able to get through this little animal's prickly defences, and it is remarkable that, in an area where hedgehogs are very seldom seen, as many as 20 of their pelts may be found near an active nest.

Pel's Fishing Owl

As the Great Grey Owl is the ghost of the vast, cold coniferous forests of the Arctic taiga, so Pel's Fishing Owl haunts the forested rivers of hot, tropical Africa. In Fishing Owl country the nights are seldom quiet: the air is vibrant with the trilling and droning of insects and the cacophony of frog sounds, and, adding to the symphony, the deep 'hoot heet… hooot, heeet' calls of the owls. The resonant notes of the male and female calling in duet, his higher pitched and hers lower pitched, may be coming from a few hundred metres or a few kilometres away and yet, such is the carrying power of the sound in the night air that, near or far, its loudness is almost the same.

One can hear the owls in their riverine habitats at any time of the year, but most often in summer, heralding the coming breeding season. The pairs space themselves out along the river-front at a density which may be as little as a kilometre or as much as four or five kilometres apart, according to the nature of the area, and their calls presumably serve to maintain the territorial status quo. The length of river-frontage a pair needs probably depends on how many fishing spots it offers, how many permanent pools there are and the availability of suitable nesting and roosting sites. Some of the rivers stop flowing during times of drought, and as the surface water recedes so pairs in poor localities have to move, until eventually groups of Pel's Fishing Owls may be found around the last of the pools.

If one has the good fortune to see a Pel's Fishing Owl at work at night, perhaps by spotlight from a boat in the Panhandle region of the Okavango Delta, the impression would be of a large, plump, hunch-backed ginger bird, perched motionless on a stump or branch that lies low over the water, head inclined forward and eyes intently watching the water below. They live on fish, hunting from the perches simply by diving in, feet first, to catch their prey. Unlike other owls their legs are unfeathered, and the soles of their feet are spiny, which enables them to hold on to their slippery victims. They also have powerful feet and long, sharp claws. Barbel are the most frequently represented prey species taken. The average catch usually weighs only a few hundred grams, though fish up to two kilograms have been caught. Their specialized diet and hunting technique do not demand silent flight or acute hearing and, perhaps because of this, they lack those downy edges to the flight feathers that allow other owl species to fly soundlessly. If one puts a Pel's Fishing Owl to flight during the day it flaps off almost as noisily as would any other bird its size.

The breeding season coincides with, or begins soon after, the peak flow of the river and the chick is raised as the water level is receding, a time when, presumably, conditions for fishing are at their most favourable. The clutches are usually produced in February to April, the eggs taking a little over a month to hatch. They are laid in a typical owl site – a hole or hollow in a large tree, often where a side branch has broken off or where several branches form a bowl. No lining is added and the eggs rest on whatever bits and pieces fill the hollow. Although two eggs are normally laid only one young is reared.

The chick starts life as a little bundle of white down, becomes buff-coloured and finally, by the time it fledges, takes on a more gingery colour. It utters a wailing soliciting sound, marvellously described in the early bird literature as 'a weird screechy howl, which rises in a nerve-shattering crescendo, to peter out like a cry of a lost soul falling into a bottomless pit'. Fanciful, but it suits the bird.

Pel's Fishing Owl was first collected in Ghana (then Gold Coast) in 1850, and was named for that country's governor, H.S. Pel. It is one of three fishing owl species found in Africa and all belong to the same genus. The other two are restricted to the large forested rivers of central and west Africa and little is known of their habits or behaviour.

The huge, ginger Pel's Fishing Owl with its seemingly empty eyes is unlikely to be mistaken for any other owl species. It is rare and uncommonly seen unless it is looked for specifically in the right habitat and at the right localities. It lives along the edges of tropical rivers and wetlands that are overhung by large shady trees. During the day it roosts out of sight in a leafy tree; at night it emerges to fish along the river, using hunting perches overlooking the water.

OWLS

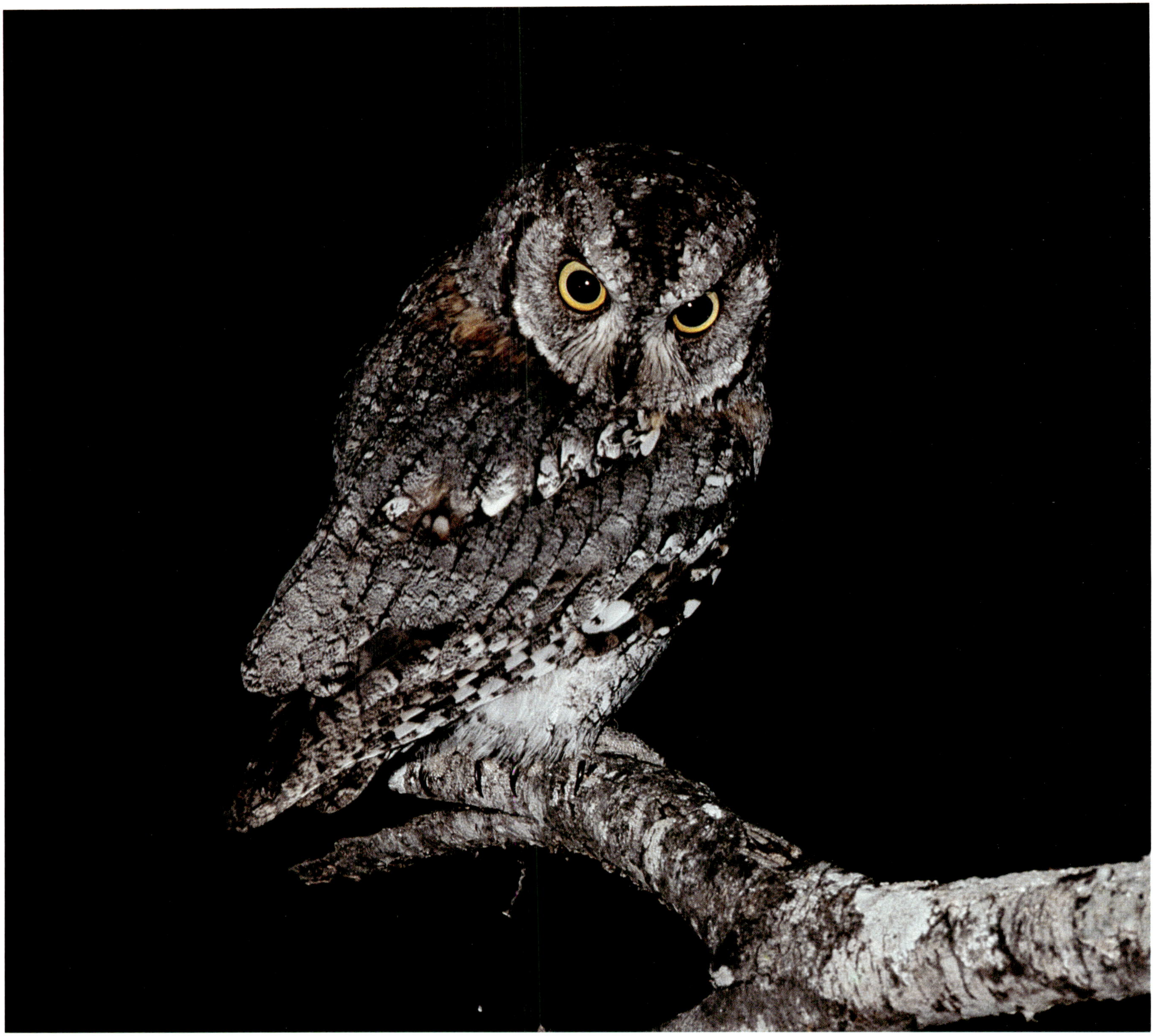

SCOPS OWL

Scops Owls are tiny creatures, weighing a mere 65 grams and, as a consequence of this and of their cryptic coloration and strictly nocturnal habits, they are extremely difficult to locate during the day. In the daylight hours they sit perfectly still – usually against the trunk of a tree where a branch comes out – and as thin as a pencil, with their feathers drawn in, their ear tufts erect and their feet moulding into the branch like a grey barnacle. Their eyes are all but closed and through the narrowest of slits the birds watch what is happening around them. If by sheer chance you happen across a roosting Scops Owl during the day it will prove to be disarmingly confiding, relying on its camouflage to escape detection. Examine its feathers closely and you will see how its dappled appearance is created by an intricate pattern of light and dark on every feather. It is just one of countless examples in nature of how natural selection has produced almost a perfect blend of a species with its background.

Like other owls, the Scops comes alive at night, when it turns into a diminutive predator of grasshoppers, beetles, crickets and other insects and arthropods that move about after dark. Their presence at these times is revealed by their call-note. The males utter a short, frog-like chirp, 'krup', repeated at five- to 10-second intervals, and it is after dark that one comes to realise Scops Owls are often common birds in many areas, quite contrary to the impression one gets during the day. In early spring and in suitable habitat one may hear four or five males calling simultaneously from different directions. The calling can go on intermittently through the night, and one can exploit the territorial behaviour of the birds to get views of them. Play a recording of the sound within hearing range of one of the calling birds and it will not be long before it comes up to investigate the source of the sound.

The Scops Owl is a savanna species, its southern African range extending across central and northern Namibia, through Botswana, into the Transvaal savanna regions and thence southwards down the eastern littoral into Zululand, Natal and the eastern Cape. It favours areas with tall, scattered trees and is particularly common in mopane woodland. Despite its numbers and wide distribution, relatively little is known of its habits and behaviour. It takes most of its prey on the ground by pouncing on it from a perch and occasionally by walking about in search of food. The nests are usually very difficult to locate as they are often sited in the hollow top of a broken-off branch, and when the female is incubating she sits tight, her camouflaged back merging with the rim. Unlike Pearlspotted Owls, Scops Owls do not normally choose closed cavities in which to nest. However, in recent years a number of boxes put up for hole-nesting birds in one of the Namibian reserves have been occupied by Scops Owls, so this preference for open-top nests is not invariable.

In the week or two before egg-laying, the Scops Owls can sometimes be heard calling softly during the day in the vicinity of the nest-to-be, and this calling may be made by the female soliciting the male. She roosts near the nest just before laying and then lays a clutch of two or three white eggs, usually in the months of September to November. During the incubation period the male is relatively quiet. He does not share in the incubation, but instead brings food to the female at intervals during the night. The eggs take about 25 days to hatch and the chicks leave the nest when they are three to four weeks old.

The Scops Owl, *Otus senegalensis*, which is found in southern Africa, extends northwards across the savannas into West Africa, overlapping there with the Palearctic Scops Owl, *Otus scops*, which breeds in southern Europe and migrates south during the winter. The two are sometimes treated as conspecific but, because their breeding ranges do not overlap and there are small differences in their size, plumage and call-notes, it is more valid to separate them. Six other species of *Otus* are also found in Africa, some of them restricted to single islands (Pemba Scops Owl and São Tomé Scops Owl) or to single forest patches (Sokoke Scops Owl).

The diminutive Scops Owl has two faces – a 'night face', illustrated here, and a 'day face'. At night it appears to be a sturdy, earless, round-faced little bird with blazing yellow eyes and a far-carrying, frog-like call. If it is disturbed during the day, however, its plumpness disappears as it draws itself in, almost to pencil thinness, sprouts long thin ears and peers out through eyes transformed into the thinnest of slits. It will sit silently, confident of its camouflage, awaiting the safety of darkness again.

Pearlspotted Owl

The Pearlspotted Owl is another 'mini-owl' of the African savanna belt and a common resident in the savannas of southern Africa. It belongs to the genus *Glaucidium*, which is also represented in Europe, Asia and North and South America. In most of these species there are two circular marks, resembling eyes, on the back of the birds' heads. The Pearlspotted Owl's 'eyes' are black, and become visible or invisible according to its mood or behaviour: if it is sitting quietly with its head hunched into its body they are not apparent, but when it is alert or agitated and looking this way and that in a typically jerky manner, they become conspicuous. The bird also has the habit of swivelling its head through 180° so that one is looking into its real eyes one moment and into its false ones the next.

Such plumage features do not come about by chance, and several explanations of their function have been offered. The one that has gained fairly general acceptance is that the false eyes offer the bird some protection against a predator which approaches from behind, and which might abandon its attack simply because it thinks it has been detected. This may be so, but nevertheless Pearlspotted Owls quite often do fall prey to other birds: to owls at night and to goshawks and sparrowhawks, and even African Hawk Eagles, during the day.

Known affectionately as 'pearlies' by today's generation of birdwatchers, these predators are more active during the day than any other owl species on the subcontinent. This is especially true in the winter months, when their movements can be followed by the chattering of birds alarming at them – bulbuls, white-eyes, sunbirds and perhaps a drongo. When agitated, the owl has the engaging habit of flicking its tail from left to right like a pendulum, and one immediately knows when it takes to flight because the chattering of the birds mobbing it suddenly assumes a more hysterical note.

A pearlie on the wing, with its dappled brown back, its rounded wings and its alternating rapid flapping and gliding flight, is strongly reminiscent of a woodpecker. In fact the nest-holes made by woodpeckers also happen to be the pearlie's favoured nest-site, and for most of the year their activities centre around the hole they have chosen. If it is a good, secure one excavated into solid wood, as those of the Bearded Woodpecker usually are, the pearlies may re-use it year after year. Good holes are often at a premium, and in between the owl's occupation there may be a succession of other residents, including rollers, Redbilled Woodhoopoes, hornbills, starlings and even the original excavators of the hole.

Pearlspotted Owls are vocally most active during the winter and spring, and while they call mainly after dark, they can often be heard during the day as well. They utter a series of piercing whistled notes (which are easy to imitate), beginning low and rising to a crescendo before tailing off. Females emit a higher-pitched sound than the males, and as the two often call at the same time, the difference is frequently noticeable. If you want to see a pearlie during the day, or at least to know if it is around, imitate its whistle and it will probably respond within seconds. Even if it does not, your efforts will be well rewarded by a mob of agitated birds arriving on the scene to scold and express their displeasure.

Pearlies nest in early summer, and in the weeks preceding egg-laying the female sits around the nest hole uttering a quiet 'peep' note, which is assumed to be a food-soliciting call. The clutch of three white, well-rounded eggs is laid (usually) during September and October, and once the female begins incubating nothing will budge her from the nest hole. She sits tight, only briefly leaving the eggs to receive food from the male, and to groom, in the evening. From this point on the male calls less frequently, and is much less obtrusive in the vicinity of the nest. He hunts from branches and takes a wide range of prey, including small rodents, beetles, frogs, crickets, small birds and, on those evenings when they emerge, termite alates. The 29-day incubation period is long for so small a bird, and the nestling period, at 31 days, even lengthier. Once the chicks begin feathering the female joins the male in obtaining food for them. Recently fledged pearlies are not down-covered but look very like the parent birds, their tender age given away by their short tails and a few stray wisps of down here and there. They beg from the parents with a sparrow-like twittering call.

---OWLS---

The Pearlspotted Owl is partly diurnal and tends to be more conspicuous than the Barred Owl which it closely resembles. Unlike the Scops Owl which closes its eyes to slits as part of its camouflage, the Pearlspotted Owl will stare in the direction of any disturbance with typical owl intensity. 'Pearlies' are among the smallest of the southern African owls: the males weigh a mere 70 grams on average, while the females are heavier and weigh approximately 90 grams.

BARRED OWL

The first Barred Owls known to science were two specimens collected in the eastern Cape some time before 1834, the year in which they were formally described. Since then many more have been collected in eastern and central Africa, but for nearly 150 years there was no further sign of the bird's existence in its type locality. Then in 1980 a freshly dead specimen was picked up near Bathurst, recognized for what it was, and sent in to the Durban Museum, where it now resides as one of the very few specimens of the eastern Cape race of the species. More sightings have been obtained here in the past few years but the bird remains elusive, and nothing is known of its population status or breeding habits.

The Barred Owls which occur in the eastern Transvaal and extend northwards into central and east Africa are larger birds with darker backs, darker barring and a different pattern of markings on their heads. A case could be made for treating the two as separate species, but more needs to be known about their behaviour before making such a decision.

Like most owls, the distinctive call of these birds reveals their presence. It is reminiscent of the piercing note of the Pearlspotted Owl but much less flamboyant and more mellow, a purring 'krrooo' sound repeated quickly six to 10 times. It sometimes extends into a faster, frequently repeated double note, 'purr-porr, purr-porr...'. Barred Owls occasionally call during the day but are usually heard only at night, and they are decidedly more nocturnal in their habits than the Pearlspotted Owl.

Because Barred and Pearlspotted Owls are similar in their general appearance, comparisons between them are inevitable. The former is larger, weighing about 120 grams, whereas pearlies average about 80 grams. However, Barred Owls have smaller feet, a characteristic associated with their mainly insectivorous diet, while pearlies take many small birds and rodents in their more diverse diet. Moreover, for some unexplained reason Barred Owls do not have false 'eyes' on the backs of their heads, which is a distinctive feature of most members of the *Glaucidium* group of owls. The preferred habitat of the two species overlaps in places, although in most areas pearlies frequent open savanna, the Barred Owls denser woodlands of tall trees or the riverine galleries fringing the larger east-flowing watercourses such as those in the eastern Transvaal. The eastern Cape birds, by contrast, live in dense *Euphorbia* bush.

Relatively little is known about the Barred Owl's nesting habits, except that it nests in holes in trees and lays two or three white eggs during September and October. It is a far scarcer and more localized species than the Pearlspotted Owl, but there are some places, such as the Moremi Wildlife Reserve in Botswana, where one can be sure to find it.

Less common and widespread than 'pearlies', Barred Owls are also more nocturnal in their habits, and they betray their presence at night by uttering a rapidly repeated growling note.

At a glance, the Barred Owl is very similar to the Pearlspotted Owl: both are small birds with disproportionately large, round heads lacking ear-tufts, and long tails. A closer look at their markings shows that their respective names are apt: the Barred Owl is, literally, barred from tail-tip to forehead, whereas the Pearlspotted Owl has spots above and streaks below.

WHITEFACED OWL

The Whitefaced Owl is the Scops Owl's big brother: another diminutive, though not quite as small a species as the Scops, it weighs about 200 grams. It has a similarly wide range across the African savanna belt, extending from West Africa as far south as Natal and the northern Cape. It is found in a diversity of habitats in southern Africa, but seems most at home in semi-arid thornveld country of scattered trees and open ground with a sparse grass cover.

These owls prey mainly on small rodents, and especially on the Multimammate Mouse. At irregular intervals these rodents undergo population irruptions and, for a few months, are abundant. The Whitefaced Owl is one of several birds of prey that appears to capitalize on this, moving according to prey availability, and breeding at high densities when the irruptions are in progress.

Although Whitefaced Owls breed mainly in early summer (August to October), they may do so at any time of the year, several pairs having been recorded breeding in close proximity to each other during rodent booms. They usually lay their eggs on the old stick nests of other birds, such as the crow or Grey Lourie, or that of the Nagapie. They may nest in the bowl of a tree where several branches converge.

The normal clutch is two or three white eggs. The female undertakes most of the incubation and, when she is sitting on the nest, all that shows are two elongated 'ears' protruding above the rim. She is fed by the male during the night, and the eggs take about 30 days to hatch. Both parents feed the chicks, which take about a month to fledge.

In some areas Whitefaced Owls are permanent residents, breeding at the same time each year, and they may use the same nest-site season after season. By contrast, in other parts of the bird's range it occurs erratically (but sometimes commonly), and there may be long intervals between these occurrences. These two contrasting lifestyles found within the same bird species make it an especially interesting subject for study.

The jovial, explosive giggle 'who-who-who-who-whe-whieuw' uttered at night by the Whitefaced Owl is usually the first indication of its presence. It lives in savanna and is common in the drier parts of its range, but, being strictly nocturnal, is not readily encountered during the day.

APPENDIX

The flight silhouettes in the appendix are shown to scale within each group; obvious sexual dimorphism has been indicated but, for reasons of space, it has not been possible to illustrate the wide variety of dark and light phase birds, and plumage development from non-adult to adult birds.

Key to distribution ranges

▢ Non-breeding range

▢ Breeding range

▢ Overlapping ranges

→ Migration routes

SECRETARYBIRD

SCIENTIFIC NAME
Sagittarius serpentarius

OTHER NAMES
Sekretarisvoël

SIZE
Length about 1,3 m
Wingspan about 2 m
Weight about 4 kg

IDENTIFICATION
Unlikely to be mistaken for any other bird of prey; crane-like on the ground, eagle-like in flight, except for long tail

HABITAT
Grassland, savanna and scrub

DISTRIBUTION
Throughout southern Africa except for most arid areas in west; extends north through Africa to edge of Sahara Desert

STATUS
Breeding resident with local movements; fairly common

HABITS
Usually in pairs; hunts by walking on the ground; roosts at night on tree-tops; sometimes soars

BREEDING
Nest a large platform of sticks on tree-top; breeds in any month; lays 1-3 eggs, white, 78 x 56 mm; incubation period about 42 days; nestling period about 82 days (variable); female incubates mostly, fed by male

FOOD
Insects, rodents, lizards, snakes, birds' eggs

VOICE
Seldom calls; a harsh croak

BEARDED VULTURE

SCIENTIFIC NAME
Gypaetus barbatus

OTHER NAMES
Lammergeier, Baardaasvoël

SIZE
Length about 1,1 m
Wingspan about 2,5 m
Weight about 6 kg

IDENTIFICATION
Very large; long dark wings, dark wedge-shaped tail; ginger underparts; white head with black mask

HABITAT
Mountains

DISTRIBUTION
In southern Africa restricted to Lesotho highlands and adjacent areas; also in East Africa, southern and eastern Europe and Asia

STATUS
Breeding resident; scarce

HABITS
Adults in pairs; immatures sometimes in groups; scavenges for carcasses from the air

BREEDING
Nest built in pothole or on ledge on high cliff; breeds in winter; lays 2 eggs, white, blotched and streaked brown, 86 x 65 mm; incubation about 57 days; nestling period 110-122 days; both sexes share duties

FOOD
Carrion, mostly domestic animals

VOICE
Seldom calls; a weak scream

PALMNUT VULTURE

SCIENTIFIC NAME
Gypohierax angolensis

OTHER NAMES
Vulturine Fish Eagle, Witaasvoël

SIZE
Length about 0,6 m
Wingspan about 1,4 m
Weight about 1,5 kg

IDENTIFICATION
Adult wholly white except for black secondaries and tail (which is white-tipped), red skin on face; immature uniform brown

HABITAT
Always associated with Raffia or Oil Palms, including those artificially established

DISTRIBUTION
Zululand (at two localities), northwards along Mozambique coast; also northern Botswana and Namibia; extends to East and West Africa

STATUS
Very localized breeding resident; rare vagrant elsewhere

HABITS
Solitary, in pairs, or in flocks farther north in Africa; feeds, roosts and nests in palm trees; scavenges on coast

BREEDING
Nest of sticks, usually in palm crown; breeds in winter; lays 1 egg, white blotched with brown; 71 x 54 mm; little else known of breeding habits

FOOD
Mainly fruit and husks of palms; also fish, insects, carrion

VOICE
Seldom calls; a repeated cawing 'kwuk'

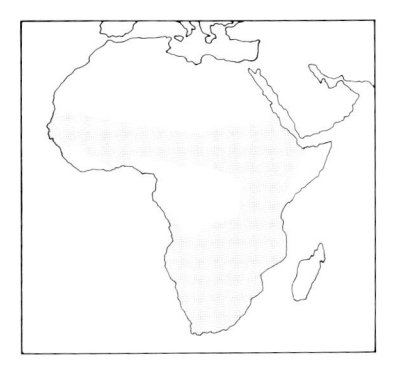

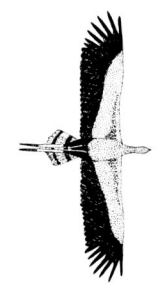

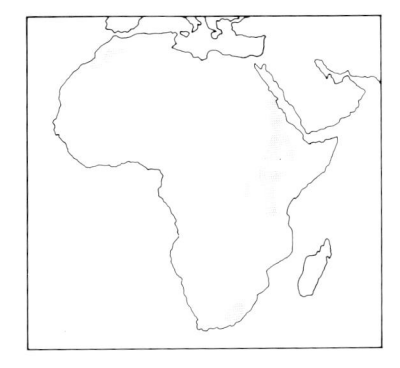

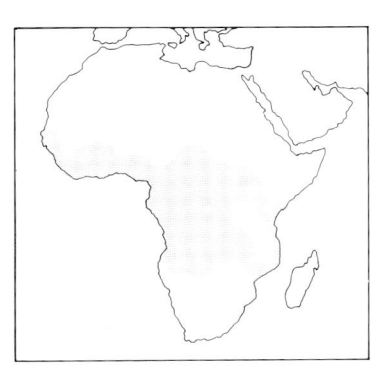

EGYPTIAN VULTURE

SCIENTIFIC NAME
Neophron percnopterus

OTHER NAMES
Egiptiese Aasvoël

SIZE
Length about 0,7 m
Wingspan about 1,6 m
Weight about 2 kg

IDENTIFICATION
Adult all white except for black primaries and secondaries, and bare yellow face; immature all brown; wedge-shaped tail distinctive

HABITAT
Semi-arid country with cliffs

DISTRIBUTION
Once widespread in southern Africa, now only in Transkei and northern Namibia; in Angola, East, West and North Africa and southern Europe to Middle East

STATUS
Rare vagrant

HABITS
Solitary or in pairs, gregarious where common; usually seen on the wing or scavenging at carcasses

BREEDING
Nest of sticks placed on ledge of cliff; lays 2 eggs, white with blotches; 66 x 50 mm; incubation about 42 days; nestling period about 77 days; both sexes share duties

FOOD
Carrion and refuse

VOICE
Seldom calls; utters mewing and whistling sounds

CAPE VULTURE

SCIENTIFIC NAME
Gyps coprotheres

OTHER NAMES
Cape Griffon Vulture, Kransaasvoël

SIZE
Length about 1,1 m
Wingspan about 2,5 m
Weight about 9 kg

IDENTIFICATION
Large; pale buffy colour with darker flight feathers on wing; no white patch on back

HABITAT
Grassland, savanna, scrub

DISTRIBUTION
Endemic to southern Africa; breeds southern Cape to northern Transvaal and adjacent Botswana; formerly Namibia and Zimbabwe

STATUS
Breeding resident; locally common

HABITS
Gregarious while foraging, breeding and roosting; breeding adults live near cliffs year-round; often roosts on pylons

BREEDING
Nests colonially on ledges of large cliffs in winter; lays 1 egg, white, 92 x 68 mm; incubation about 56 days; nestling period about 140 days; both sexes share duties

FOOD
Carrion

VOICE
Noisy at colonies and while feeding; squealing and hissing

HOODED VULTURE

SCIENTIFIC NAME
Necrosyrtes monachus

OTHER NAMES
Monnikaasvoël

SIZE
Length about 0,7 m
Wingspan about 1,7 m
Weight about 2 kg

IDENTIFICATION
Adults and young uniform dark brown; adult has downy white head; face can flush red

HABITAT
Savanna

DISTRIBUTION
Northern Namibia, Botswana, Zimbabwe, eastern Transvaal, Mozambique; mainly in large reserves. Also in central, East and West Africa

STATUS
Breeding resident; locally common

HABITS
Solitary, in pairs, or occasionally in groups; usually seen at carcasses, perched in trees or in flight

BREEDING
Nest of sticks in fork of leafy tree; lays 1 egg, white, sometimes blotched, 73 x 54 mm; incubation about 51 days; nestling period about 110 days; both sexes share duties

FOOD
Carrion and refuse

VOICE
Seldom calls; utters squeals at carcasses

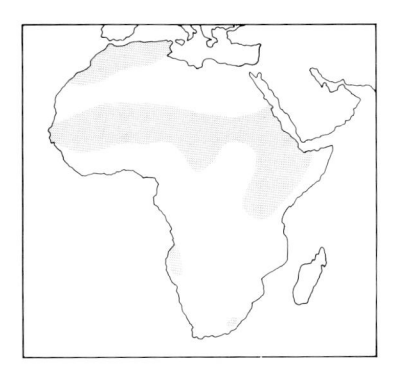

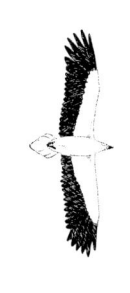

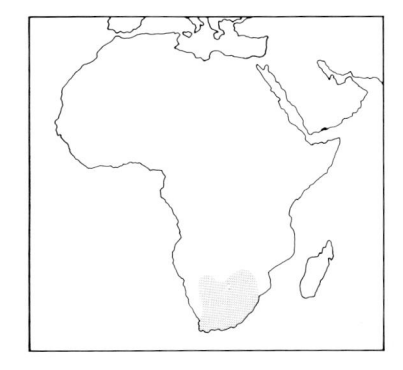

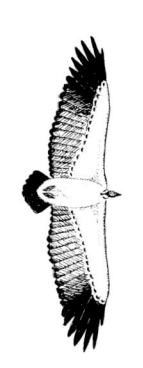

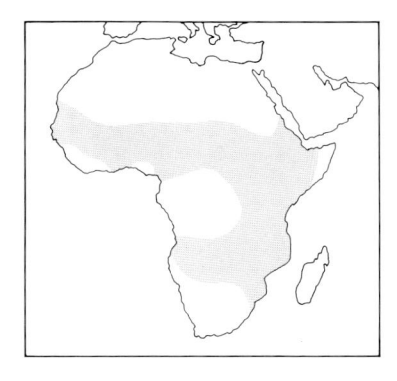

WHITEBACKED VULTURE

SCIENTIFIC NAME
Gyps africanus

OTHER NAMES
Witrugaasvoël

SIZE
Length about 1 m
Wingspan about 2,2 m
Weight about 5 kg

IDENTIFICATION
Smaller than similar Cape Vulture; adults have conspicuous white back

HABITAT
Savanna

DISTRIBUTION
Zululand, northern Cape and Transvaal northwards through Botswana, Zimbabwe and northern Namibia to East and West Africa

STATUS
Breeding resident; commonest vulture in southern Africa

HABITS
Gregarious while foraging, breeding and roosting; often in hundreds at carcasses

BREEDING
Nest of sticks on tree-top; colonies of 5-20 pairs in neighbouring trees; breeds in winter; lays 1 egg, white, 89 x 66 mm; incubation about 56 days; nestling period about 126 days; both sexes share duties

FOOD
Carrion

VOICE
Noisy while feeding; hissing and squealing

LAPPETFACED VULTURE

SCIENTIFIC NAME
Torgos tracheliotus

OTHER NAMES
Black Vulture, Swartaasvoël

SIZE
Length about 1 m
Wingspan about 2,6 m
Weight about 7 kg

IDENTIFICATION
Large; mainly black, with white leggings, ruff and underwing stripe; adult has bare loose-skinned red face (lappet)

HABITAT
Desert and arid savanna

DISTRIBUTION
Zululand, northern Cape, Transvaal and Namibia northwards through Botswana, Zimbabwe and Mozambique to East and West Africa

STATUS
Scarce, local breeding resident; vagrants occur widely

HABITS
Solitary or in small groups; usually seen soaring or at carcasses

BREEDING
Large nest of sticks on tree-top; sometimes loosely colonial; breeds in winter; lays 1 egg, white, often blotched, 93 x 71 mm; incubation about 56 days; nestling period about 126 days; both sexes share duties

FOOD
Carrion; may kill small animals

VOICE
Seldom heard; occasionally yelps

WHITEHEADED VULTURE

SCIENTIFIC NAME
Trigonoceps occipitalis

OTHER NAMES
Witkopaasvoël

SIZE
Length about 0,8 m
Wingspan about 2 m
Weight about 4 kg

IDENTIFICATION
Mainly black, with white head, belly and underwing stripe; female has white secondaries; immature browner than adult

HABITAT
Savanna

DISTRIBUTION
Zululand, eastern Transvaal, Mozambique, western Zimbabwe, Botswana and northern Namibia extending northwards to East and West Africa

STATUS
Breeding resident; scarce (found mostly in large reserves)

HABITS
Solitary or in pairs; usually seen soaring or at carcasses; territorial

BREEDING
Large nest of sticks on tree-top; always solitary; breeds in winter; lays 1 egg, white, sometimes blotched, 87 x 67 mm; both sexes share duties

FOOD
Carrion, especially smaller animals; may kill for itself

VOICE
Seldom calls; a chittering noise

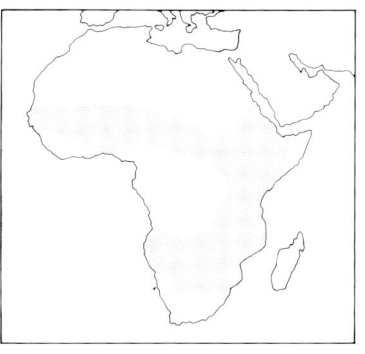

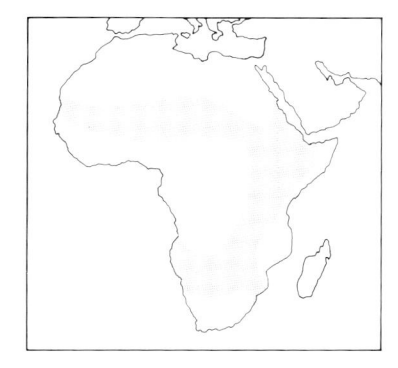

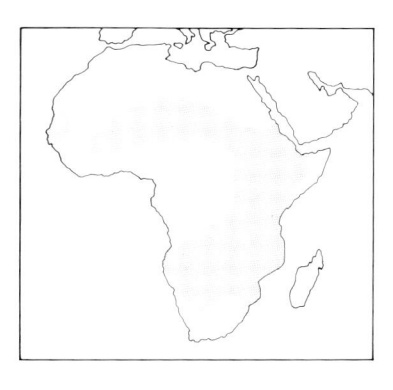

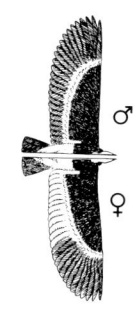

BLACK KITE

SCIENTIFIC NAME
Milvus migrans

OTHER NAMES
Yellowbilled Kite, Geelbekwou

SIZE
Length about 0,5 m
Wingspan about 1,3 m
Weight about 0,8 kg

IDENTIFICATION
Entirely brown with long wings and forked tail; yellow bill in one race, black bill in other

HABITAT
Diverse – forest-edge to desert-edge but requires trees

DISTRIBUTION
Throughout southern Africa extending northwards to Europe and Asia

STATUS
Breeding migrant (one race), non-breeding migrant (other race); both common

HABITS
Solitary, in pairs or in flocks, sometimes hundreds; scavenges from the wing

BREEDING
Nest of sticks in fork of tree; breeds in early summer; lays 2-3 eggs, white blotched with red, 54 x 40 mm; incubation about 31 days; nestling period about 45 days; both sexes share duties

FOOD
Carrion, termites and other insects

VOICE
A mewing whistle

BLACKSHOULDERED KITE

SCIENTIFIC NAME
Elanus caeruleus

OTHER NAMES
Blackwinged Kite, Blouvalk

SIZE
Length about 0,3 m
Wingspan about 0,7 m
Weight about 0,25 kg

IDENTIFICATION
White head, front and tail; grey above with black shoulders and wingtips; brilliant red eye; immature washed with brown

HABITAT
Savanna, grassland, scrub

DISTRIBUTION
Throughout southern Africa, extending northwards through Africa to southern Europe

STATUS
Breeding resident with local movements; common

HABITS
Solitary or in pairs; often roosts colonially; hunts from perches or by hovering, often along road edges; wags tail

BREEDING
Small nest of sticks in tree or bush; breeds any time, but mostly in autumn or spring; lays 3-5 eggs, pale brown, 40 x 31 mm; incubation about 31 days; nestling period about 35 days; female incubates, fed by male

FOOD
Mainly small rodents; rarely lizards and small birds

VOICE
A range of whistles

CUCKOO HAWK

SCIENTIFIC NAME
Aviceda cuculoides

OTHER NAMES
Cuckoo Falcon, Koekoekvalk

SIZE
Length about 0,4 m
Wingspan about 0,9 m
Weight about 0,6 kg

IDENTIFICATION
Adult has grey back, breast, and head, barred belly and tail, distinctive crest, rufous underwing; immature brown above and white below with bold spots

HABITAT
Tall woodland, including plantations; forest edge

DISTRIBUTION
Eastern Cape northwards through Natal, Mozambique, eastern Transvaal, Zimbabwe and northern Botswana and Namibia; extends to West Africa

STATUS
Breeding resident with local movements; scarce

HABITS
Solitary or in pairs; forages in tree-tops, on branches and on the ground; sometimes seen soaring

BREEDING
Small nest of leafy branches high up in fork of tree; breeds in early summer; lays 2 eggs, white with red blotches, 43 x 35 mm; incubation about 33 days; nestling period about 30 days; both sexes share duties

FOOD
Mainly insects (grasshoppers); also chameleons, lizards, rodents, small birds

VOICE
A plaintive whistle and a treble-noted 'tickey-to-you'

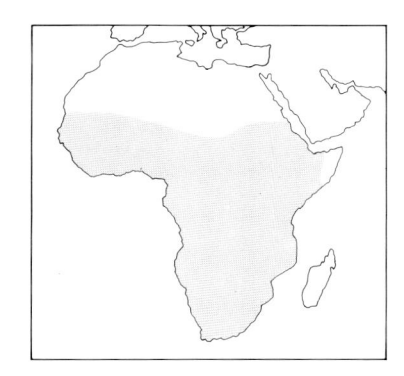

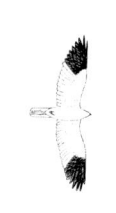

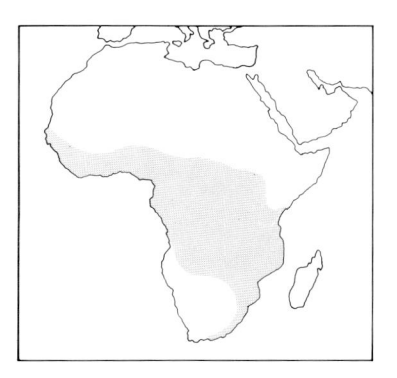

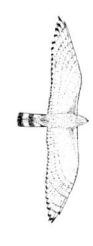

BAT HAWK

SCIENTIFIC NAME
Macheiramphus alcinus

OTHER NAMES
Vlermuisvalk

SIZE
Length about 0,5 m
Wingspan about 0,9 m
Weight about 0,65 kg

IDENTIFICATION
Wholly dark brown with white nuchal patches, white eyelids and variable amount of white on breast (under-feathers showing through)

HABITAT
Tropical savanna

DISTRIBUTION
Zululand, Mozambique, eastern Transvaal, Zimbabwe, northern Botswana and Namibia extending northwards to central and West Africa; also in Asia

STATUS
Breeding resident; rare

HABITS
Solitary or in pairs; forages on the wing at dawn and dusk; roosts in tall foliaged trees

BREEDING
Stick nest on lateral branch of large tree; breeds in early summer; lays 1 egg, white, 62 x 46 mm; incubation about 42 days; nestling period about 67 days; both sexes share duties

FOOD
Mainly bats; also small birds

VOICE
Mellow whistling, much like call of Water Dikkop; also kekking note

HONEY BUZZARD

SCIENTIFIC NAME
Pernis apivorus

OTHER NAMES
Wespedief

SIZE
Length about 0,6 m
Wingspan about 1,4 m
Weight about 0,7 kg

IDENTIFICATION
Very variable, from pale, unmarked birds to dark individuals; told by tail barring: two narrow bars near body and one broad terminal bar

HABITAT
Woodland, including plantations; forest edge

DISTRIBUTION
Eastern half of southern Africa; extends northwards through Africa into Europe, where it breeds

STATUS
Non-breeding visitor to southern Africa (November to April); rare

HABITS
Solitary or loosely associated groups during migration; forages in trees and on the ground

BREEDING
Does not breed in southern Africa

FOOD
Mainly wasps and their larvae and pupae; also other insects, small birds and fruit

VOICE
Seldom calls in non-breeding range; a buzzard-like 'peeeoo' in Europe

BLACK EAGLE

SCIENTIFIC NAME
Aquila verreauxii

OTHER NAMES
Verreaux's Eagle, Witkruisarend

SIZE
Length about 0,9 m
Wingspan about 2,3 m
Weight about 4 kg

IDENTIFICATION
Adult unmistakable: jet black except for white back and V on shoulders, white panels in outer wing; immature streaked brown

HABITAT
Mountains, hills and koppies

DISTRIBUTION
Throughout southern Africa except for flat country; commonest in arid areas; extends northwards to Red Sea and Arabian Peninsula

STATUS
Breeding resident; locally common

HABITS
Usually in pairs; seen flying or perched on rocks and cliffs; hunts on the wing; often soars

BREEDING
Large stick nest on cliff ledge; breeds in winter; lays 2 eggs, white speckled with red, 75 x 58 mm; incubation about 44 days; nestling period about 95 days; female incubates, fed by male

FOOD
Mainly dassies; sometimes other mammals, birds and reptiles

VOICE
Seldom calls; a ringing 'keeeooo'

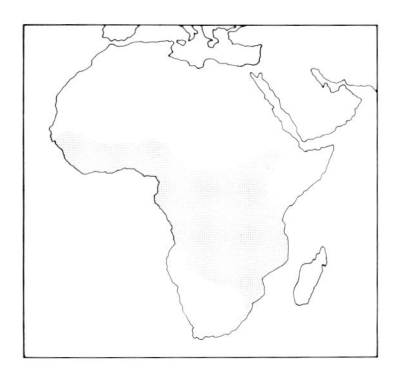

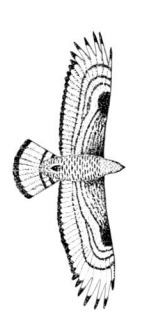

TAWNY EAGLE

SCIENTIFIC NAME
Aquila rapax

OTHER NAMES
Roofarend

SIZE
Length about 0,7 m
Wingspan about 1,8 m
Weight about 2,3 kg

IDENTIFICATION
Variable tawny brown colour, female usually darker than male; distinguishable by large size and shape

HABITAT
Savanna, especially thornveld

DISTRIBUTION
From northern Cape and Zululand northwards through Namibia, Botswana, Transvaal, Zimbabwe and Mozambique into central, north-east and West Africa

STATUS
Breeding resident; locally common, especially in large reserves

HABITS
Usually in pairs; often seen soaring while searching for food; kills own prey but also pirates other raptors' and scavenges carrion

BREEDING
Large stick nest on tree-top; breeds in winter; lays 2 eggs, white, 70 x 55 mm; incubation about 42 days; nestling period about 84 days; female incubates, fed by male

FOOD
Diverse – small mammals, birds, reptiles, fish, carrion

VOICE
Seldom calls; a harsh, barking 'kyow'

STEPPE EAGLE

SCIENTIFIC NAME
Aquila nipalensis

OTHER NAMES
Steppe-arend

SIZE
Length about 0,8 m
Wingspan about 2 m
Weight about 3 kg

IDENTIFICATION
Adult uniform dark brown; immature has pale rump, pale panel in outer wing and pale lines running along wing

HABITAT
Savanna

DISTRIBUTION
From northern Cape, Transvaal and Zululand northwards to East and West Africa; breeds in eastern Europe and Russia

STATUS
Non-breeding visitor to southern Africa (October to March); usually scarce

HABITS
Solitary, in small groups or occasionally in flocks; often with Milvus kites; usually found foraging on the ground

BREEDING
Does not breed in southern Africa

FOOD
Mainly termites in non-breeding range

VOICE
Seldom calls in non-breeding range; a crow-like croak in Europe

WAHLBERG'S EAGLE

SCIENTIFIC NAME
Aquila wahlbergi

OTHER NAMES
Bruinarend

SIZE
Length about 0,6 m
Wingspan about 1,3 m
Weight about 1,1 kg

IDENTIFICATION
Variable, from creamy white to dark brown, mainly medium brown; small crest; immature like adult

HABITAT
Savanna

DISTRIBUTION
Northern Natal, Transvaal, northern Botswana and Namibia, Zimbabwe and Mozambique, extending northwards to East and West Africa

STATUS
A breeding visitor to southern Africa (August to April); common

HABITS
Usually in pairs; hunts on the wing; often soars; perches in tall trees

BREEDING
Nest of sticks in fork of tall tree; breeds in early summer; lays 1-2 eggs, white variably marked with brown, 62 x 49 mm; incubation about 44 days; nestling period about 70 days; incubation mainly by female, fed by male

FOOD
Diverse – small mammals, birds, reptiles and insects

VOICE
Often calls; a shrill, repeated 'kyip' while perched and 'kleeeeu' in flight

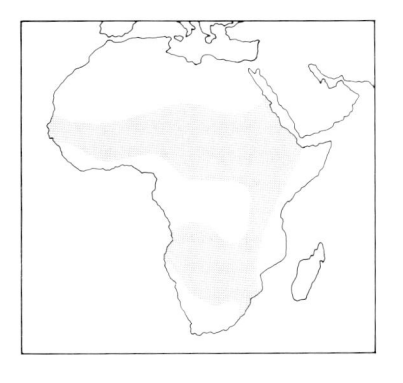

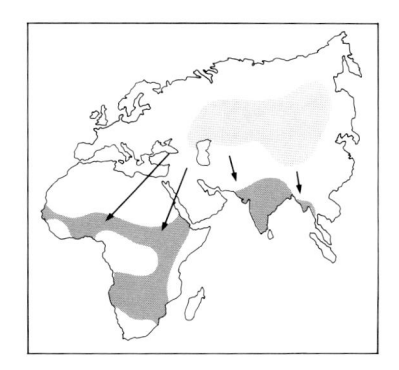

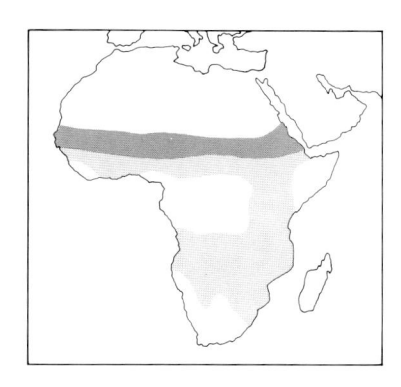

pale form

dark form

BOOTED EAGLE

SCIENTIFIC NAME
Hieraaetus pennatus

OTHER NAMES
Dwergarend

SIZE
Length about 0,5 m
Wingspan about 1,2 m
Weight about 1 kg

IDENTIFICATION
Two colour forms - pale brown and dark brown; both have distinct 'booted' tarsi and white patches on leading edge of wing close to body; immature more rufous

HABITAT
Breeds in semi-arid mountains; at other times may be found virtually anywhere

DISTRIBUTION
May occur anywhere in southern Africa but only known to breed in southern and western Cape and northern Namibia; also breeds in southern and eastern Europe

STATUS
Breeding resident with local movements; European birds visit in summer

HABITS
Solitary, or in pairs while breeding; hunts from the wing; often soars

BREEDING
Nest of sticks on cliff ledge, often behind bush; breeds in early summer; lays 2 eggs, white, 54 x 44 mm; incubation about 40 days; nestling period about 54 days; female incubates, fed by male

FOOD
Mainly birds, also lizards and rodents

VOICE
Noisy while breeding, otherwise silent; rapid 'pipipipi' and a repeated 'kyip'

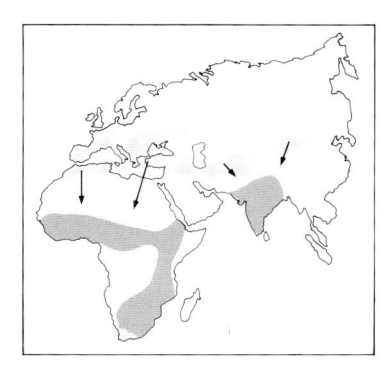

pale form
dark form

LESSER SPOTTED EAGLE

SCIENTIFIC NAME
Aquila pomarina

OTHER NAMES
Gevlekte Arend

SIZE
Length about 0,6 m
Wingspan about 1,4 m
Weight about 1,5 kg

IDENTIFICATION
Adult uniform dark brown; distinguishable by narrow leggings ('stovepipes'); immature has pale rump, outer wing panel and line along wing

HABITAT
Savanna

DISTRIBUTION
Zululand and eastern Transvaal northwards through Zimbabwe, northern Botswana and northern Namibia extending to East Africa; breeds in eastern Europe

STATUS
Non-breeding visitor to southern Africa (October to March); scarce

HABITS
Solitary, occasionally in flocks, sometimes with Steppe Eagles; forages mainly on the ground

BREEDING
Does not breed in southern Africa

FOOD
Mainly termites in non-breeding range

VOICE
Seldom calls in non-breeding range; a high-pitched repeated bark

AFRICAN HAWK EAGLE

SCIENTIFIC NAME
Hieraaetus spilogaster

OTHER NAMES
Bonelli's Eagle (Europe), Grootjagarend

SIZE
Length about 0,7 m
Wingspan about 1,6 m
Weight about 1,5 kg

IDENTIFICATION
Adult blackish above, white below, streaked with black, (female more than male); immature streaked brown

HABITAT
Savanna

DISTRIBUTION
Northern half of southern Africa extending northwards to East and West Africa; other races occur in southern Europe and Asia

STATUS
Breeding resident; fairly common

HABITS
Usually in pairs, often soaring together, or perched in tall trees; hunts from the wing

BREEDING
Large nest of sticks in fork of tall tree; breeds in winter; lays 2 eggs, white blotched with red, 65 x 51 mm; incubation about 43 days; nestling period about 68 days; female incubates, fed by male

FOOD
Mainly gamebirds; also small mammals, especially squirrels

VOICE
Seldom calls; a ringing 'klu-klu-klu-kluee' and yelping

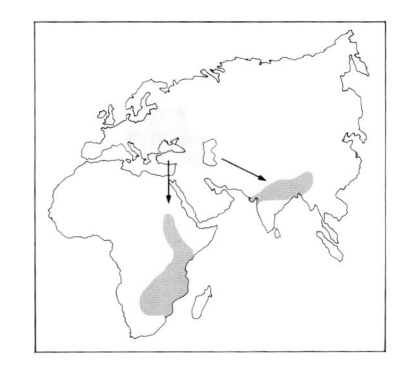

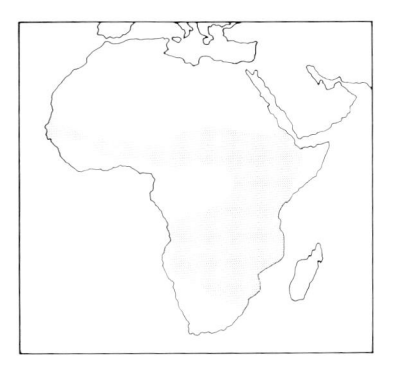

APPENDIX

AYRES' EAGLE

SCIENTIFIC NAME
Hieraaetus ayresii

OTHER NAMES
Ayres' Hawk Eagle, Kleinjagarend

SIZE
Length about 0,5 m
Wingspan about 1,2 m
Weight about 0,9 kg

IDENTIFICATION
Adults blackish above, white below heavily blotched with black, sometimes almost all black; often has black 'hood'; immature streaked brown

HABITAT
Tall woodland and forest edge

DISTRIBUTION
Northern and eastern Transvaal, Mozambique, Zimbabwe and northern Botswana; extends northwards to central, East and West Africa

STATUS
Mainly a non-breeding visitor (September to April); also breeds in northern and eastern Zimbabwe; rare

HABITS
Solitary, or in pairs while breeding; often soaring; a dashing hunter, chasing birds on the wing

BREEDING
Nest of sticks in fork of tall tree; breeds in winter; lays 1 egg, white, 56 x 44 mm; incubation about 45 days; nestling period about 75 days; female incubates, fed by male

FOOD
Mainly small birds

VOICE
Seldom calls outside breeding period; a melodious repeated whistle

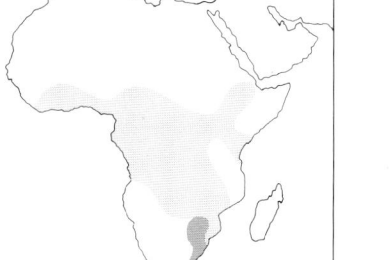

LONGCRESTED EAGLE

SCIENTIFIC NAME
Lophaetus occipitalis

OTHER NAMES
Langkuifarend

SIZE
Length about 0,6 m
Wingspan about 1,3 m
Weight about 1,3 kg

IDENTIFICATION
Dark brown except white wing panels and leggings; long floppy crest distinctive; immature like adult

HABITAT
Tall woodland, especially plantations, and forest edge

DISTRIBUTION
Eastern Cape northwards through Natal, Mozambique, eastern Transvaal, Zimbabwe and northern Botswana and Namibia into central, East and West Africa

STATUS
Breeding resident with local movements; fairly common

HABITS
Solitary or in pairs; hunts from perches over open ground, often using telephone poles; often soars

BREEDING
Nest of sticks in fork of tall tree; breeds any month but mainly early summer; lays 2 eggs, white blotched with red, 59 x 48 mm; incubation about 42 days; nestling period about 56 days; female incubates mostly, fed by male

FOOD
Mainly rodents, especially Vlei Rat

VOICE
Noisy, calls in flight and while perched; shrill 'keeee-eh' and repeated 'kik'

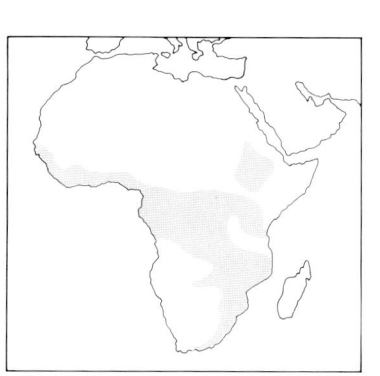

CROWNED EAGLE

SCIENTIFIC NAME
Stephanoaetus coronatus

OTHER NAMES
Kroonarend

SIZE
Length about 0,9 m
Wingspan about 2 m
Weight about 3,8 kg

IDENTIFICATION
Adults very dark, slate-black above, barred black and rufous below, barred underwings and tail; immature quite different, grey above and cream below

HABITAT
Forests and plantations

DISTRIBUTION
From eastern Cape northwards through Natal, eastern Transvaal, Mozambique and Zimbabwe into central, East and West Africa

STATUS
Breeding resident; locally common

HABITS
Usually in pairs; often soars and calls over forest; hunts from perches in forest and from the wing

BREEDING
Large nest of sticks in fork of tall tree; breeds in summer; lays 2 eggs, white sparsely speckled, 69 x 55 mm; incubation about 50 days; nestling period about 110 days; female incubates, fed by male

FOOD
Mammals, especially dassies, monkeys and young antelope

VOICE
Noisy year-round; a ringing 'koowie' repeated many times

MARTIAL EAGLE

Scientific Name
Polemaetus bellicosus

Other Names
Breëkoparend

Size
Length about 0,8 m
Wingspan about 2,3 m
Weight about 4,5 kg

Identification
Adults dark brown above, including head and chest, white below with dark spots; underwing dark; immature grey above and white below

Habitat
Diverse – savanna, grassland and scrub

Distribution
Throughout southern Africa, extending northwards to north-east and West Africa

Status
Breeding resident; rare to scarce

Habits
Solitary or in pairs; soars at great height; hunts from the wing and from perches

Breeding
Large nest of sticks in fork of tall tree; breeds in winter; lays 1 egg, white, sometimes speckled, 80 x 63 mm; incubation about 48 days; nestling period about 100 days; female incubates, fed by male

Food
Diverse – gamebirds, mammals (especially mongoose) and monitor lizards

Voice
Seldom calls; fluted 'ku-wee-oh' and repeated 'kwi'

WESTERN BANDED SNAKE EAGLE

Scientific Name
Circaetus cinerascens

Other Names
Banded Snake Eagle, Enkelbandslangarend

Size
Length about 0,6 m
Wingspan about 1,5 m
Weight not known

Identification
Adult uniform greyish brown except for faintly barred belly and one broad white bar on black tail; immature browner and lacking tail bar

Habitat
Riverine and swamp woodland

Distribution
Northern Namibia, northern Botswana and northern Zimbabwe; extends to East and West Africa

Status
Breeding resident; scarce

Habits
Solitary, or in pairs while breeding; perches for long periods inside trees watching for prey; sometimes soars

Breeding
Small nest of sticks hidden inside creeper-covered tree; breeds in late summer; lays 1 egg, white, 71 x 55 mm; little else known of breeding habits

Food
Snakes, frogs, fish, insects, rodents

Voice
Noisy; call similar to Southern Banded Snake Eagle but louder

BROWN SNAKE EAGLE

Scientific Name
Circaetus cinereus

Other Names
Bruinslangarend

Size
Length about 0,7 m
Wingspan about 2 m
Weight about 2 kg

Identification
Uniform dark brown except underwings which have white primaries and secondaries and tail which has narrow white bars; immature like adult but mottled in front

Habitat
Savanna

Distribution
Natal, eastern Transvaal and northern half of southern Africa extending northwards to north-east and West Africa

Status
Breeding resident with local movements; fairly common

Habits
Solitary, or in pairs while breeding; hunts from high perches, especially electricity pylons; often soars

Breeding
Small nest of sticks on tree-top; breeds in midsummer; lays 1 egg, white, 76 x 61 mm; incubation about 50 days; nestling period about 105 days; female incubates, fed by male

Food
Snakes, occasionally other small animals

Voice
Seldom heard; harsh, repeated 'hok'

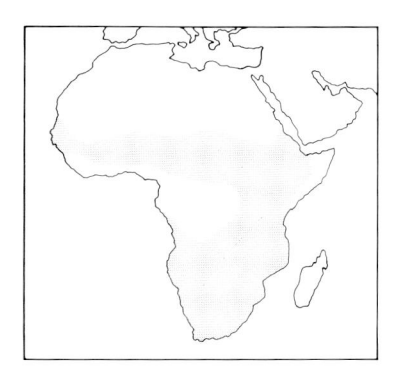

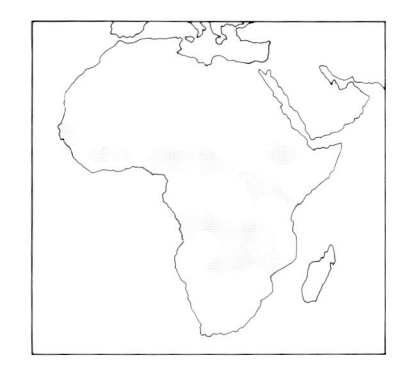

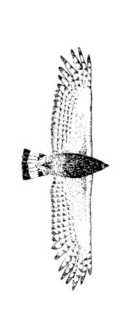

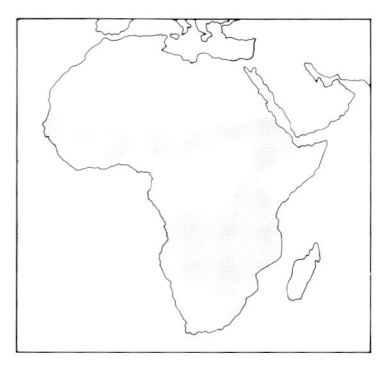

BLACKBREASTED SNAKE EAGLE

SCIENTIFIC NAME
Circaetus gallicus

OTHER NAMES
Shorttoed Eagle (Europe), Swartborsslangarend

SIZE
Length about 0,7 m
Wingspan about 1,9 m
Weight about 1,6 kg

IDENTIFICATION
Adult has black back, head and breast, white underparts, including entire underwing; tail barred; immature uniform pale rufous brown

HABITAT
Savanna, grassland, semi-desert

DISTRIBUTION
From central Cape northwards through to north-east Africa; a second race breeds in North Africa and southern and eastern Europe

STATUS
Breeding resident with local movements; fairly common

HABITS
Solitary, or in pairs while breeding; roosts communally in places; hunts from high perches or while hovering

BREEDING
Small nest of sticks on tree-top; breeds in winter; lays 1 egg, white, 73 x 57 mm; incubation about 52 days; nestling period about 90 days; female incubates, fed by male

FOOD
Snakes, occasionally other small animals

VOICE
Seldom heard; a melodious whistling in flight

SOUTHERN BANDED SNAKE EAGLE

SCIENTIFIC NAME
Circaetus fasciolatus

OTHER NAMES
Fasciated Snake Eagle, Dubbelbandslangarend

SIZE
Length about 0,6 m
Wingspan about 1,6 m
Weight about 1 kg

IDENTIFICATION
Adult uniform greyish brown except for barred belly and tail (with two white bars); immature similar but darker brown

HABITAT
Riverine woodland and coastal forest

DISTRIBUTION
Zululand northwards through Mozambique and adjacent low-lying Zimbabwe to coastal East Africa

STATUS
Breeding resident; scarce

HABITS
Solitary, or in pairs while breeding; hunts from perches, including telephone poles and dead trees; soars at times

BREEDING
Small nest of sticks hidden in creeper-covered forest tree; breeds in early summer; lays 1 egg, white; little else known of breeding habits

FOOD
Snakes; also frogs, lizards, insects, rodents

VOICE
Noisy; a loud crowing 'ko-ko-ko-kaau'

BATELEUR

SCIENTIFIC NAME
Terathopius ecaudatus

OTHER NAMES
Berghaan

SIZE
Length about 0,7 m
Wingspan about 1,8 m
Weight about 2,2 kg

IDENTIFICATION
Mainly black with greyish shoulder and chestnut back and tail; very short tail; underwing mainly white; female has white underwing with flight feathers narrowly tipped black; immature uniform brown

HABITAT
Savanna

DISTRIBUTION
Zululand, eastern Transvaal northwards through Mozambique, Zimbabwe, Botswana and northern Namibia to East and West Africa

STATUS
Breeding resident; scarce or absent outside large reserves, where often common

HABITS
Usually in pairs; flies with low soaring flight for most of day; scavenges at carcasses

BREEDING
Nest of sticks in fork of tall tree; breeds in midsummer; lays 1 egg, white, 79 x 63 mm; incubation about 55 days; nestling period about 110 days (variable); both sexes share duties

FOOD
Diverse – mainly carrion; also small birds, animals, reptiles

VOICE
Seldom heard; a loud barking 'kaw-ow'

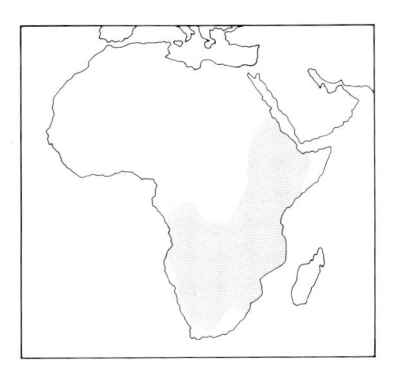

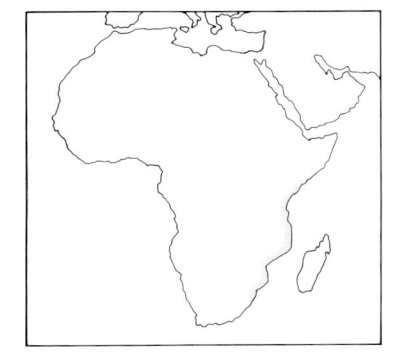

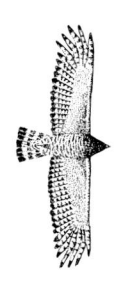

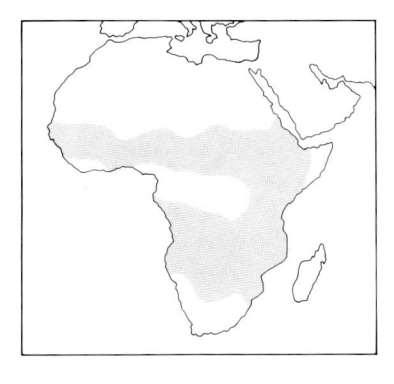

APPENDIX

AFRICAN FISH EAGLE

SCIENTIFIC NAME
Haliaeetus vocifer

OTHER NAMES
Fish Eagle, Visarend

SIZE
Length about 0,7 m
Wingspan about 2,1 m
Weight about 3 kg

IDENTIFICATION
Adult unmistakable with white head, chest and tail, chestnut body and shoulders and black wings with chestnut coverts; immature streaky shades of brown and white

HABITAT
Large rivers, dams, lakes, estuaries and lagoons

DISTRIBUTION
Most of southern Africa outside of the arid regions; extends to central, East and West Africa

STATUS
Breeding resident; common in suitable areas

HABITS
Usually in pairs; perches on tall trees overlooking water; often soars and calls on the wing

BREEDING
Large nest of sticks in tall tree; breeds in winter; lays 2 eggs, white, 70 x 54 mm; incubation about 43 days; nestling period about 70 days; both sexes share duties but female does more

FOOD
Mainly fish; also waterbirds and small mammals

VOICE
Noisy all year; well-known ringing 'WHOW, kyow kow-kow' call

STEPPE BUZZARD

SCIENTIFIC NAME
Buteo buteo

OTHER NAMES
Bruinjakkalsvoël

SIZE
Length about 0,5 m
Wingspan about 1,2 m
Weight about 0,7 kg

IDENTIFICATION
Variable brown, streaked and barred in front, with paler chest area; immature and adult fairly similar

HABITAT
Grassland, savanna, scrub

DISTRIBUTION
Throughout southern Africa except most arid parts; extends northwards through Africa to breeding grounds in Eurasia

STATUS
Non-breeding visitor to southern Africa (October to April); common

HABITS
Solitary in non-breeding range (except on migration); hunts from perches, often using telephone poles; often soars

BREEDING
Does not breed in southern Africa

FOOD
Rodents, insects, small birds, lizards

VOICE
Seldom calls in non-breeding range; a mewing 'kee-oo'

FOREST BUZZARD

SCIENTIFIC NAME
Buteo trizonatus

OTHER NAMES
Mountain Buzzard, Bosjakkalsvoël

SIZE
Length about 0,5 m
Wingspan about 1,2 m
Weight about 0,7 kg

IDENTIFICATION
Variable brown, streaked and blotched in front (blotches and absence of barring distinguishes from Steppe Buzzard); immature much like adult

HABITAT
Plantations and forest edge

DISTRIBUTION
Southern Cape extending northwards through Natal into eastern Transvaal; another race in East Africa

STATUS
Breeding resident; locally common

HABITS
Solitary or in pairs; usually seen hunting from perch inside tree; often soars above forest

BREEDING
Nest of sticks in tall tree; breeds in early summer; lays 2 eggs, greenish white speckled red, 56 x 43 mm; incubation about 50 days

FOOD
Rodents, lizards, small birds, insects

VOICE
A typical buzzard-like mewing 'keee-oo'

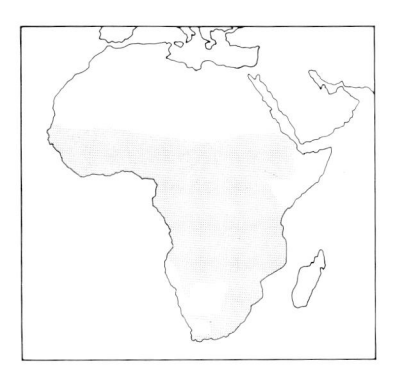

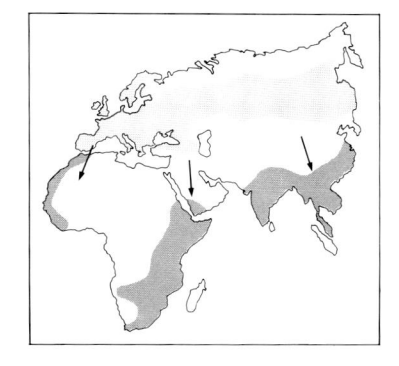

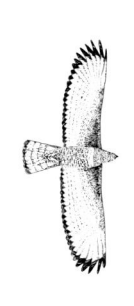

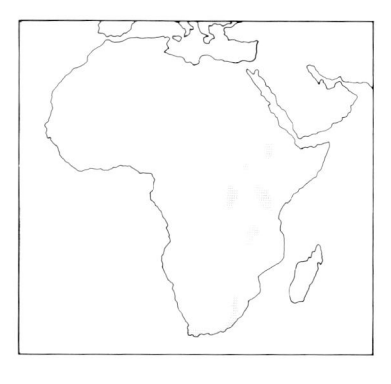

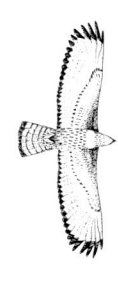

APPENDIX

LONGLEGGED BUZZARD

SCIENTIFIC NAME
Buteo rufinus

OTHER NAMES
Langbeenjakkalsvoël

SIZE
Length about 0,6 m
Wingspan about 1,3 m
Weight about 1,1 kg

IDENTIFICATION
Variable brown, with paler head and almost unbarred tail; distinguishable from Steppe Buzzard by larger size and different flight shape

HABITAT
Semi-arid savanna

DISTRIBUTION
A non-breeding visitor to savanna areas north of equator; a rare vagrant to southern Africa; breeds in eastern Europe and Mediterranean countries

STATUS
See above

HABITS
Solitary in non-breeding grounds; hunts from perches

BREEDING
Does not breed in southern Africa

FOOD
Small mammals and reptiles

VOICE
Seldom calls in non-breeding range; a typical buzzard-like mewing

AUGUR BUZZARD

SCIENTIFIC NAME
Buteo augur

OTHER NAMES
Witborsjakkalsvoël

SIZE
Length about 0,5 m
Wingspan about 1,2 m
Weight about 1 kg

IDENTIFICATION
Adult black above and white below with rufous tail; immature streaked pale brown

HABITAT
Mountainous and hilly country

DISTRIBUTION
Zimbabwe and central Namibia northwards to southern Tanzania

STATUS
Breeding resident; locally common

HABITS
Solitary or in pairs; soars and hunts from perches on rocks and trees

BREEDING
Nest of sticks on cliff ledge, often behind bush; breeds in late winter; lays 2 eggs, white, variably marked; 57 x 46 mm; incubation about 40 days; nestling period about 49 days

FOOD
Mainly rodents and lizards; also small birds, insects

VOICE
A yelping, repeated 'kow'

JACKAL BUZZARD

SCIENTIFIC NAME
Buteo rufofuscus

OTHER NAMES
Rooiborsjakkalsvoël

SIZE
Length about 0,5 m
Wingspan about 1,2 m
Weight about 1 kg

IDENTIFICATION
Adult unmistakable with bold black, white and rufous colouring; immature streaked pale brown

HABITAT
Mountainous and hilly country

DISTRIBUTION
Endemic to southern Africa, from southern Cape north to northern Transvaal and southern Namibia

STATUS
Breeding resident; locally common

HABITS
Solitary or in pairs; often found perched on telephone poles; hovers above ridges and often soars

BREEDING
Nest of sticks on cliff ledge or in tree; breeds in late winter; lays 2 eggs, white, variably marked, 60 x 47 mm; incubation about 40 days; nestling period about 50 days; both sexes share duties

FOOD
Mainly rodents and lizards, but may eat any small prey

VOICE
A high-pitched yelping 'kweeya'

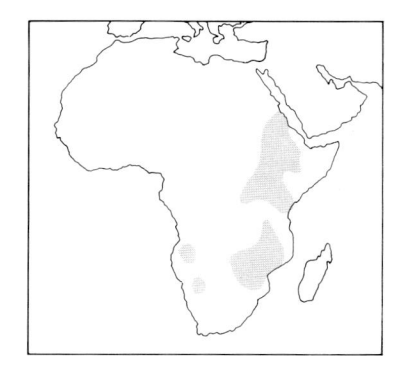

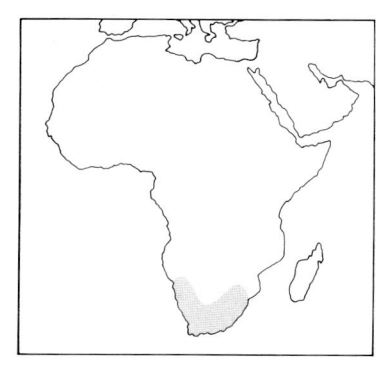

APPENDIX

LIZARD BUZZARD

SCIENTIFIC NAME
Kaupifalco monogrammicus

OTHER NAMES
Akkedisvalk

SIZE
Length about 0,4 m
Wingspan about 0,6 m
Weight about 0,3 kg

IDENTIFICATION
Grey above and below with barred grey and white belly, white throat crossed by vertical black stripe, boldly barred tail; immature like adult

HABITAT
Savanna and forest edge

DISTRIBUTION
Zululand northwards through Transvaal, eastern Botswana, Mozambique, Zimbabwe and northern Namibia to East and West Africa

STATUS
Breeding resident with winter influx; locally common

HABITS
Solitary, or in pairs while breeding; sluggish in habits, perches for long periods, watching ground; soars and calls in flight

BREEDING
Nest of sticks in fork of tree; breeds in early summer; lays 2 eggs, white, 45 x 36 mm; incubation about 33 days; nestling period about 40 days; female incubates, fed by male

FOOD
Mainly lizards and insects; also rodents, frogs, birds

VOICE
Noisy while breeding; a melodious, repeated whistle

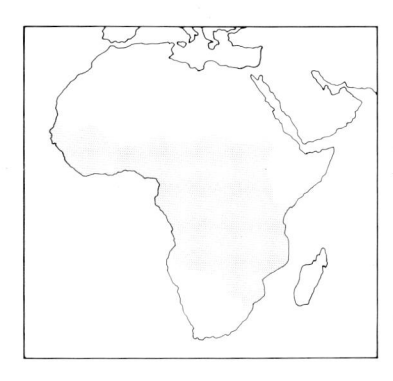

REDBREASTED SPARROWHAWK

SCIENTIFIC NAME
Accipiter rufiventris

OTHER NAMES
Rooiborssperwer

SIZE
Length about 0,4 m
Wingspan about 0,6 m
Weight about 0,2 kg

IDENTIFICATION
Slate grey above, uniform rufous below, barred black and white tail; yellow eye-ring; immature mottled in front

HABITAT
Montane grassland with forest or plantations

DISTRIBUTION
South-western Cape, eastwards through Cape to Natal, eastern Transvaal and eastern Zimbabwe; extends to north-east Africa

STATUS
Breeding resident; scarce to locally common

HABITS
Solitary or in pairs; secretive and usually seen soaring or flying over open ground while hunting; roosts and nests in tall trees

BREEDING
Nest of sticks in fork of tall tree; breeds in early summer; lays 3-4 eggs, white blotched with brown, 41 x 32 mm; incubation about 34 days; nestling period about 35 days; female incubates, fed by male

FOOD
Mainly small birds; occasionally rodents and insects

VOICE
Seldom calls outside breeding period; a piping, repeated 'kew'

OVAMBO SPARROWHAWK

SCIENTIFIC NAME
Accipiter ovampensis

OTHER NAMES
Ovambosperwer

SIZE
Length about 0,4 m
Wingspan about 0,6 m
Weight about 0,2 kg

IDENTIFICATION
Overall grey, barred grey and white in front, barred tail, no white on rump; immature either streaked buffy brown or rufous brown, with pale eyebrow

HABITAT
Mosaic of open ground and tall woodland or plantations

DISTRIBUTION
Zululand northwards through eastern and central Transvaal, Zimbabwe, northern Botswana and Namibia to central, East and West Africa

STATUS
Breeding resident; rare to locally common

HABITS
Solitary or in pairs; secretive; soars above breeding area; hunts on the wing and from perches

BREEDING
Nest of sticks in fork of tall tree; breeds in early summer; lays 2-5 eggs, white variably marked with brown, 41 x 33 mm; incubation about 34 days; nestling period about 33 days; female incubates, fed by male

FOOD
Exclusively small birds

VOICE
Seldom calls ouside breeding period; a piping, repeated 'keep'

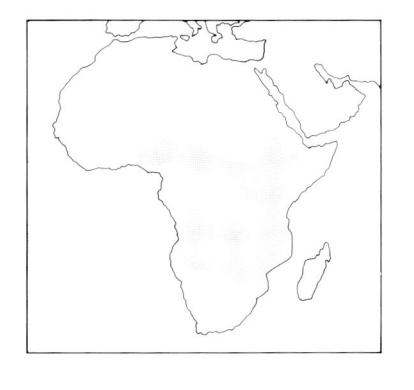

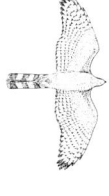

APPENDIX

LITTLE SPARROWHAWK

SCIENTIFIC NAME
Accipiter minullus

OTHER NAMES
Kleinsperwer

SIZE
Length about 0,25 m
Wingspan about 0,4 m
Weight about 0,1 kg

IDENTIFICATION
Adult grey above, white below finely barred with rufous; black tail with two central white spots; immature brown above, white below with large spots

HABITAT
Savanna, forest and plantations

DISTRIBUTION
Southern Cape, extending eastwards through Natal, Mozambique, to Transvaal, Zimbabwe, Botswana and northern Namibia; ranges to north-east Africa

STATUS
Breeding resident; locally common

HABITS
Solitary or in pairs; secretive; hunts from perches in cover; sometimes soars

BREEDING
Small nest of sticks in fork of tree; breeds in early summer; lays 2 eggs, white, 35 x 28 mm; incubation about 32 days; nestling period about 27 days; female incubates, fed by male

FOOD
Mainly small birds, rarely insects and small mammals

VOICE
Seldom calls outside breeding period; repeated shrill 'kik'

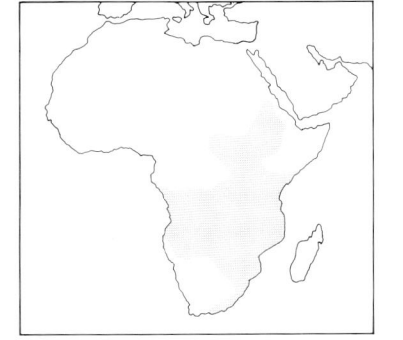

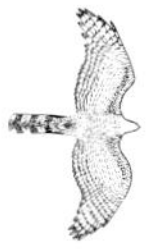

BLACK SPARROWHAWK

SCIENTIFIC NAME
Accipiter melanoleucus

OTHER NAMES
Great Sparrowhawk, Swartsperwer

SIZE
Length about 0,5 m
Wingspan about 1 m
Weight about 0,75 kg

IDENTIFICATION
Adult wholly black above and white below with variable amount of black on chest and flanks; immature streaked rufous brown

HABITAT
Forest, plantations and tall woodland

DISTRIBUTION
Southern Cape, extending eastwards to Natal and north through Transvaal, Mozambique, Zimbabwe and northern Botswana to north-east and West Africa

STATUS
Breeding resident; scarce to locally common

HABITS
Solitary or in pairs; noisy at breeding site; soars and hunts by hot pursuit

BREEDING
Nest of sticks in fork of tall tree; breeds in late winter; lays 3-4 eggs, white, 56 x 44 mm; incubation about 37 days; nestling period about 42 days; female incubates, fed by male

FOOD
Mainly doves and gamebirds, rarely non-bird prey

VOICE
Noisy while breeding; loud, repeated 'kyip'

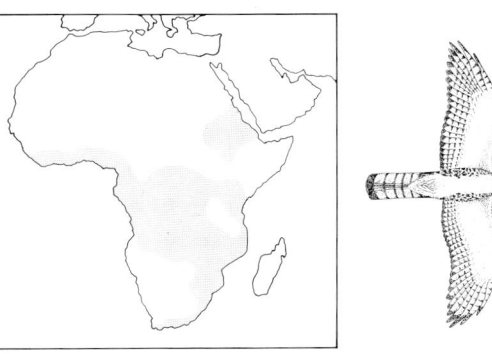

PALE CHANTING GOSHAWK

SCIENTIFIC NAME
Melierax canorus

OTHER NAMES
Bleeksingvalk

SIZE
Length about 0,5 m
Wingspan about 1 m
Weight about 0,75 kg

IDENTIFICATION
Adult light grey except for finely barred black and white belly, white rump, barred tail, white secondaries and black primaries; immature streaked and barred pale brown

HABITAT
Arid savanna, scrub and semi-desert

DISTRIBUTION
Central Cape north through western Transvaal, southern Botswana and Namibia; another race found in north-east Africa

STATUS
Breeding resident; common

HABITS
Solitary or in pairs; hunts from perches, often on telephone poles; conspicuous and confiding

BREEDING
Nest of sticks in tree or shrub; breeds in early summer; lays 1-2 eggs, white, 57 x 44 mm; incubation about 37 days; nestling period about 52 days; female incubates mostly, fed by male

FOOD
Diverse – birds, especially gamebirds, mammals, reptiles, insects, carrion

VOICE
Noisy; a melodious chanting whistle

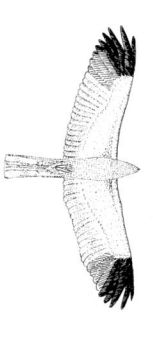

Dark Chanting Goshawk

SCIENTIFIC NAME
Melierax metabates

OTHER NAMES
Donkersingvalk

SIZE
Length about 0,5 m
Wingspan about 1 m
Weight about 0,7 kg

IDENTIFICATION
Like Pale Chanting Goshawk but darker grey, has grey (not white) rump and grey secondaries; immature brown with barred underparts

HABITAT
Tall woodland and savanna

DISTRIBUTION
Zululand, eastern Transvaal, Mozambique, Zimbabwe and northern Botswana and Namibia; extends to East and West Africa

STATUS
Breeding resident; fairly common

HABITS
Solitary or in pairs; hunts from perches; soars

BREEDING
Nest of sticks in fork of tall tree; breeds in early summer; lays 1-2 eggs, white, 53 x 42 mm; breeding habits poorly known

FOOD
Diverse – birds, mammals, insects, reptiles

VOICE
Seldom heard; a high-pitched chanting whistle

Little Banded Goshawk

SCIENTIFIC NAME
Accipiter badius

OTHER NAMES
Shikra, Gebande Sperwer

SIZE
Length about 0,3 m
Wingspan about 0,65 m
Weight about 0,13 kg

IDENTIFICATION
Adult grey above with white chest finely barred with rufous; tail barred (except for central tail feathers); immature brown, streaked and barred below

HABITAT
Savanna

DISTRIBUTION
Zululand north through Mozambique and Zimbabwe, eastern and northern Transvaal, Botswana, northern Namibia to East and West Africa; also Asia

STATUS
Breeding resident with local movements; common

HABITS
Solitary, or in pairs while breeding; hunts from perches in trees, sometimes telephone poles; soars

BREEDING
Nest of sticks in fork of tall tree; breeds in early summer; lays 2-3 eggs, white variably marked with brown, 37 x 30 mm; incubation about 30 days; nestling period about 32 days; female incubates, fed by male

FOOD
Lizards, insects, small birds, rodents

VOICE
Noisy before breeding; various whistling notes; characteristic 'kli-vit'

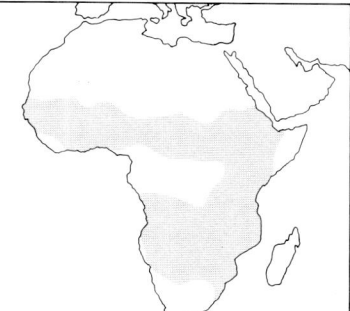

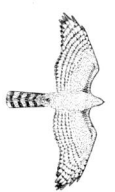

African Goshawk

SCIENTIFIC NAME
Accipiter tachiro

OTHER NAMES
Afrikaanse Sperwer

SIZE
Length about 0,4 m
Wingspan about 0,7 m
Weight about 0,35 kg

IDENTIFICATION
Adult brown (female) or grey (male) above, white barred with brown below; tail barred with two white spots above; immature brown above, white below with bold spots

HABITAT
Forest and forest edge; plantations

DISTRIBUTION
Southern and eastern Cape, Natal, eastern Transvaal, Mozambique, Zimbabwe, northern Botswana and Namibia; ranges to north-east and West Africa

STATUS
Breeding resident; common

HABITS
Solitary or in pairs; secretive, usually detected only by call; soars above forest; hunts from perches

BREEDING
Nest of sticks in fork of tall tree; breeds in early summer; lays 2-3 eggs, white, 45 x 36 mm; incubation about 30 days; nestling period about 35 days; female incubates, fed by male

FOOD
Mainly small birds; also rodents, lizards, insects

VOICE
Noisy throughout year; calls a single 'krit' in flight and when perched, especially in early morning

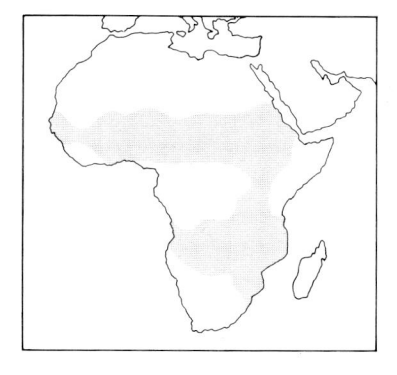

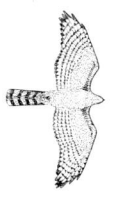

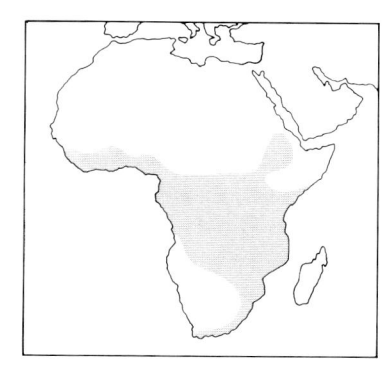

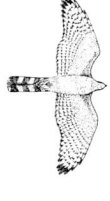

APPENDIX

GABAR GOSHAWK

SCIENTIFIC NAME
Micronisus gabar

OTHER NAMES
Witkruissperwer, Kleinsingvalk

SIZE
Length about 0,3 m
Wingspan about 0,6 m
Weight about 0,17 kg

IDENTIFICATION
Adult blue-grey above, grey head and chest, grey and white barred belly; also a wholly black melanistic form; immature streaked and barred brown

HABITAT
Savanna, especially semi-arid thornveld

DISTRIBUTION
From central Cape and northern Natal northwards through Namibia, Botswana, Zimbabwe and Mozambique to East and West Africa

STATUS
Breeding resident; common

HABITS
Solitary or in pairs; hunts on the wing; soars; perches high in trees

BREEDING
Nest of sticks festooned with cobweb in fork of tree; breeds in early summer; lays 2-4 eggs, white, 40 x 31 mm; incubation about 34 days; nestling period about 35 days; female incubates, fed by male

FOOD
Diverse – birds, lizards, rodents, insects

VOICE
Noisy before breeding; a shrill, repeated 'pi'

EUROPEAN MARSH HARRIER

SCIENTIFIC NAME
Circus aeruginosus

OTHER NAMES
Europese Vleivalk

SIZE
Length about 0,5 m
Wingspan about 1,2 m
Weight about 0,65 kg

IDENTIFICATION
Female chocolate brown with cream cap, nape, shoulder edge; male has tail, most of upperwing grey, and pale head; unbarred tail diagnostic

HABITAT
Vleis and wet grassland

DISTRIBUTION
Natal, Transvaal and Zimbabwe where it is a rare vagrant; winters in East and West Africa and breeds in Eurasia

STATUS
Non-breeding vagrant; usually rare, occasionally fairly numerous

HABITS
Solitary; hunts with a slow bouyant flight, somersaulting into grass for prey; often perches on fence posts

BREEDING
Does not breed in southern Africa

FOOD
Frogs, birds, rodents, reptiles

VOICE
Silent in non-breeding grounds; a chattering call in Europe

AFRICAN MARSH HARRIER

SCIENTIFIC NAME
Circus ranivorus

OTHER NAMES
Afrikaanse Vleivalk

SIZE
Length about 0,5 m
Wingspan about 1 m
Weight about 0,5 kg

IDENTIFICATION
Variable streaky brown, with barred tail; often has pale area on chest; immature darker than adult

HABITAT
Vleis and reedbeds

DISTRIBUTION
Throughout southern Africa in suitable habitat, thus absent from most of Namibia, Botswana and northern Cape

STATUS
Breeding resident; locally common

HABITS
Solitary or in pairs; often seen flying buoyantly above vlei, head down, wings angled upwards; soars

BREEDING
Nest of sticks and weed stems built close to ground hidden in reeds or sedge; breeds in any month, but mostly in early summer; lays 3-4 eggs, white, 47 x 37 mm; incubation, by female, about 35 days; nestling period about 38 days

FOOD
Rodents, birds, frogs, insects, reptiles

VOICE
A chattering call while breeding

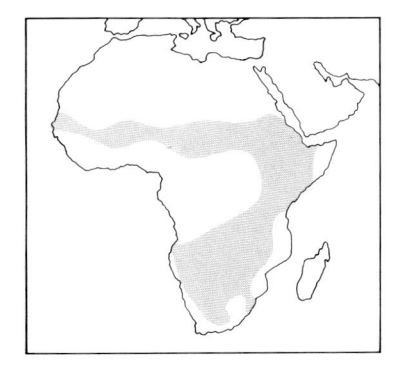

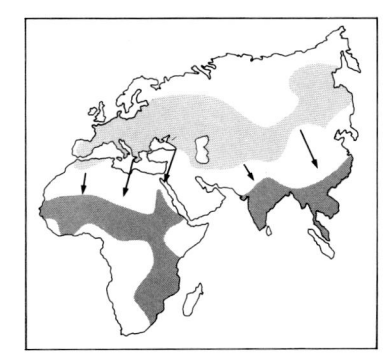

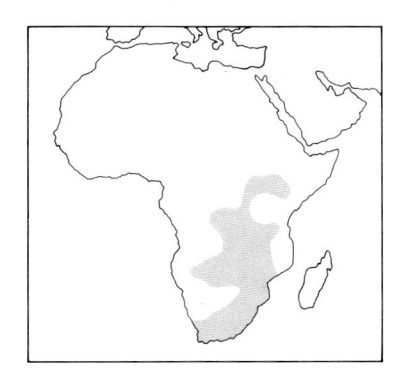

BLACK HARRIER

SCIENTIFIC NAME
Circus maurus

OTHER NAMES
Swartvleivalk

SIZE
Length about 0,5 m
Wingspan about 1,1 m
Weight not known

IDENTIFICATION
Black with conspicuous white rump, white in underwing, and black and white barred tail; immature browner and mottled

HABITAT
Karoo scrub, grassland and fynbos

DISTRIBUTION
Endemic to southern Africa, breeding mainly in southern Cape, and ranging north to southern Namibia and Transvaal in non-breeding period

STATUS
Breeding resident with local movements; scarce to locally common

HABITS
Solitary, or in pairs while breeding; flies with typical harrier buoyancy; often hunts along road verges

BREEDING
Nest of weed stems hidden in scrub; breeds in early summer; lays 3-4 eggs, white, 47 x 37 mm; incubation about 34 days; nestling period about 36 days; female incubates, fed by male

FOOD
Birds, rodents, frogs, insects

VOICE
A chattering call and shrill whistle while breeding

MONTAGU'S HARRIER

SCIENTIFIC NAME
Circus pygargus

OTHER NAMES
Blouvleivalk

SIZE
Length about 0,45 m
Wingspan about 1,1 m
Weight about 0,3 kg

IDENTIFICATION
Male blue-grey above, on head and chest; white below, streaked rufous; black wingtips and wingbar; female brown, streaked below; immature plain rufous below

HABITAT
Savanna, grassland and scrub

DISTRIBUTION
Winters in Africa, extending as far south as the north-eastern Cape; breeds in Eurasia

STATUS
A non-breeding visitor to southern Africa (October to April); scarce or rare

HABITS
Solitary, or in small groups during migration; flies with typical harrier buoyancy; hunts on the wing

BREEDING
Does not breed in southern Africa

FOOD
Rodents, frogs, insects, small birds

VOICE
Silent in non-breeding grounds; a chattering call in Europe

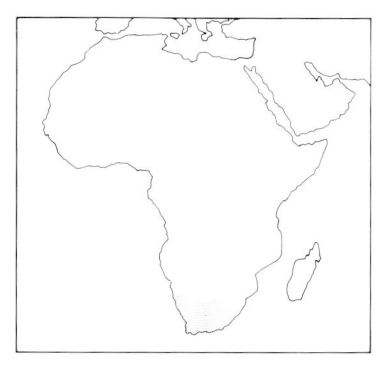

PALLID HARRIER

SCIENTIFIC NAME
Circus macrourus

OTHER NAMES
Witborspaddavreter

SIZE
Length about 0,45 m
Wingspan about 1,1 m
Weight about 0,35 kg

IDENTIFICATION
Male pale grey above and white below, with black wingtips; female brown, streaked below; immature plain brown below

HABITAT
Savanna, grassland and scrub

DISTRIBUTION
Winters in Africa, extending as far south as southern Cape; breeds in eastern Europe

STATUS
A non-breeding visitor to southern Africa (October to April); scarce or rare

HABITS
Solitary, but may roost communally; flies with typical harrier buoyancy; hunts on the wing

BREEDING
Does not breed in southern Africa

FOOD
Rodents, frogs, birds, lizards, insects

VOICE
Silent in non-breeding grounds; a chattering call in Europe

GYMNOGENE

SCIENTIFIC NAME
Polyboroides typus

OTHER NAMES
Banded Harrier Hawk, Kaalwangvalk

SIZE
Length about 0,6 m
Wingspan about 1,4 m
Weight about 0,75 kg

IDENTIFICATION
Adult grey, with black tail cut by one white bar, and black flight feathers; bare yellow face; immature variable streaky brown

HABITAT
Diverse – kloofs, mountains, riparian woodland, savanna

DISTRIBUTION
From southern Cape eastwards to Natal, north through Transvaal to Botswana, northern Namibia, Zimbabwe and Mozambique; north to Sahara Desert

STATUS
Breeding resident; fairly common

HABITS
Solitary, or in pairs while breeding; hunts by searching tree trunks and cliffs for prey; floppy flight

BREEDING
Nest of sticks on cliff ledge or in fork of tree; breeds in early summer; lays 2 eggs, white blotched with red-brown, 56 x 44 mm; incubation about 36 days; nestling period about 49 days; both sexes share duties

FOOD
Lizards, birds, rodents, insects

VOICE
A plaintive whistle

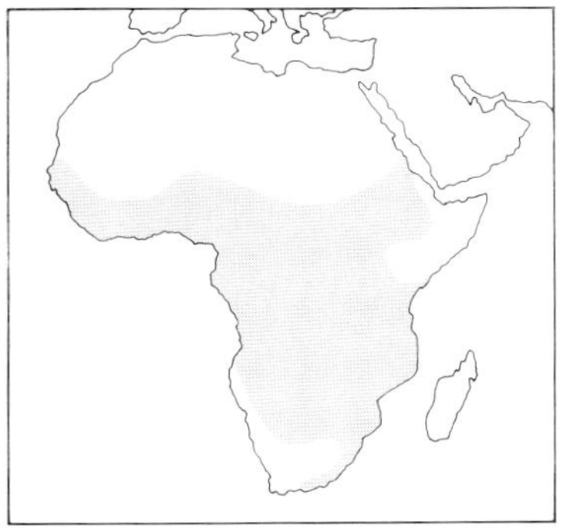

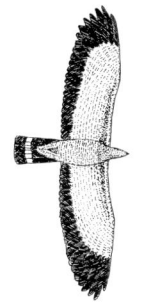

OSPREY

SCIENTIFIC NAME
Pandion haliaetus

OTHER NAMES
Fish Hawk, Visvalk

SIZE
Length about 0,6 m
Wingspan about 1,6 m
Weight about 1,5 kg

IDENTIFICATION
Above dark brown, below white; has white crown and black mask through eye; barred underwing and tail with black carpal joint

HABITAT
Lakes, dams, pans, estuaries

DISTRIBUTION
Virtually world-wide in distribution, a non-breeding migrant to Africa from Europe ranging to southern Cape; may occur in any suitable habitat

STATUS
A non-breeding visitor (August to May), some overwinter and occasionally breed; scarce

HABITS
Solitary; seen perching around and flying about waterbodies; hovers

BREEDING
Nest of sticks in tall tree near water; breeds in early summer; lays 2 eggs, white blotched with red, 61 x 44 mm; incubation about 37 days; nestling period about 55 days; both sexes share duties

FOOD
Fish

VOICE
Seldom heard; a plaintive whistle

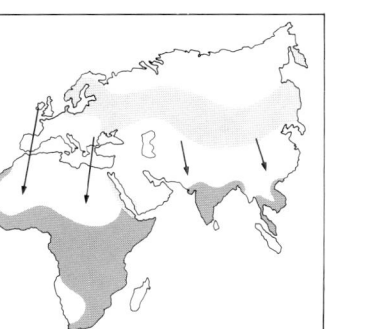

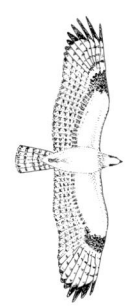

PEREGRINE FALCON

SCIENTIFIC NAME
Falco peregrinus

OTHER NAMES
African Peregrine, Swerfvalk

SIZE
Length about 0,35 m
Wingspan about 0,9 m
Weight about 0,6 kg

IDENTIFICATION
Slate grey above, with black head and moustache stripes, white front finely barred with black on the belly; immature brown above, with black head and streaked front

HABITAT
Hunts anywhere but confined while breeding to mountains and ravines with cliffs

DISTRIBUTION
Throughout southern Africa but breeding birds more restricted (see above); different races occur in most parts of the world

STATUS
Breeding resident (African race), non-breeding migrant (European race); both scarce

HABITS
Solitary, or in pairs while breeding; hunts by high-speed stoops on prey; perches on cliffs and in tall dead trees

BREEDING
No nest built; lays on cliff ledge, usually overhung; breeds in early summer; lays 3 eggs, buffy brown, 51 x 41 mm; incubation about 30 days; nestling period about 40 days; incubation mainly by female

FOOD
Mostly birds, especially doves and pigeons

VOICE
Raucous, repeated 'kack' alarm call; whining 'waaik' begging call

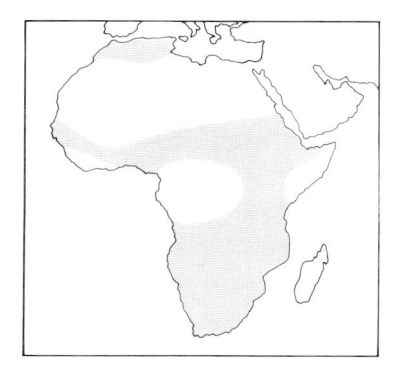

LANNER FALCON

SCIENTIFIC NAME
Falco biarmicus

OTHER NAMES
Lanner, Edelvalk

SIZE
Length about 0,4 m
Wingspan about 1 m
Weight about 0,6 kg

IDENTIFICATION
Slate grey above, with black head and moustache stripes, rufous crown and buffy front; immature brown above, rufous crown, white front streaked with dark brown

HABITAT
Diverse – flat or mountainous country in arid or wet environments

DISTRIBUTION
Throughout southern Africa; ranges to North Africa and Middle East

STATUS
Breeding resident; common

HABITS
Solitary, or in pairs while breeding; hunts by stooping on aerial prey, by pursuit and from perches

BREEDING
No nest built; lays on cliff ledge or old stick nest of crow or raptor; breeds in late winter to spring; lays 2-5 eggs, brownish, 52 x 41 mm; incubation about 32 days; nestling period about 42 days; sexes share duties

FOOD
Mainly birds, especially pigeons; also rodents and lizards

VOICE
Raucous, repeated 'kack' alarm; also whining

EUROPEAN HOBBY

SCIENTIFIC NAME
Falco subbuteo

OTHER NAMES
Hobby Falcon, Europese Boomvalk

SIZE
Length about 0,3 m
Wingspan about 0,9 m
Weight about 0,2 kg

IDENTIFICATION
Head, moustache stripes and upperparts blackish; front white, heavily streaked black; thighs and vent rufous; immature lacks rufous vent

HABITAT
Diverse – grassland, savanna, forest edge; often near water

DISTRIBUTION
Natal northwards and across to central and northern Namibia; winters in Africa south of Equator; breeds in Eurasia

STATUS
Non-breeding migrant (October to March); scarce to locally common

HABITS
Solitary in winter quarters, occasionally scattered birds together; hunts by aerial pursuit, especially at dusk

BREEDING
Does not breed in southern Africa

FOOD
Insects, small birds, bats

VOICE
Silent in wintering grounds; a shrill, repeated 'kew' in Europe

AFRICAN HOBBY

SCIENTIFIC NAME
Falco cuvieri

OTHER NAMES
African Hobby Falcon, Afrikaanse Boomvalk

SIZE
Length about 0,3 m
Wingspan about 0,9 m
Weight about 0,2 kg

IDENTIFICATION
Head, moustache stripes and upperparts blackish; front warm rufous, finely streaked with black; immature has more heavily streaked front

HABITAT
Tropical savanna, forest clearings, riverine fringe

DISTRIBUTION
Northern Transvaal northwards to Zimbabwe, northern Botswana and northern Namibia; vagrants to eastern Cape; ranges to central and West Africa

STATUS
Breeding visitor (October to March); rare

HABITS
Solitary, or in pairs when breeding; hunts by aerial pursuit, especially at dusk

BREEDING
No nest built; lays on old crow or raptor stick nest in tree; breeds in early summer; lays 3 eggs, buffy brown, 39 x 31 mm; little else known of breeding habits

FOOD
Insects, small birds, bats

VOICE
A shrill, repeated 'kik'

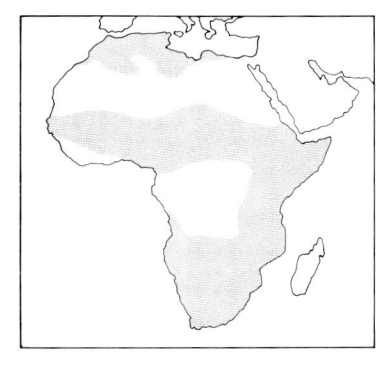

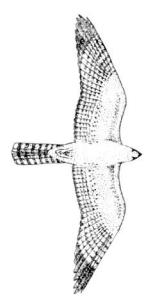

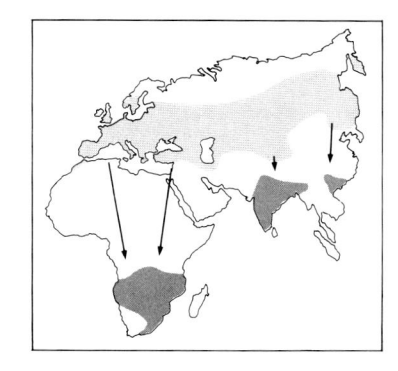

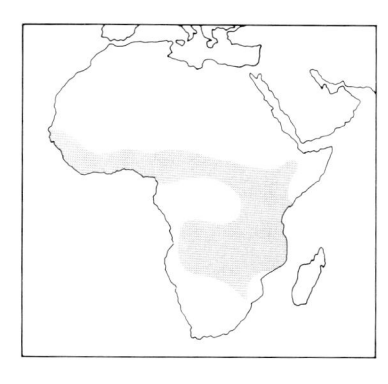

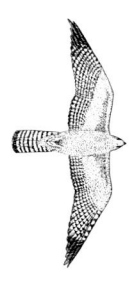

APPENDIX

TAITA FALCON

SCIENTIFIC NAME
Falco fasciinucha

OTHER NAMES
Teita Falcon, Taitavalk

SIZE
Length about 0,3 m
Wingspan about 0,6 m
Weight about 0,25 kg

IDENTIFICATION
Slate-grey above, black head with rufous nuchal patches, white throat, rufous front; immature browner

HABITAT
Cliffs overlooking or surrounded by mature woodland

DISTRIBUTION
Northern and eastern Zimbabwe; ranges northwards discontinuously to Ethiopia

STATUS
Breeding resident; rare and localized

HABITS
Solitary or in pairs; lives on cliffs; hunts by high-speed stoops on aerial prey

BREEDING
No nest built; lays in pothole on cliff; breeds in early summer; lays 3-4 eggs, brown, 43 x 35 mm; incubation about 26 days; nestling period about 35 days; incubation mainly by female

FOOD
Mostly small birds; also insects

VOICE
Noisy, repeated 'kek' alarm call

REDNECKED FALCON

SCIENTIFIC NAME
Falco chicquera

OTHER NAMES
Rufousnecked Falcon, Rooinekvalk

SIZE
Length about 0,3 m
Wingspan about 0,6 m
Weight about 0,2 kg

IDENTIFICATION
Blue-grey above, barred black; rufous head, black moustache stripe; front white, washed buff on chest and barred black on belly; immature has brown head

HABITAT
Semi-arid or arid thornveld; open palm savanna in Zambia

DISTRIBUTION
Namibia, Botswana, northern Cape; a second race ranges from Mozambique to East Africa

STATUS
Breeding resident and nomad; rare to locally common

HABITS
Solitary, or in pairs while breeding; hunts by aerial pursuit; perches in tree canopies

BREEDING
No nest built; lays on old crow or raptor stick nest in tree; breeds in early summer; lays 3-4 eggs, brownish, 44 x 33 mm; incubation about 33 days; nestling period about 35 days; female incubates, fed by male

FOOD
Mainly small birds, occasionally lizards or rodents

VOICE
High-pitched, rasping 'yak, yak, yak...'

ELEONORA'S FALCON

SCIENTIFIC NAME
Falco eleonorae

OTHER NAMES
Eleonoravalk

SIZE
Length about 0,4 m
Wingspan about 1,2 m
Weight about 0,37 kg

IDENTIFICATION
Head, moustache stripe, upperparts sooty brown; throat and cheek white; front rufous, streaked with black; rare dark phase is entirely sooty brown

HABITAT
Tropical savanna

DISTRIBUTION
Vagrant to Mozambique coastal belt; normally overwinters in Madagascar and breeds on some Mediterranean islands

STATUS
Non-breeding vagrant; rare

HABITS
Solitary or in groups; hunts insects and small birds by aerial pursuit

BREEDING
Does not breed in southern Africa

FOOD
Insects in wintering grounds; small birds while breeding

VOICE
Silent in wintering grounds; a shrill, repeated 'ki' in breeding areas

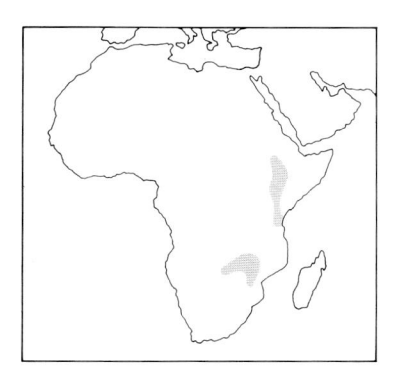

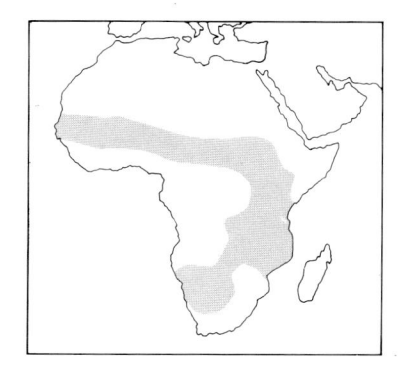

SOOTY FALCON

SCIENTIFIC NAME
Falco concolor

OTHER NAMES
Roetvalk

SIZE
Length about 0,35 m
Wingspan about 1 m
Weight about 0,32 kg

IDENTIFICATION
Wholly slate-grey with yellow bare parts; slimmer and longer-winged than Grey Kestrel

HABITAT
Tall trees bordering on clearings; often near water

DISTRIBUTION
Natal coast, Zululand, Mozambique (regular); vagrants elsewhere; overwinters mainly in Madagascar; breeds in North Africa and Middle East

STATUS
Non-breeding visitor (December to March); rare

HABITS
Solitary or in small groups; perches high up; hunts by aerial pursuit, especially at dusk

BREEDING
Does not breed in southern Africa

FOOD
Insects, small birds, bats

VOICE
Silent in wintering grounds; a shrill, repeated 'kilik' in breeding area

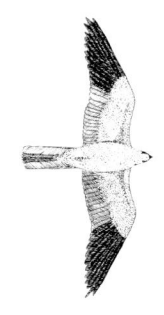

GREY KESTREL

SCIENTIFIC NAME
Falco ardosiaceus

OTHER NAMES
Donker Grysvalk

SIZE
Length about 0,3 m
Wingspan about 0,7 m
Weight about 0,24 kg

IDENTIFICATION
Wholly slate-grey except for bare parts which are yellow; wings faintly barred; sexes and immature alike

HABITAT
Tropical savanna and forest clearings

DISTRIBUTION
Northern Namibia; ranges northwards through central and West Africa

STATUS
Resident? scarce to rare

HABITS
Solitary or in pairs; hunts from perches, taking prey on the ground

BREEDING
Not recorded in southern Africa; nests inside Hamerkop nests elsewhere; lays 3-5 eggs, brownish, 41 x 33 mm; little else known of breeding habits

FOOD
Lizards, rodents, small birds, insects

VOICE
Shrill, repeated 'keek'

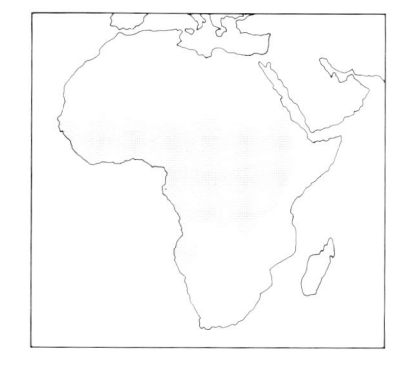

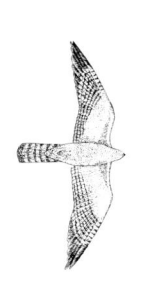

WESTERN REDFOOTED KESTREL

SCIENTIFIC NAME
Falco vespertinus

OTHER NAMES
Western Redfooted Falcon, Westelike Rooipootvalk

SIZE
Length about 0,3 m
Wingspan about 0,7 m
Weight about 0,16 kg

IDENTIFICATION
Male wholly dark grey with rufous thighs, red bare parts; female orange-brown front and crown; grey, barred black wings, tail and back; black eye-mask

HABITAT
Semi-arid savanna

DISTRIBUTION
Namibia, Botswana, western Transvaal and Zimbabwe; breeds in eastern Europe and Russia

STATUS
Non-breeding migrant; scarce

HABITS
In groups, often associated with other migrant kestrels; hunts insects from perches and by hovering

BREEDING
Does not breed in southern Africa

FOOD
Insects, especially grasshoppers and locusts

VOICE
Silent, except at communal roosts; shrill, repeated 'kee'

Eastern Redfooted Kestrel

SCIENTIFIC NAME
Falco amurensis

OTHER NAMES
Eastern Redfooted Falcon, Oostelike Rooipootvalk

SIZE
Length about 0,3 m
Wingspan about 0,7 m
Weight about 0,15 kg

IDENTIFICATION
Male wholly grey except for rufous thighs and white underwing coverts; bare parts red; female barred grey above, white blotched with black below; black eye-mask

HABITAT
Grassland and savanna

DISTRIBUTION
Eastern Cape, northwards through Natal, Orange Free State, Transvaal, Zimbabwe and Zambia; breeds from eastern Siberia to China

STATUS
Non-breeding migrant; common

HABITS
Gregarious; roosts communally in trees, sometimes in thousands; hunts by hovering or from perches

BREEDING
Does not breed in southern Africa

FOOD
Insects, especially grasshoppers and locusts

VOICE
Silent, except at communal roosts; a shrill, repeated 'kee'

Rock Kestrel

SCIENTIFIC NAME
Falco tinnunculus

OTHER NAMES
Kestrel or Common Kestrel, Rooivalk

SIZE
Length about 0,3 m
Wingspan about 0,7 m
Weight about 0,2 kg

IDENTIFICATION
Rufous body and wings spotted and streaked black; grey head and tail which has black terminal bar, tipped white; yellow bare parts

HABITAT
Grassland, scrub and savanna, especially where cliffs occur

DISTRIBUTION
Throughout southern Africa; other races occur elsewhere in Africa and in Europe and Asia

STATUS
Breeding resident with local movements; common

HABITS
Solitary or in pairs; hunts by hovering or from perches, often alongside roads

BREEDING
No nest built; lays in pothole on cliff or on old nest of crow; breeds in early summer; lays 3-4 eggs, warm brown, 39 x 33 mm; incubation about 30 days; nestling period about 35 days; incubation mainly by female

FOOD
Insects, rodents, lizards, small birds

VOICE
Shrill, repeated 'kee'; also 'kik-kik-kik…' alarm call, and melodious trill

Lesser Kestrel

SCIENTIFIC NAME
Falco naumanni

OTHER NAMES
Kleinrooivalk

SIZE
Length about 0,3 m
Wingspan about 0,6 m
Weight about 0,13 kg

IDENTIFICATION
Males rufous above with grey head and tail, buff below, lightly spotted; black terminal tail bar; female and immature pale brown streaked with darker brown

HABITAT
Grassland and open savanna

DISTRIBUTION
Most of southern Africa except arid west and eastern littoral; winters throughout Africa and breeds in Palearctic

STATUS
Non-breeding migrant (November to March); common

HABITS
Gregarious; hunts during day in small flocks and roosts at night in trees in large flocks; hunts from perches and by hovering

BREEDING
Does not breed in southern Africa

FOOD
Insects, especially grasshoppers and locusts

VOICE
Silent, except at roosts; a shrill twittering

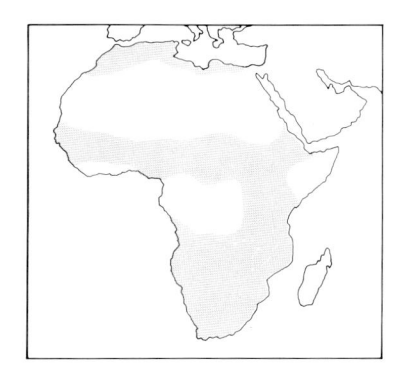

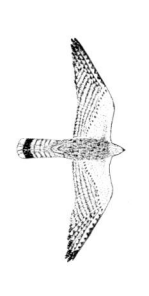

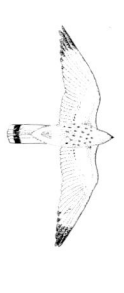

Greater Kestrel

Scientific Name
Falco rupicoloides

Other Names
White-eyed Kestrel, Grootrooivalk

Size
Length about 0,35 m
Wingspan about 0,9 m
Weight about 0,25 kg

Identification
Sandy-brown barred above and streaked below with black; tail grey with black bars; eye white in adult, but brown in immature

Habitat
Desert, semi-arid savanna, grassland

Distribution
Namibia, Botswana, Cape interior to western Zimbabwe, Transvaal, Orange Free State and northern Natal; ranges discontinuously to north-east Africa

Status
Breeding resident with local movements; common

Habits
Solitary or in pairs; hunts from perches and by hovering

Breeding
No nest built; lays in old stick nest of crow or raptor in trees; breeds in early summer; lays 3-5 eggs, brownish buff, 42 x 34 mm; incubation, by female, about 32 days; nestling period about 30 days

Food
Insects, rodents, lizards, small birds

Voice
A trilling, repeated 'kwirr'

Dickinson's Kestrel

Scientific Name
Falco dickinsoni

Other Names
Dickinsonse Grysvalk

Size
Length about 0,3 m
Wingspan about 0,7 m
Weight about 0,2 kg

Identification
Two-tone grey: pale on head and rump and dark on rest of body; bare parts yellow

Habitat
Savanna, especially where large baobabs or tall palms occur

Distribution
Mozambique, northern Transvaal, Zimbabwe, northern Botswana and Namibia

Status
Breeding resident; scarce

Habits
Solitary or in pairs; hunts from perches, taking prey on the ground

Breeding
No nest built; uses natural hole in baobab or palm, or old Hamerkop nest; breeds in early summer; lays 3-4 brownish eggs, 39 x 31 mm; nestling period about 35 days

Food
Lizards, rodents, small birds, insects

Voice
Shrill, high-pitched, repeated 'kik'

Pygmy Falcon

Scientific Name
Polihierax semitorquatus

Other Names
Dwergvalk

Size
Length about 0,2 m
Wingspan about 0,3 m
Weight about 0,06 kg

Identification
White in front, dove-grey above; female has russet back; bare parts orange; immature buffier than adult

Habitat
Semi-arid savanna and scrub provided Sociable Weaver nests are present

Distribution
Northern Cape, western Transvaal, southern Botswana and interior of Namibia

Status
Breeding resident; fairly common

Habits
Solitary or in pairs; always associated with Sociable Weaver nests; hunts from perches; flight woodpecker-like

Breeding
No nest built; uses Sociable Weaver nest chamber; breeds in summer; lays 2-4 eggs, white, 28 x 23 mm; incubation about 30 days; nestling period about 28 days; female incubates mostly, fed by male

Food
Lizards and insects, occasionally small birds

Voice
Shrill, chirping, repeated 'ki'

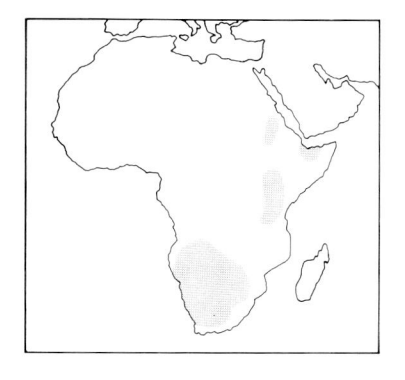

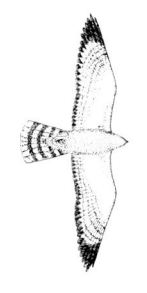

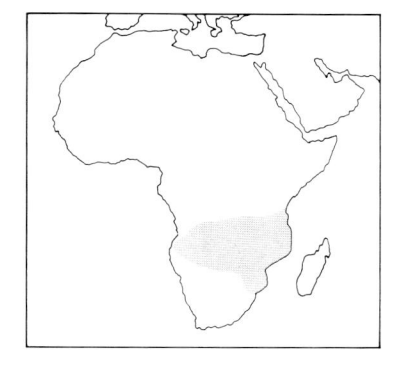

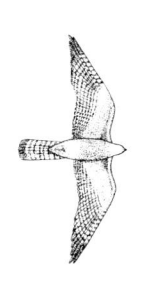

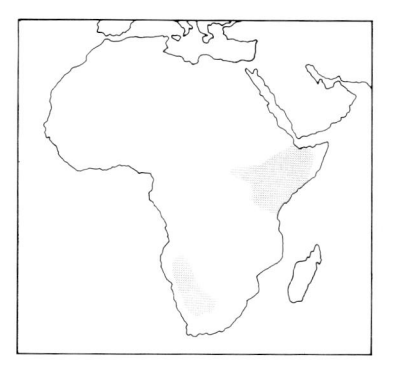

BARN OWL

SCIENTIFIC NAME
Tyto alba

OTHER NAMES
Nonnetjie-uil

SIZE
Length about 0,3 m
Wingspan about 0,9 m
Weight about 0,3 kg

IDENTIFICATION
Buffy grey above with light spots, white below with small dark spots; white heart-shaped face; immature darker than adult

HABITAT
Diverse – desert, semi-arid scrub and savanna, grassland

DISTRIBUTION
Virtually world-wide; occurs throughout southern Africa and through most of Africa

STATUS
Breeding resident with local movements; common

HABITS
Usually in pairs; seen by day only if flushed from roost site; at night detected by shrill call; flies with slow wingbeats and glides

BREEDING
No nest built; lays in a variety of holes and cavities; breeds any month, but mostly in autumn; lays 2-12 eggs, white, 39 x 31 mm; incubation about 31 days; nestling period about 50 days

FOOD
Mainly small rodents

VOICE
Noisy at night; a thin, shrill screech

GRASS OWL

SCIENTIFIC NAME
Tyto capensis

OTHER NAMES
Grasuil

SIZE
Length about 0,3 m
Wingspan about 0,9 m
Weight about 0,4 kg

IDENTIFICATION
Brown above and white below, spotted with brown; large white heart-shaped face; immature buffier below

HABITAT
Rank grass along vleis and streams

DISTRIBUTION
From eastern Cape to Zimbabwe and north to East Africa; also in northern Namibia

STATUS
Breeding resident with local movements; scarce

HABITS
Strictly nocturnal; roosts in grass and not easily flushed; hunts in flight at night

BREEDING
Nest a pad of grass hidden in vegetation on the ground; breeds mostly in autumn; lays 3-5 eggs, white, 42 x 34 mm; incubation about 32 days; nestling period about 35 days; female incubates, fed by male

FOOD
Mainly small rodents

VOICE
A frog-like clicking

WOOD OWL

SCIENTIFIC NAME
Strix woodfordii

OTHER NAMES
Woodford's Owl, Bosuil

SIZE
Length about 0,3 m
Wingspan about 0,8 m
Weight about 0,3 kg

IDENTIFICATION
Rufous brown, speckled above and barred below, whitish face and eyebrows

HABITAT
Forests, riverine galleries and tall woodland

DISTRIBUTION
Southern Cape east to Natal coastal belt, Mozambique, eastern Transvaal, eastern and northern Zimbabwe to northern Botswana and Namibia; extends to West Africa

STATUS
Breeding resident; common

HABITS
In pairs; strictly nocturnal; seldom flushed during day when hidden in vegetation

BREEDING
No nest built; lays in hole in tree; breeds in early summer; lays 2 eggs, white, 43 x 38 mm; incubation about 31 days; nestling period about 35 days; female incubates, fed by male

FOOD
Insects, rodents, small birds

VOICE
Often calls at night; a cheery hoot

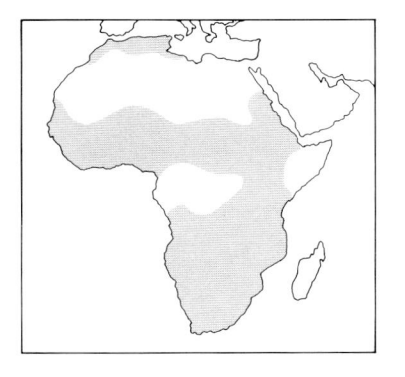

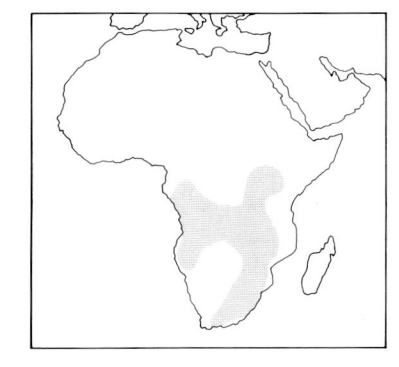

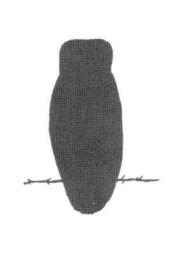

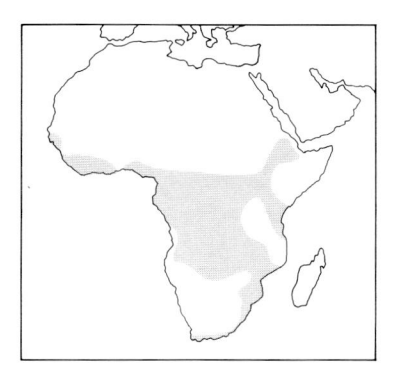

MARSH OWL

SCIENTIFIC NAME
Asio capensis

OTHER NAMES
Vlei-uil

SIZE
Length about 0,35 m
Wingspan about 0,9 m
Weight about 0,3 kg

IDENTIFICATION
Uniform brown except for paler face with black rim and tawny panel in outer wing; eyes dark brown

HABITAT
Temporary and permanent vleis in grassland and savanna

DISTRIBUTION
Southern Cape eastwards to Natal, then north to Mozambique, Zimbabwe, eastern Botswana and northern Namibia; ranges to central Africa

STATUS
Breeding resident with local movements; common

HABITS
Hides in grass during the day, but emerges to hunt in evening and morning; flight slow flapping with glides; often perches on fence posts

BREEDING
Nest a pad of grass close to ground hidden in vegetation; breeds any month, but mostly in autumn; lays 4 eggs, white, 40 x 34 mm; incubation about 28 days; nestling period about 35 days

FOOD
Insects, rodents, small birds

VOICE
Often calls; a short, rasping 'gggk' repeated three or four times

CAPE EAGLE OWL

SCIENTIFIC NAME
Bubo capensis

OTHER NAMES
Mackinder's Eagle Owl, Kaapse Ooruil

SIZE
Length about 0,5 m
Wingspan about 1,2 m
Weight about 1,2 kg

IDENTIFICATION
Brown mottled with tawny above; breast white, heavily blotched with dark brown and tawny; prominent ear tufts; orange eyes; Zimbabwe race larger

HABITAT
Rocky hills and ravines in grassland, scrub, fynbos

DISTRIBUTION
Western, southern and eastern Cape, Natal, eastern Transvaal, eastern Zimbabwe; southern edge of Namibia; ranges to north-east Africa

STATUS
Breeding resident; rare to fairly common

HABITS
Solitary or in pairs; entirely nocturnal; roosts amongst rocks during day; hunts from perches at night

BREEDING
No nest built; lays on the ground, usually on an overhung cliff ledge; breeds in winter; lays 2-3 eggs, white, 53 x 45 mm (larger in Zimbabwe); incubation about 35 days; nestling period about 75 days

FOOD
Diverse – rodents, hares, dassies, birds, insects

VOICE
A loud triple-noted hoot

SPOTTED EAGLE OWL

SCIENTIFIC NAME
Bubo africanus

OTHER NAMES
Gevlekte Ooruil

SIZE
Length about 0,45 m
Wingspan about 1 m
Weight about 0,7 kg

IDENTIFICATION
Grey above, spotted and streaked with white; white below with grey barring; prominent ear tufts; yellow eyes

HABITAT
Diverse – grassland, scrub, rocky hills; suburban gardens

DISTRIBUTION
Throughout southern Africa; extends north to East and West Africa

STATUS
Breeding resident; common

HABITS
Solitary or in pairs; roosts during day in sheltered spot; active at night, often hunting along roads and often perched on telephone poles

BREEDING
No nest built; lays on ground, in tree hollow, on Hamerkop nest, etc; breeds in early summer; lays 2-4 eggs, white, 49 x 41 mm; incubation about 31 days; nestling period about 49 days; female incubates, fed by male

FOOD
Diverse – rodents, birds, insects, frogs

VOICE
Two- or three-syllabled hoots

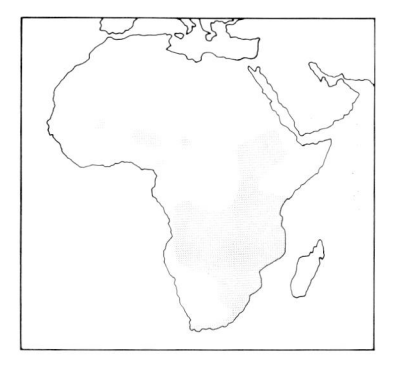

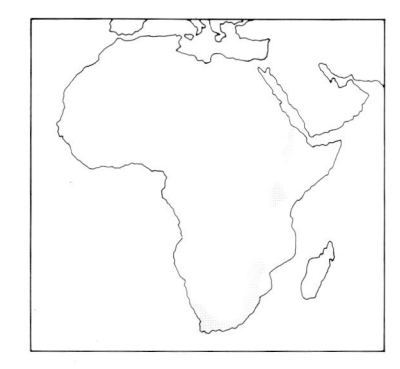

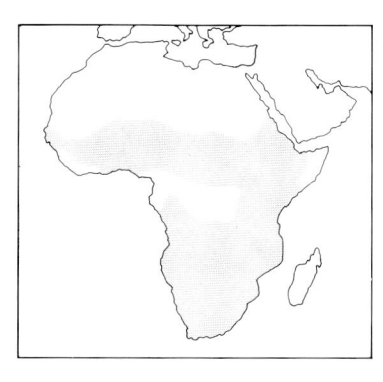

GIANT EAGLE OWL

SCIENTIFIC NAME
Bubo lacteus

OTHER NAMES
Milky Eagle Owl, Verreaux's Eagle Owl, Reuse Ooruil

SIZE
Length about 0,6 m
Wingspan about 1,4 m
Weight about 2 kg

IDENTIFICATION
Buffy grey above, finely barred grey and white below, whitish face rimmed with black; prominent ear tufts; dark brown eyes and pink eyelids

HABITAT
Savanna

DISTRIBUTION
Northern Cape across to Zululand, northwards through Namibia, Botswana, Zimbabwe and Mozambique to East and West Africa; vagrant to southern Cape

STATUS
Breeding resident with local movement; scarce to common

HABITS
Solitary or in pairs; roosts during day in large, leafy trees; hunts at night from perches; a formidable predator

BREEDING
No nest built; lays in old eagle, hawk and other stick nests, occasionally in tree hollow; breeds in winter; lays 2 eggs, white, 63 x 51 mm; incubation about 33 days; nestling period about 60 days

FOOD
Mammals, especially hedgehogs, medium-sized birds, insects, frogs

VOICE
Deep, grunting hoot

PEL'S FISHING OWL

SCIENTIFIC NAME
Scotopelia peli

OTHER NAMES
Visuil

SIZE
Length about 0,6 m
Wingspan about 1,5 m
Weight about 2,1 kg

IDENTIFICATION
Overall ginger colour, darker above than below, streaked and barred with dark brown; no ear tufts; eyes dark brown; large

HABITAT
Galleries of forest along rivers and lake edges

DISTRIBUTION
Zululand northwards through Mozambique, eastern Transvaal, eastern and northern Zimbabwe and northern Botswana and Namibia; ranges to central Africa

STATUS
Breeding resident; rare to locally common

HABITS
Solitary or in pairs; roosts during the day in heavily foliaged trees; at night hunts along rivers from overhanging perches

BREEDING
No nest built; lays in hole in large tree; breeds in late summer; lays 2 eggs, white, 62 x 52 mm; incubation about 35 days; nestling period about 70 days; female incubates, fed by male

FOOD
Mainly fish; also crabs, frogs, etc

VOICE
Deep, resonant hoot

SCOPS OWL

SCIENTIFIC NAME
Otus senegalensis

OTHER NAMES
Skopsuil

SIZE
Length about 0,2 m
Wingspan about 0,4 m
Weight about 0,06 kg

IDENTIFICATION
Very small; grey below, streaked with black; brown or grey above, spotted white; conspicuous ear tufts; cryptic

HABITAT
Savanna

DISTRIBUTION
Eastern Cape (rare), eastwards through Natal, Mozambique, Transvaal, Zimbabwe, northern Botswana and Namibia; extends to East and West Africa

STATUS
Breeding resident; locally common

HABITS
Solitary or in pairs; sits against tree trunks during the day, difficult to locate; vocal at night; hunts from perches

BREEDING
No nest built; lays in tree hollows, usually open above; breeds in early summer; lays 2-3 eggs, white, 30 x 25 mm; incubation about 25 days; nestling period about 25 days; female incubates, fed by male

FOOD
Insects

VOICE
Noisy at night during summer; a distinctive 'krup'

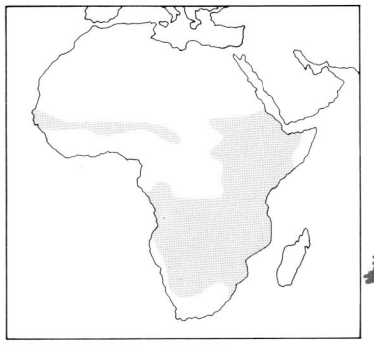

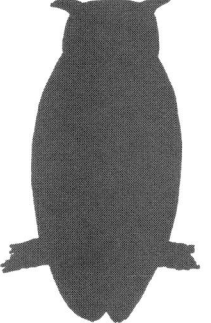

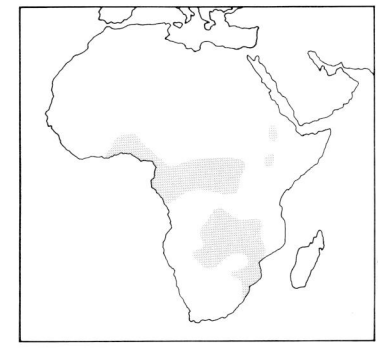

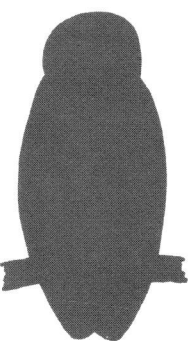

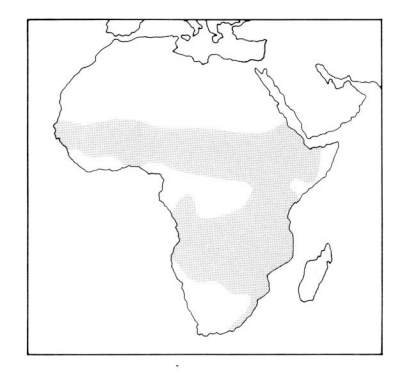

PEARLSPOTTED OWL

SCIENTIFIC NAME
Glaucidium perlatum

OTHER NAMES
Witkoluil

SIZE
Length about 0,2 m
Wingspan about 0,4 m
Weight about 0,08 kg

IDENTIFICATION
Brown above with white spots; white below, streaked with brown; no ear tufts, but has 'false' black eyes on back of head

HABITAT
Savanna

DISTRIBUTION
Northern Cape, Zululand and central Transvaal, northwards to East and West Africa

STATUS
Breeding resident; common

HABITS
Solitary or in pairs; a noisy, conspicuous little owl, often active during the day; hunts from perches

BREEDING
No nest built; lays in holes in trees, especially woodpecker holes; breeds in early summer; lays 3 eggs, white, 31 x 26 mm; incubation about 29 days; nestling period about 30 days; female incubates, fed by male

FOOD
Diverse – insects, small birds, rodents

VOICE
Noisy during most of the the year; a series of piercing whistled notes

BARRED OWL

SCIENTIFIC NAME
Glaucidium capense

OTHER NAMES
Gebande Uil

SIZE
Length about 0,2 m
Wingspan about 0,45 m
Weight about 0,12 kg

IDENTIFICATION
Brown, finely barred white, on back, head and chest; white underparts, spotted with brown; no ear tufts and no 'false' eyes

HABITAT
Tall woodland, riparian and coastal bush

DISTRIBUTION
Eastern Cape (rare), Zululand north through Mozambique, eastern Transvaal, Zimbabwe and northern Botswana and Namibia; extends to Kenya

STATUS
Breeding resident; rare to locally common

HABITS
Solitary or in pairs; less diurnal than Pearlspotted Owl and not easily located during the day; hunts from perches

BREEDING
No nest built; lays in smallish natural holes in trees; breeds in early summer; lays 2-3 eggs, white, 33 x 27 mm; little else known about breeding habits

FOOD
Mainly insects

VOICE
A distinctive double-noted purring call

WHITEFACED OWL

SCIENTIFIC NAME
Otus leucotis

OTHER NAMES
Whitefaced Scops Owl, Witwanguil

SIZE
Length about 0,25 m
Wingspan about 0,5 m
Weight about 0,22 kg

IDENTIFICATION
Small; grey above, finely streaked with black; white below, finely streaked; white face, rimmed with black; orange eyes; prominent ear tufts

HABITAT
Savanna, especially thornveld

DISTRIBUTION
Northern half of southern Africa ranging northwards to East and West Africa

STATUS
Breeding resident with local movements; locally common

HABITS
Solitary or in pairs; roosts during day and is active at night; hunts from perches and on the ground

BREEDING
No nest built; lays on stick nests (e.g. crows') or in hollow in tree; breeds in any month, but mainly in early summer; lays 2-3 eggs, white, 39 x 32 mm; incubation about 30 days; nestling period about 30 days

FOOD
Mainly small rodents; also insects, birds, spiders, etc

VOICE
Briefly vocal before breeding; a series of rapid hoots

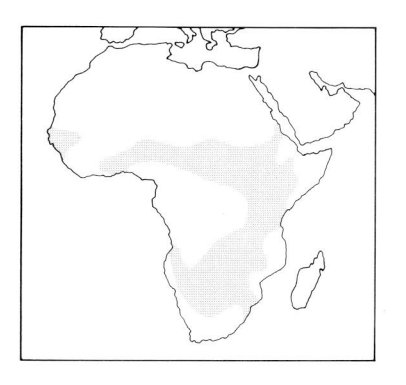

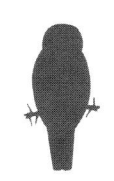

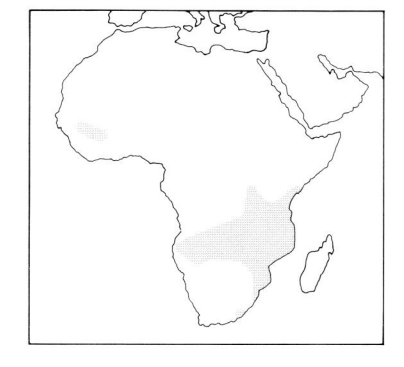

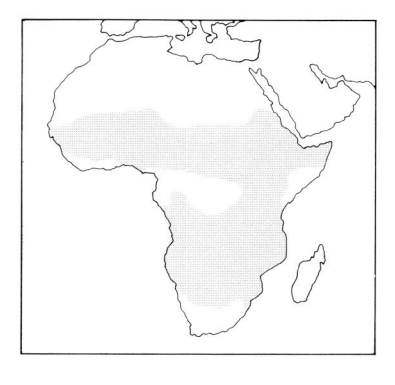

Further Reading

Brown, L.H. 1970.
African birds of prey.
London: Collins.

Brown, L.H. 1980.
The African Fish Eagle.
Cape Town: Purnell.

Brown, L.H. and Amadon, D. 1968.
Eagles, Hawks and Falcons of the world.
Feltham: Country Life.

Brown, L.H., Urban, E.K. and Newman, K.B. 1982.
The birds of Africa, vol. 1.
London: Academic Press.

Finch-Davies, C.G. and Kemp, A.C. 1980.
The birds of prey of southern Africa.
Johannesburg: Winchester Press.

Fry, C.H., Keith, S. and Urban, E.K. 1988.
The birds of Africa, vol. 3.
London: Academic Press.

Kemp, A.C. (ed.). 1978.
Proceedings of a symposium on African predatory birds.
Pretoria: Transvaal Museum.

Kemp, A.C. and Calburn, S. 1987.
The owls of southern Africa.
Cape Town: Struik Winchester.

Maclean, G.L. 1984.
Roberts' birds of southern Africa.
Cape Town: John Voelcker Bird Book Fund.

Mendelsohn, J.M. and Sapsford, C.W. (eds.). 1984.
Proceedings of the second symposium on African predatory birds.
Durban: Natal Bird Club.

Mundy, P.J. 1982.
The comparative biology of southern African vultures.
Johannesburg: Vulture Study Group.

Newton, I. 1979.
Population ecology of raptors.
Berkhamstead: Poyser.

Steyn, P. 1973.
Eagle days.
Johannesburg: Purnell.

Steyn, P. 1982.
Birds of prey of southern Africa.
Cape Town: David Philip.

Steyn, P. 1984.
A delight of owls.
Cape Town: David Philip.

Tarboton, W.R. and Allan, D.G. 1984.
The status and conservation of birds of prey in the Transvaal.
Transvaal Museum Monograph 3.

GLOSSARY

Arboreal Living in trees
Biome A region defined by its biotic community
Breeding season Months in which egg-laying has been recorded
Cainism Process in which first-hatched chick kills younger sibling
Call Vocalization
Carrion Dead and rotting flesh
Cere Bare, coloured skin at the base of the bill (see illustration)
Clutch A set of eggs laid, and incubated simultaneously
Colonial Roosting, feeding or nesting in close proximity
Coverts Group of feathers covering either base of major flight feathers or other area or structure (e.g. the ear)
Crepuscular Active at dawn and dusk
Crest Elongated feathers on forehead, crown or nape
Crop A thin-walled extensible pouch in the oesophagus used for temporary food storage
Crown Top of head (see illustration)
Dimorphism The occurrence in a species of two distinct types of individual
Diurnal Active during the day
Endemic Restricted to a certain region, and found nowhere else
Extralimital Beyond the borders of southern Africa
Falconry The use of trained birds of prey for hunting wild quarry
Fledgling A young bird that has recently left the nest
Forage Look or hunt for food
Forest A woodland of tall, evergreen trees with a closed canopy
Gape The basal opening of the bill (see illustration)
Generic Of a genus, a classifying term between family and species

Grassland Area devoid of woody plants and dominated by grass species
Gregarious Living together in groups or flocks
Habitat A particular environment inhabited by a particular species
Immature Bird that has moulted from juvenile plumage but has not attained adult plumage
Incubation The process whereby heat is applied to an egg, usually by the parent sitting on it, to promote embryonic development
Irruption A rapid expansion of a species' normal range
Jizz A word coined to refer to a bird's characteristic posture and behaviour
Juvenile The first full-feathered plumage of a young bird
Local movements Short migrations
Melanistic Black or blackish in colour
Migrant A species that undertakes usually long-distance flights from its wintering to breeding areas
Montane Pertaining to highland areas
Neoteny The persistence of juvenile features in the adult form of an animal
Nestling A young bird that has not yet left the nest
Nocturnal Active at night
Nomadic Descriptive of movements of a species that are not seasonal or cyclic

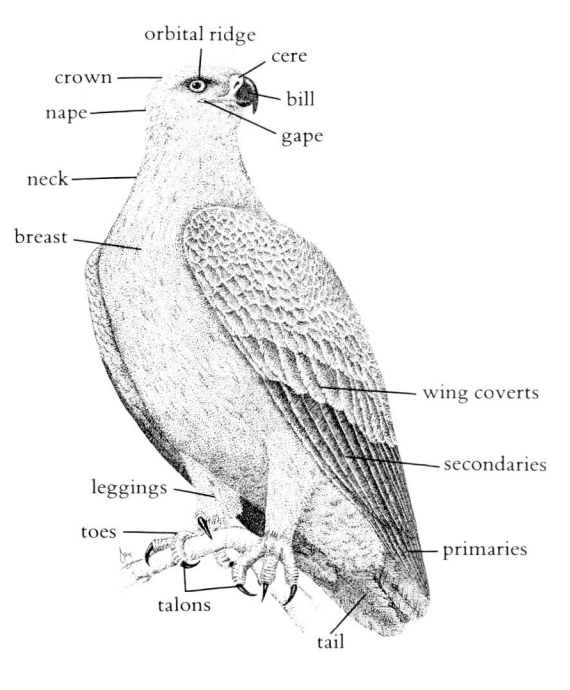

Ossuary Collection of skeletal fragments, usually at nest or roost
Overwinter To spend winter in the subregion instead of migrating to breeding grounds
Palearctic North Africa, Greenland, Europe, Asia north of the Himalayas, southern China and South East Asia
Plumage The feather covering of a bird
Primaries The outermost major flight feathers of the wing (see illustration)
Race Subspecies; a geographical population of a species
Range Distribution
Raptor Bird of prey
Remiges Flight feathers (i.e. primaries and secondaries)
Resident Species not prone to migration, remaining in the same area year-round
Roost A place where bird/s regularly rest, usually at night
Savanna A grassland with scattered trees, usually less than 50 per cent tree cover
Scrub An area dominated by low woody plants
Secondaries Longest wing-feathers, from mid-wing to the base of the wing (see illustration)
South African Red Data Book of Birds A published list of bird species regarded as threatened in South Africa
Talons The claws of a bird of prey (see illustration)
Tarsus The lower part of the leg, just above the foot
Taxonomy Scientific classification
Terminal At end or tip of structure
Terrestrial Living on land
Territory Area defended by a bird or pair of birds
Vagrant Rare and accidental to the region
Wing panel Pale area at the base of the primaries, which is a useful field identification character for some species
Woodland Area dominated by deciduous trees; usually more than 50 per cent canopy cover

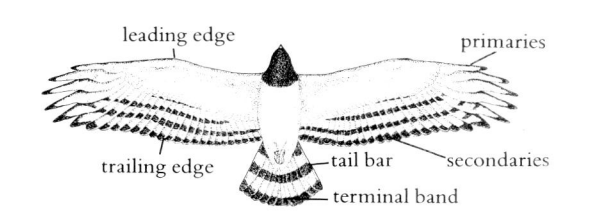

INDEXES

GENERAL

A
Ayres, Thomas 65, 122

B
badgers, honey *see* ratels
Bazas 42
Bee-eater, European 138
bishopbirds 125
'blushing' in birds of prey 133
Borassus palm 150
Brown, Leslie 65, 149
bulbuls 188
    Blackeyed 117
'Buzzard' 88

C
'Cain-and-Abel' struggle 49 *see also* cainism
cainism 36, 49, 52, 56, 58, 83, 91, 93, 94, 96, 183
Cariamidiae 11
cobras 166
cormorants 8, 63
Crane family 11
crows 149, 150, 161, 183, 192
    Black 144
    Pied 144
cuckoo 104

D
Desert, Namib 29, 104, 109, 144, 150, 161, 170
Dickinson, Dr 164
dimorphism 103, 106-8, 109, 117, 138, 158, 161, 164
doves 104
drongos 183, 188
    Squaretailed 117

E
Eagle
    Bald 47, 85
    Beaudouin's Snake 76
    Shorttoed 76
eggshell thinning 83, 142
Etosha 52

F
falconry 106, 142, 144
Food items
    amphibians 60, 176, 178
        frogs 56, 60, 73, 76, 91, 117, 125, 164, 173, 181, 188
    arthropods 187
    birds 12, 34, 42, 44, 52, 55, 56, 58, 60, 65, 71, 79, 83, 91, 93, 94, 99, 100, 103, 104, 106, 108, 109, 113, 114, 117, 118, 121, 125, 132, 141, 144, 148, 149, 150, 152, 153, 154, 158, 164, 173, 175, 176, 178, 181, 183, 188, 190
        bee-eaters 153
        bulbuls 103, 117, 149
        buntings 58
        canaries 100
        chickens, domestic 61, 71, 144, 183
        crakes 153
        cuckoos 44
        doves 44, 65, 100, 106, 117, 118, 142, 150
            Laughing 65, 113
        ducks 125
        egrets 133
        Falcon, Lanner 181
        finches 150
        gamebirds 56, 61, 71, 93, 181
            francolins 52, 61, 71, 106, 144
                Crested 118
            guineafowl 52, 61, 71
                Helmeted 70, 106, 113
            sandgrouse 144
        herons 133
        hoopoes 153
        hornbills 81
            Yellowbilled 113
        korhaans
            Black 109
            Redcrested 109
        larks 58, 100, 132, 146, 150
            Stark's 150

Food items: birds *(cont.)*
        longclaws 100
        martins 44
        nightjars 44
        owls
            Barn 183
            Grass 183
            Marsh 183
            Spotted Eagle 183, 188
            Wood 66
        pigeons 65, 142, 144
            Rock 175
        pipits 100, 103, 132, 146, 153
        quails 132
        queleas 60, 132, 144
        rollers 153
            Lilacbreasted 81
        sandgrouse
        shrikes, Longtailed 81
        snipe 173
        sparrows 118
        starlings 58
            Redwinged 149
        swallows 44, 146, 153
            European 146
        swifts 44, 133, 149
            Alpine 100
        thrushes 118
        Trogon, Narina 117
        wagtails 153
        warblers 153
        waxbills 104, 114
        weavers 103, 114, 118, 133
    birds' eggs 12, 132, 133
    bones 15, 16
    carrion 16, 18, 22, 25, 26, 27, 29, 30, 34, 81, 94
    fish 18, 73, 83, 125, 137, 138, 181, 184
        barbel 184
        mullet 138
        Tiger 183
    fruit 66, 133
    insects 18, 33, 34, 42, 66, 73, 76, 79, 88, 91, 93, 94, 96, 104, 109, 113, 114, 117, 118, 132, 141, 144, 146, 148, 153, 154, 155, 157, 158, 161, 164, 166, 173, 175, 176, 178, 181, 187, 190
        beetles 132, 173, 175, 176, 181, 187, 188
        caterpillars 42, 155

INDEX

Food items: insects *(cont.)*
    cicada beetles 114
    crickets 155, 157, 166, 175, 181, 187, 188
    dragonflies 146
    grasshoppers 12, 42, 96, 132, 154, 155, 157, 158, 161, 173, 175, 181, 187
    hover-moths 146, 148
    locusts 155
    mantids 42
    moths 117
    termites 52, 55, 60, 148, 154, 181, 188
    wasps 45
  mammals 55, 56, 60, 61, 71, 109, 113, 118, 183
    antelope 68
      bushbuck 68
      dik-dik 71
      impala 71
    bats 33, 44, 133, 146, 148
    dassies 48-9, 61, 68, 71, 93, 178
    elephants 52
    hares 56, 81
      rock 178
      scrub 61, 93, 178
    hedgehog 183
    mongooses 30, 71
      banded 71
      dwarf 113
      yellow 52
    monkeys 68
      Samango 68
    rodents 12, 18, 33, 42, 56, 58, 66, 76, 87, 88, 91, 93, 94, 96, 99, 109, 117, 121, 125, 132, 144, 154, 158, 170, 173, 175, 176, 178, 181, 188, 190, 192
      dormice 133
      gerbils 109
      mice 60, 66, 79, 109, 113, 133
        Multimammate Mouse 39, 170, 192
        Three-striped Mouse 39
      rats 60, 66
        Vlei Rat 39, 66, 125, 173
      squirrels 113
        bush 56
        forest 117
        ground 52, 60, 71
    suricates 52, 71
    voles 60
  molluscs 18
    crabs 18, 178, 181
    snails 18
  palm fruit 18
  refuse 34
  reptiles 33, 52, 55, 60, 66, 71, 73, 87, 93, 99, 114, 118, 121, 132, 176, 181
    chameleons 42, 91, 117

Food items: reptiles *(cont.)*
    geckoes 114
    lizards 12, 42, 56, 58, 79, 81, 88, 91, 94, 96, 104, 109, 113, 117, 132, 133, 144, 154, 158, 164, 166
      Cape Rough-scaled 114
    monitor lizards 52, 71
    snakes 12, 52, 56, 73, 75, 76, 79, 96, 109, 113
      cobras 76
      herald snake 73
      mambas 75
    water monitors 73

G

Game Reserve, Umfolozi 29
geckoes, barking 109
Geese, Egyptian 106
Griffon, Ruppell's 22
Gruidae 11

H

Hamerkop 154, 164, 170, 181, 183
Harrier
  Hen 131
  Northern 131
Hawk, Marsh *see* Harrier, Northern
herons 8, 83
hornbills 188
  Ground 88, 113

J

Jackal 81
  Blackbacked 94

K

Kalahari 29, 104, 109, 166
Karoo 71, 72, 94, 100, 109, 126
kingfisher 138
Kite, Red 34
kites, 'milvus' 34, 36

L

'landing lights' 58, 65
lions 27

Livingstone, David 164
Louries, Grey 183, 192

M

melanism 103, 118
mimicry 42
Moremi Wildlife Reserve 190
Museum
  Durban 190
  South African 175

N

nagapie 192
Namaqualand 109
National Park
  Hwange 52, 71, 104
  Kalahari Gemsbok 18, 52, 81, 183
  Kruger 52, 60, 61, 71, 81, 83, 88, 118, 150, 164, 175
  Matobo 48, 61, 93
neoteny 100

O

'Old Whitey' 65
ossuaries 178
Owl
  Eurasian Eagle 183
  Great Grey 184
  Palearctic Scops 187
  Pemba Scops 187
  Sao Tome Scops 187
  Sokoke Scops 187

P

Pan-African Ornithological Congress (1957) 149
Pel, Governor H.S. 184
Peregrine, Peale's 142
persecution of birds 8-9, 68, 71, 83
poisoning of birds 8, 22, 29, 36, 52, 81, 82, 83, 94, 132, 138, 142

R

Raphia palms 18
ratels 109, 113
ravens 149

Reserve, Moremi Wildlife 190
'ringtails' 128-9, 131, 132
Roberts' *Birds of South Africa* 96, 122
Robin
    Chorister 68
    Natal 68
rollers 188
rooks 155

S

shrikes 8, 166
sibling aggression 12, 16, 58, 61, 66, 91, 94, 96, 133, 183 *see also* cainism
size difference between sexes *see* dimorphism
Smith, Andrew 175

South African Red Data Book of Birds 9, 25, 66, 79, 100, 125, 173
sparrowhawk 175
    European 100
starlings 188
Stork, Black 138
sunbirds 188
swallows 146
swifts 149

T

'Turkey Buzzards' *see* Hornbills, Ground

V

vultures, griffon 15

W

warblers 8
Watson, Rick 81
weavers
    Lesser Masked 118
    Sociable 166, 181, 183
    Spottedbacked 118
wetlands 125
white-eyes 188
widowbirds 125
Woodford, Colonel 175
Woodhoopoe, Redbilled 188
Woodpecker, Bearded 188

COMMON NAMES

Page references in **bold type** denote main species entries and photographs; page references in *italic type* denote additional photographs

A

Accipiters 42, 99

B

Bateleur 8, 26, 30, 36, 47, 52, 75, **81-2**, 94, 203
Buzzard
    Augur **93**, 94, 205
    Forest 87, **91**, 204
    Honey 33, **45**, 87, 198
    Jackal 8, *87*, 93, **94**, 205
    Lizard 87, **96**, 118, 206
    Longlegged 8, **92**, 205
    Mountain *see* Buzzard, Forest
    Steppe 8, 45, 55, *86-7*, 87, **88**, 91, 92, 204
    'Wasp' *see* Buzzard, Honey
Buzzards 87-96

E

Eagle 11, 12
    African Fish 18, *46-7*, 47, 68, 76, **83**, 138, 204
    African Hawk **61**, 65, 106, 188, 200

    Ayres' *47*, 58, 61, **65**, 201
    Ayres' Hawk *see* Eagle, Ayres'
    Black **48-9**, 144, 198
    Bonelli's *see* Eagle, African Hawk
    Booted 47, **58**, 65, 138, 200
    Crowned *2*, 47, **68**, 96, 201
    Fish *see* Eagle, African Fish
    Harrier *see* Snake Eagle
    Lesser Spotted 55, **60**, 200
    Longcrested 47, **66**, 106, 201
    Martial 47, **71-2**, 76, 202
    Shorttoed *see* Snake Eagle, Blackbreasted
    Steppe **55**, 60, 199
    Tawny 36, **52**, 55, 199
    Verreaux's *see* Eagle, Black
    Vulturine Fish *see* Vulture, Palmnut
    Wahlberg's 8, 20, **56**, 60, 183, 199
Eagles 8, 47-83

F

Falcon
    African Hobby *see* Hobby, African
    Cuckoo *see* Hawk, Cuckoo
    Eastern Redfooted *see* Kestrel, Eastern Redfooted

    Eleonora's 8, **152**, 213
    Hobby *see* Hobby, European
    Horsbrugh's *see* Falcon, Rednecked
    Lanner *4*, *140-1*, **144**, 146, 212
    Peregrine 8, **142**, 144, 146, 149, 211
    Pygmy 8, 104, **166**, 216
    Redfooted *see* Kestrel, Eastern Redfooted
    Rednecked **150**, 213
    Rufousnecked *see* Falcon, Rednecked
    Sooty 146, 152, **153**, 154, 164, 214
    Taita **149**, 213
    Teita *see* Falcon, Taita
    Western Redfooted *see* Kestrel, Western Redfooted
Falconidae 141-166
Falconiformes 8, 11, 169
Falcons 8, 65
Falcons and Kestrels 141-166

G

Goshawk
    African 42, *99*, 103, 104, 114, **117**, 208
    Dark Chanting 109, **113**, 208
    Gabar 103, 104, 114, **118**, 209
    Little Banded 103, 104, **114**, 208

INDEX

Goshawk *(cont.)*
    Pale Chanting **109**, 113, 207
Goshawks 42, 65, 79, 96, 188
Goshawks and Sparrowhawks 99-118
Gymnogene 45, 106, 121, **133**, 211

H

Harrier
    African Marsh *1*, *6-7*, *120-1*, 121, 122, **125**, 126, 209
    Banded *see* Gymnogene
    Black 8, 121, **126**, *129*, 210
    European Marsh **122**, 209
    Montagu's *121*, *128-9*, **131**, 132, 210
    Pallid 131, **132**, 210
    Steppe *see* Harrier, Pallid
Harriers and Allied Species 121-133
Hawk
    Banded Harrier *see* Gymnogene
    Bat 33, **44**, 146, 198
    Cuckoo *32-3*, 33, **42**, 79, 197
    Fish *see* Osprey
Hawks 88
Hawks, Chanting 96, 118
Hobbies 141
Hobby
    African 146, **148**, 212
    European **146**, 148, 153, 157, 212

K

Kestrel *see* Kestrel, Rock
Kestrel
    Common *see* Kestrel, Rock
    Dickinson's 154, **164**, 216
    Eastern Redfooted 146, 155, **157**, 158, 215
    Greater *141*, 160, **161**, 216
    Grey 153, **154**, 164, 214
    Lesser 8, 155, 157, 158, **160**, 215
    Rock **158**, 160, 215
    Western Redfooted **155**, 157, 158, 214
    White-eyed *see* Kestrel, Greater

Kestrels and Falcons 141-166
Kite
    Black 8, 33, **34-6**, 55, 197
    Blackshouldered 33, **39**, 76, 96, 114, 192, 197
    Blackwinged *see* Kite, Blackshouldered
    Yellowbilled 8, *33*, 36, *37 see also* Kite, Black
Kites 8, 42, 161
Kites and Allied Species 33-45, 47, 87

L

Lammergeier *see* Vulture, Bearded
Lanner *see* Falcon, Lanner

O

Osprey 8, *136-7*, **137-8**, 211
Owl
    Barn 8, **170**, 173, 217
    Barred **190**, 220
    Cape Eagle *9*, *169*, **178**, 218
    Giant Eagle 106, **183**, 219
    Grass **173**, 176, 217
    Mackinder's Eagle *see* Owl, Cape Eagle
    Marsh 173, **176**, 218
    Milky Eagle *see* Owl, Giant Eagle
    Pearlspotted 187, **188**, 190, 220
    Pel's Fishing **184**, 219
    Scops 8, **187**, 192, 219
    Spotted Eagle *168-9*, 178, **181**, 218
    Verreaux's Eagle *see* Owl, Giant Eagle
    Whitefaced **192**, 220
    Whitefaced Scops *see* Owl, Whitefaced
    Wood **175**, 217
    Woodford's *see* Owl, Wood
Owls 8, 141, 169-192

P

'pearlie' *see* Owl, Pearlspotted
Peregrine, African *see* Falcon, Peregrine

R

'ringtails' 131, 132

S

Secretarybird *10-11*, **11-12**, 161, 194
Shikra *see* Goshawk, Little Banded
'shortwings' *see* Accipiters
Snake Eagle
    Banded *see* Snake Eagle, Western Banded
    Blackbreasted 8, 75, **76**, 203
    Brown 8, **75**, 76, 96, 202
    Fasciated *see* Snake Eagle, Southern Banded
    Smaller Banded *see* Snake Eagle, Western Banded
    Southern Banded **79**, 203
    Western Banded **73**, 79, 202
Snake Eagles 47, 75
Sparrowhawk
    Black 61, *98-9*, 103, **106-8**, 207
    Great *see* Sparrowhawk, Black
    Little 103, **104**, 114, 207
    Ovambo **103**, 104, 106, 114, 206
    Redbreasted **100**, 206
Sparrowhawks and Goshawks 99-118, 188
Strigiformes 8, 169-192

T

'Turmvalke' *see* Kestrel, Rock

V

Vulture
    Bearded *14-15*, 15, **16**, 194
    Black *see* Vulture, Lappetfaced
    Cape 8, 15, 16, **21-2**, 27, 30, 195
    Cape Griffon *see* Vulture, Cape
    Egyptian 9, 18, **20**, 25, 195
    Hooded **25**, 26, 195
    Lappetfaced 15, 25, 26, **29**, 30, 196
    Palmnut 15, **18**, 20, 25, 194
    Whitebacked *15*, 15, **26-7**, 29, 30, 196
    Whiteheaded 25, 26, 29, **30**, 196
Vultures 8, 15-30, 47, 52

Scientific Names

A

Accipiter
  badius 208
  melanoleucus 207
  minullus 207
  ovampensis 206
  rufiventris 206
  tachiro 208
Aquila 47
  nipalensis 199
  pomarina 200
  rapax 199
  verreauxii 198
  wahlbergi 199
Asio capensis 218
Aviceda cuculoides 197

B

Bubo
  africanus 218
  capensis 218
  lacteus 183, 219
Buteo 88, 91
  augur 205
  buteo 88, 91, 204
  buteo buteo 88, 91
  buteo vulpinus 88
  rufinus 205
  rufofuscus 205
  tachardus 91
  trizonatus 91, 204

C

Circaetus 75
  cinerascens 202
  cinereus 202
  fasciolatus 203
  gallicus 203
Circus
  aeruginosus 209
  macrourus 210
  maurus 210
  pygargus 210
  ranivorus 209

E

Elanus caeruleus 197

F

Falco
  amurensis 215
  ardosiaceus 214
  biarmicus 212
  chicquera 150, 213
  chicquera horsbrughi 150
  chicquera ruficollis 150
  concolor 214
  cuvieri 212
  dickinsoni 216
  eleonorae 213
  fasciinucha 213
  naumanni 215
  peregrinus 211
  peregrinus anatum 142
  rupicoloides 216
  subbuteo 212
  tinnunculus 158, 215
  vespertinus 214

G

Glaucidium 188, 190
  capense 220
  perlatum 220

Gypaetus barbatus 194
Gypohierax angolensis 18, 194
Gyps
  africanus 196
  coprotheres 195

H

Haliaeetus 47
  vocifer 204
Hieraaetus 47
  ayresii 201
  pennatus 200
  spilogaster 61, 200

K

Kaupifalco monogrammicus 96, 206

L

Lophaetus occipitalis 201

M

Macheiramphus alcinus 198
Melierax
  canorus 207
  metabates 208
Micronisus gabar 209
Milvus 33, 34
  migrans 197

N

Necrosyrtes monachus 195
Neophron percnopterus 195

O

Otus 187
  leucotis 220
  scops 187
  senegalensis 187, 219

P

Pandion haliaetus 211
Peregrinus falco minor 142
Pernis apivorus 198
Polemaetus bellicosus 202
Polihierax semitorquatus 216
Polyboroides typus 211

S

Sagittarius serpentarius 194
Scotopelia peli 219
Stephanoaetus coronatus 201
Strix woodfordii 175, 217

T

Terathopius ecaudatus 203
Torgos tracheliotus 196
Trigonoceps occipitalis 196
Tyto 173
  alba 217
  capensis 217